George Lambert

Around the Globe and through Bible Lands

George Lambert

Around the Globe and through Bible Lands

ISBN/EAN: 9783337170707

Printed in Europe, USA, Canada, Australia, Japan

Cover: Foto ©Andreas Hilbeck / pixelio.de

More available books at **www.hansebooks.com**

Around the Globe

and through

Bible Lands.

Notes and Observations

On the Various Countries Through Which the Writer Traveled.

ILLUSTRATED.

BY GEORGE LAMBERT.

FROM THE PRESS OF
MENNONITE PUBLISHING COMPANY.
ELKHART, INDIANA.

Entered according to Act of Congress, in the year 1896, by GEORGE LAMBERT, in the office of the Librarian of Congress, at Washington. All rights reserved.

Dedication.

To my beloved wife, the choice of my youth, and the best gift of God to man,

To our children which God gave us and who stood by us so faithfully during these wanderings,

To my friends who encouraged me during my travels, and to those requesting and urging the publication of this book,

I affectionately dedicate the same.

George Lambert.

PREFACE.

GREETING:—Why another book meets you in the open field, among thousands of others, and which, like others, must stand on its own merits, is, Inasmuch as the author believes that as every man in this world has his own special calling, duty or mission to fulfill, so have also the good books that have been handed down to us; and by the grace of God, they have been the means of enlightening, instructing and educating the human family, and of bringing them into a closer relationship with each other in this world of Christian usefulness.

This work treats on foreign mission lands, mission work and other topics of interest to Bible students in general as they are observed by those visiting these countries. It is an act of charity and Christian kindness to be interested in our brethren beyond the seas; and though they are of different nationality, and many of them far inferior in intelligence, science, arts and education to the civilized Christian nations, we ought to remember that they are our brethren, for He "hath made of one blood all nations of men for to dwell on all the face of the earth."

There is no closer relation existing anywhere than the relation between the Christian church at home and Christian missions in foreign lands. Hence, all should learn to know more about them and become personally interested in the great mission work of this Christian nation. There is no closer relation existing anywhere than the relation between the Bible and Bible lands, and these are so closely interwoven that traces confirming the truth of the teachings of God's Holy Word, are seen on every hand. The writer has given briefly the facts as he observed them during his travels, to the best of his knowledge, without the least exaggeration, with notes, references, extracts and statistics, as he has found them accurate, interesting and beneficial.

The author is greatly indebted to different guide-books: Murray's Handbook on Japan, Madras Publications on India and Bible Lands, Baedeker on Lower Egypt, Baedeker's Palestine and Syria, and especially to the "Journeys of Jesus" by Dr. Addison D. Crabtre, from which, through the kindness of the Mennonite Publishing Company, he has been permitted to use a number of illustrations. All of these works are considered very reliable.

As the author has been permitted to visit a number of missions in foreign lands, and has seen the need of making special efforts to aid these institutions in their work of Christianizing these heathen countries, and since many appeals for help were made to him, it is his sincere purpose and desire to set apart a certain percentage of the proceeds from the sale of this book for foreign missions, as the Lord may direct.

It is the prayer of the author that these lines, as they go out on their mission, may be the means of creating a deeper interest in the hearts of the readers, and aid them by imparting such knowledge as will inspire them to look up and reach out, under the blessing of God, to greater usefulness.

GEORGE LAMBERT,

Elkhart, Indiana.

TABLE OF CONTENTS.

CHAPTER I. INTRODUCTION................................... 14

CHAPTER II.—PASSPORTS AND MONEYS.—Table of Foreign Moneys—Sample Passport—Table of Comparative Time........ 17

CHAPTER III.—LEAVING HOME.—Farewell—Fears for Safe Return—Accompanied to Chicago by a Friend—Chicago Mission—Salt Lake—Mountains and Deserts—Our Western Metropolis—Chinatown—Starting for the Land of the Rising Sun—Good Byes—Music—Golden Gate............................... 25

CHAPTER IV.—OUT ON THE DEEP.—Ship Rolls—Seasickness—Missionaries—Tourists—The Ship like a Country Town—Farm Yard—Honolulu—Queen's Palace—Productions—Water Melons—Leprosy—Leper Doctor—Part Forever—Doctors as Missionaries—Natives—Out on the Deep—Sea Rough—Waves Mountain High—Crossing the Meridian—Torpedo Lines—Turtle Soup—Native Boats... 28

CHAPTER V.—YOKOHAMA AND KAMAKURA.—Main Sea Port—Jinrikishas—Kamakura—Gods of War—Daibutsu—Dimensions of this Idol—Goddess of Mercy—"Where is your God?"—"I See It"—Learn to Know Thyself............................... 39

CHAPTER VI.—TOKIO.—A Missionary's Statement—The War Spirit—Shaven Eyebrows and Blackened Teeth—Visits through Tokio—Japanese Dinner with Chopsticks—Women Bought and Sold—Legalized Prostitution—Bath Rooms—Crematory—Products—Fujiyama—Manner of Constructing Buildings—Cemeteries—Idols—Women as Slaves............................ 46

CHAPTER VII.—KOBE, NAGASAKI AND HONG KONG.—Widowed Mother and Child—Kobe—Inland Sea—Nagasaki—City of the Dead—Child taken from its Mother—War Vessels—Services on board Ship—Hong Kong—Seamen's Mission—Street Sights.. 61

CHAPTER VIII. SINGAPORE AND COLOMBO.—Services on board Ship—Singapore—Sea Shells—All kinds of Work done on the Streets—Chats with People of Different Nationalities—Poor Meals—Mission Service—Penang—Island of Sumatra—Colombo. 66

TABLE OF CONTENTS.

CHAPTER IX.—MADRAS.—Transferred to the Khedive—Sailing on Bay of Bengal—Population of Madras—Seat of Government—Compared with other Nations—Ninety to Ninety-five per cent. Poor People—Women carrying Brick and Mortar—Ear, Nose, and Neck Jewels—Low Wages—Buildings—Bungals—Huts—Penitentiary—An American in Prison—Dangers of our Young People.. 72

CHAPTER X.—MISSION WORK.—Missionaries—Fifteen Dollars Per Year Furnishes All—Who were the Men of God—Theosophy Missions—Castes—Christmas Songs—Meeting of Missionaries—Rev. Halicham Bannagee................................. 80

CHAPTER XI.—MADRAS TO CALCUTTA.—Meeting the American Party—Services on Board—Hugli River—The immense Wash of the Hugli River—Sagar Island—Dangerous Passage—Jungles—Met many Ships and Boats—Calcutta............... 89

CHAPTER XII.—CALCUTTA.—City of Palaces—"A Globe Trotter"—Bathing in the Sacred River—Mission Service—Burning Gnatt—Infant Weddings—Widowhood—Tombstone of an American, and a Brother's Words........................... 92

CHAPTER XIII.—BENARES.—Railroad Accommodations—A Nice Country—Temples and Mosques—Bloody Sacrifices—Monkey Temple—Animal Worship—Pilgrims—The Treacherous Lie—A Hindoo Saying—"Sons of the Ganges"—Distances and Fares—Disgraceful Carvings—Dancing Girls..................... 100

CHAPTER XIV.—ALLAHABAD.—Junction of Sacred Rivers—Thousands of Pilgrims—Banners and Flags Floating—Underground Temple—Suicide—Brahmans Drowning—Prayag—India Productions and Animals—English Officers—Forts—Soldiers... 108

CHAPTER XV.—BOMBAY.—Population—Streets—Buildings—Missions—Hospital for Aged Bullocks—Ant Feeding—Child Widows—Elephanta Caves............................... 114

CHAPTER XVI.—PARSEES.—Principal Merchants—Worship the Four Elements—Child Training—Marriage—Marriageable Age—Marriage Fund—Funeral—Preparing the Dead—"Towers of Silence"... 122

CHAPTER XVII.—BOMBAY TO EGYPT.—Farewell to India—War Vessels—Rev. and Mrs. Hazen—Arabian Sea—Aden—Red Sea in Sight—Bible Lands—Crossing of the Israelites—Mount Sinai—Suez—The Canal—Short cut Around the Globe—Bitter Lake—Crocodile Lake and Ismalia........................ 139

CHAPTER XVIII.—THE LAND OF THE PHARAOHS.—Mixed Population Streets Crowded—Water Carriers—Turbans—Ornaments—Veiling of Women (Single, Married)—Child Carrying—Water Fountain—Moslem's Prayer............................ 151

CHAPTER XIX.—DERVISHES AND THE TOMBS.—Dancing and Howling Dervishes and Mode of Worship—Citadel—Tombs of the Mamelukes—Khalifs—Mosque of Sultan Hasan—Tombs of the Khedives—Island of Roida—Coptic Church—Holy Family Sheltered—Joseph's Well—American Mission................. 160

CHAPTER XX.—THE PYRAMIDS, AND UP THE NILE.—Pyramids—Sphinx—Memphis—Up the Nile Water Wheels—Working in the Fields—Necropolis Ramses II.—Sakkara—Apis Tombs—Sacred Bulls—Passage to the Tombs Monster Coffins—Mariette Lasting Impressions............................ 170

CHAPTER XXI.—MUSEUM OF GIZEH AND HELIOPOLIS.—Museum—Egyptian Collections—Coffins—Mummies Different Necropoles—Ancient Jewelry—Ornaments Obelisk of Heliopolis—Virgin and Child Hid—Palm Trees—Land of Goshen—Canals—Railroad Cut... 182

CHAPTER XXII.—PORT SAID, EGYPT, TO JOPPA, PALESTINE.—History—Sailing for Joppa—Land in View—Joppa Sea Port—Passport Hotels—House of Simon the Tanner—Plain of Sharon Flowers and Productions—Railroad—Stations—Orange Groves Jerusalem Confusion............................ 187

CHAPTER XXIII. JERUSALEM AND ITS HISTORY.—Visitor's First Impression Interest Grows—Jerusalem not a Place of Amusement—King David's Reign Character of the City Ancient Walls—Mount Zion—Solomon's Reign—The City Beautified Jerusalem Destroyed and Rebuilt 200

CHAPTER XXIV.—JERUSALEM FROM HEZEKIAH'S REIGN TO THE PRESENT TIME. Jews Carried into Captivity—Solomon—Treasures Stolen from Temple and Carried to Babylon Temple Burned—Jews Return—Destruction and Bloodshed Herod Captured the City—The City Enriched Time of Christ—Was Taken by the Persians—Fell to the Egyptians Saladin Captured the City—Kharezmians Took it by Storm—Under Turkish Rule. 207

CHAPTER XXV. SOLOMON'S TEMPLE. City Walls—Pools Houses—Streets—Climate—Its Water Supply—Population—Mosque of Omar or Solomon's Temple—Mount Moriah—Rock in Interior—From where Christ Drove the Changers—Abraham and Melchizedek Sacrificing—Well of Souls—Golden Nails—Blowing the Trumpet—Calling to Judgment—Wire Rope across the Valley—Vaults—Stables of Solomon....................... 210

CHAPTER XXVI.—CALVARY AND TOMB OF CHRIST.—Jews' Wailing Place—Chanting—Immense Stones—Golgotha—Grotto of Jeremiah—The Cross Conquered the World—Dearest Spot on Earth—Rent in the Rock—Consoling Angel—Turkish Officials—Different Chapels—Decoration......................... 223

CHAPTER XXVII.—EASTER IN JERUSALEM.—Exciting Scenes—Easter Festival—Grand Mass—Good Friday—Holy Fire—Immense Crowds—Church Illuminated—Fighting and Accidents—Rough Mannered Officials—Wildest Confusion—Turning Somersaults 234

CHAPTER XXVIII.—MISSIONS, AND JEWISH PASSOVER.—Missions—German and English Services—Jewish Passover—Two Million Souls—Passover Services in Every House—Messiah Comes—Wine and Unleavened Bread—Greek Foot-washing—Latin Foot-washing—St. Stephens' Gate—Pool of Bethesda—Via Dolorosa—Ecce Homo Arch—House of Dives—Bathing the Stones with Tears.. 240

CHAPTER XXIX.—STREETS AND SHOPS.—Streets—Lanes—Grain Markets—Bazaars—Jewish Quarters—Shops—Castle of David—Jaffa Gate—Valley of Hinnom—Burial Grounds—Gihon—Official Buildings—Hospitals—Zion's Gate—Coenaculum—Tombs of Kings, David and Solomon—Outpouring of the Holy Ghost—Washing of the Apostles' Feet—Last Supper—House of Caiaphas 252

CHAPTER XXX.—A WALK TO GETHSEMANE.—Valley of Kidron—Beggars—Lepers—Hospital—List of Lepers—Stephen Stoned—Virgin's Tomb—Cavern of Agony—Gethsemane—Sorrowful Event—Affecting Scenes in the Garden—Mount of Olives—Trees and Shrubs... 260

CHAPTER XXXI.—MOUNT OF OLIVES AND SURROUNDINGS.—Church of the Lord's Prayer—Ascension—Great Ingathering—Russian Building—Valley of Jehoshaphat—Resurrection—Absalom's Tomb—Grotto of St. James—Village of Siloah—Pool of Siloah—St. Mary's Well.. 270

CHAPTER XXXII.—A VISIT TO BETHLEHEM.—"Hill of Evil Counsel"—Tree on which Judas Hanged Himself—Boundary Line—Well of Magi—Rachel's Tomb—Bethlehem—Naomi—Ruth—Boaz—David Anointed—Church of the Nativity—Manger—"Milk Grotto"—David's Well—Shepherd's Field—Cave of Adullam 280

CHAPTER XXXIII.—FROM JERUSALEM DOWN TO JERICHO.—Bethany—Home of Jesus—House of Mary and Martha—Lazarus' Tomb—Stone of Rest—Apostles' Springs—"Valley of Achor"—Way of Blood—Modern Jericho—Balsam Gardens.............. 291

CHAPTER XXXIV. — JERICHO, JORDAN, AND DEAD SEA. — Jericho—Thorns—Balm of Gilead—Apples of Sodom—Elisha's Spring—House of Rahab—Forty Days' Fast—Robbers—Jordan—Man Drowned Bathing in Jordan—Dead Sea—Camels—Mountains of Moab—American Party.......................... 300

CHAPTER XXXV.—HEBRON AND CAVE OF MACHPELAH.— Solomon's Pools—Aqueducts—Tomb of the Prophet Jonah—Valley of Eschol—History of Hebron—Great Stones—Tombs of Abraham, Isaac and Jacob with their Wives—Jewish Prayer—"Christians." "Dogs"—Missions—Pilgrimages................. 313

CHAPTER XXXVI.—EMMAUS AND SAMUEL'S TOMB.— Tombs—Rough Roads—Samuel's Tomb—Christ met the Disciples—Emmaus—Lord made Himself Known—Stone Structure—Mountains and Ravines—Brooks—Where David Slew the Giant—Return to Jerusalem—Leaving the Holy City................. 320

CHAPTER XXXVII. - MOUNT CARMEL. Leaving Joppa—Haifa (Acre)—Mount Carmel—Elijah's Castle—Phœnicia—Baal Worshipers... 328

CHAPTER XXXVIII.—TYRE AND SIDON.—Ancient Ruins—Bible Times—Crowning City—Robbed of Its Treasures—Top of a Rock—Zarephath... 334

CHAPTER XXXIX.—NAZARETH AND HILLS OF GALILEE.— Kishon—Home of Zebedee—Nazareth—Home of Jesus—Sheep and Goats—Streets—St. Mary's Well—Mount Tabor—Hills of Galilee—Bedouin Camps—Tiberas—Sea of Galilee—A Night of Misery... 338

CHAPTER XL.— SEA OF GALILEE AND ADJACENT POINTS.— Gennesaret—Description—Magdala—Capernaum—Chorazin—Bethsaida—Sea of Galilee—Plain of the Five Thousand—Cana of the Bible—Saul's Battle-ground—Arabs Plowing............ 346

CHAPTER XLI.—BEIRUT AND DAMASCUS.— Beirut—Diligence—Railroad—Lebanon Mountains—Mount Hermon—Druses—Massacring Maronites—European Commission—Damascus—History 354

CHAPTER XLII.— DAMASCUS.—Population—Naaman—Saul's Conversion—Street called Straight—House of Ananias—Tomb of St. George—Window from which Paul Escaped—Visitors in Damascus—Dogs—Moneys—Over the Lebanon Mountains by Moon Light—Turkish Funeral................................ 360

CHAPTER XLIII. BEIRUT TO SMYRNA AND EPHESUS.—Tripoli—Orange Mart—Island of Cyprus—Larnaka—Simasol—Man Overboard—Island of Rhodes—Carrying their Beds—Island of Chios—Smyrna—By Train to Ephesus........................ 367

TABLE OF CONTENTS.

CHAPTER XLIV.—EPHESUS.—Temple of Diana—Paul in Ephesus
—Home of St. John—Tomb of St. Luke—Ruins of Marble—
Modern Ephesus—Leaving for Greece.......................... 374

CHAPTER XLV.—ATHENS, GREECE.—Paul in Athens—Mars
Hill—The Unknown God—New Doctrine—Paul's Success....... 381

CHAPTER XLVI.—ATHENS AND CORINTH.—Grecian Funeral—
Priest Begging Alms—King's Gardens and Palace—Tour to
Corinth—Corinthian Canal—Paul at Corinth 387

CHAPTER XLVII.— FROM CORINTH TO NAPLES, ITALY.—
Harvest in Greece—Patres—Business Houses open on Sunday—
A Fight—Out on the Deep—American Party—Island Cofu—
Brindisi, Italy—Country—Naples—Mount Vesuvius—Pompeii—
Election—Funeral procession—Tour to Rome................. 394

CHAPTER XLVIII.—ANCIENT ROME. — Center of the Ancient
World—Other Nations Robbed of their Treasures—Paul in Rome
—Puteoli—Three Taverns—Paul's Imprisonment.............. 401

CHAPTER XLIX.—MODERN ROME.—Art Productions—Great
Cathedrals—St. Peter's Church—Ancient Ruins............... 407

CHAPTER L.— HOMEWARD BOUND. — Florence, Italy —Basel,
Switzerland — Paris, France — London, England — Crossing the
Atlantic—New York, U. S. A—Home....................... 410

CHAPTER I.

INTRODUCTION.

 A FEW years ago, in the heart of the Rocky Mountains, a gentleman encountered a French priest, his locks completely white with age, traveling apparently for pleasure. Astonished at the sight, he ventured to inquire what had induced him at this time of life to go so far from home.

"'Tis very easily explained," replied the priest. "Six months ago I was apparently about to die. One night I dreamed that I was already in God's presence and that He spoke to me these words: "My child, how did you like the beautiful world I gave you to dwell in?" I made no answer, in fact I was too mortified to make an intelligent reply. For think of it, I, who had preached for fifty years continually of a better world, had never examined this one at all. Awaking from my dream I made a vow to God, that if He gave me back my health, I would devote some months, at least, to seeing and admiring His works. So here I am making a tour of the world."

Many have been the number, during the last twenty years, who have made this tour, and given the benefit of their experiences to others, who could not make the trip for themselves. Those who make these circuits, however, often have varied experiences, and are required to endure exposure in many ways, and to practice self-denials that are not always pleasant. They are frequently in danger; they are overtaken by storms both on land and sea; they may often be obliged to elbow their way through difficulties and unpleasant crowds in both heathen and in Bible lands, while others are in their homes enjoying the comforts of life, reading, and improving their minds from the trying experiences of those who have traveled, and have given to the world what they saw and heard, and in this way their work has proved a blessing both at home and abroad.

All of us cannot, it is true, make these extended trips, but during the years and centuries that have passed since the first man made the tour around the world, traveling has become comparatively easy, and ocean voyages have to a great extent lost their terrors on account of the immense steamships and the complete system of navigation.

"Man is wonderfully and fearfully made," and while the works of the Most High are marvelous in the creation of all things, man is the greatest of all. Men differ in their qualities, graces, temperaments and dispositions, being born and brought up in different homes and under different influences; while the great God, the Father of all, is not partial, but gives to all a talent or more and calls them to their particular work and mission. To Him be all honor and glory.

Ever since the author was a boy and had learned that the world was so great and contained so many different people (with so many different modes of living) many of whom worship and serve dumb idols instead of the true and living God, he longed to visit, see and hear them. To the sorrow of his heart he has seen and heard, and therefore knows that these things are even so. Many, even the great majority of the people, do not know or hear of the Bible, or of Christ as the Saviour of the world. Since the writer first learned in early youth of the land in which the men of the Bible lived and suffered, the land in which Christ performed His mission, and the hallowed grounds upon which His holy feet trod, he has had a longing desire to visit that country; and this has seemed to be his strongest inclination in connection with ministerial work.

At last, by the providence of God, the writer believes, and the aid of a good wife and children, the way was opened for him to make the great tour around the world, and he here gives the readers some of the information gathered, which he hopes will prove interesting and instructive.

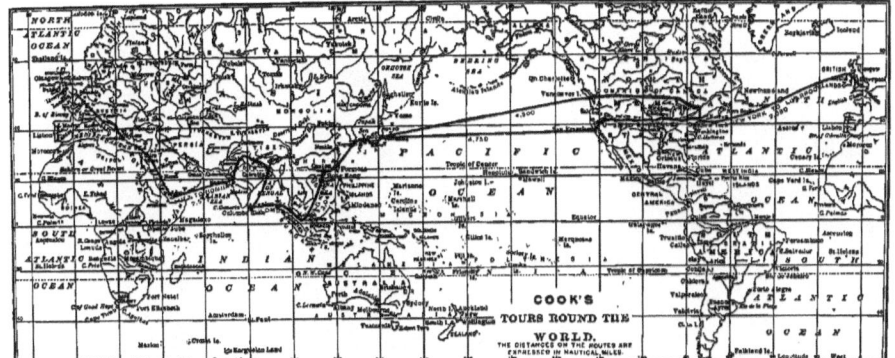

CHAPTER II.

Passports and Moneys.

BOVE all things it is necessary to learn in advance what the necessities are for a tour of this kind. Those who wish a more extensive outline and information are referred to Thos. Cook & Son, 262 Broadway, New York, where all the information on the subject of traveling, carrying money, the banking system in foreign lands, and also the circular note and letter of credit system, can be obtained. The latter is a very good way to carry money without being in danger of losing it or of being robbed. Any amount of money can be drawn and also exchanged in any country or main city in the world.

PASSPORTS.

It is of great importance to have a passport for identification at post offices, banks, and before officials in foreign lands and in crossing the lines and being admitted into some of the public places.

In Turkey it is impossible to travel into the interior without a passport, and a man is always credited for carrying one.

A passport can be obtained by applying to the Secretary of State at Washington, D. C. A blank will be sent to you together with instructions how to fill it out; and by having it acknowledged before a Justice of the Peace or

Notary Public, and returned with one dollar included for the fee, you will receive your passport, which is an honorable document for one to carry. We will here give a complete copy of the passport which we carried.

FOREIGN MONEYS.

JAPAN.

10 rin = 1 sen.
100 sen = 1 yen.

The currency consists of the following silver: 1 yen, 50 sen, 20 sen, 10 sen and 5 sen.

Copper: 2 sen, 1 sen, 5 rin and 1 rin. The yen is worth in exchange about 54 cents, United States money. Mexican silver dollars can be used at the treaty ports.

CHINA.

In the interior of China the only currency consists of brass coins, called cash, with a square hole in the center through which they are strung. Mexican and English dollars are used in the treaty ports, but going through the country each is exchanged for from 1,000 to 1,200 cash; a few dollars' worth make a load for a coolie. Mexican and English dollars are the same in value as the Japanese yen.

TABLES OF FOREIGN MONEYS.

EGYPT.

Monetary Unit—the Piastre of 40 Paras.

```
                              s.   d.
1 piastre            nearly   0   2½
100 piastres = 1 Egyptian
  pound                      20    6
English sovereign  =  97 piastres
  20 paras.
French napoleon = about 77.6 pias.
```

TURKEY.

Monetary Unit—the Piastre of 40 Paras.

```
                              s.   d.
1 piastre            nearly   0   2¼
20    "      =    1 silver
                  medjidie =  3    4
100 piastres = 1 gold medjidie
  or Turkish pound =         18    0
```

GOOD ONLY FOR
TWO YEARS FROM DATE.

DEPARTMENT OF STATE,

To all to whom these presents shall come Greeting:

I, the undersigned, Secretary of State of the United States of America, hereby request all whom it may concern to permit George Lambert a Citizen of the United States safely and freely to pass, and in case of need to give him all lawful Aid and Protection.

DESCRIPTION,
Age, 41 years.
Stature, 5 ft., 8½ in., Eng.
Forehead, high.
Eyes, grey.
Nose, straight.
Mouth, medium.
Chin, medium.
Hair, brown.
Complexion, fair.
Face, medium.

Signature of
the Bearer.

Geo. Lambert.

{ SEAL. }

Given under my hand and the Seal of the Department of State, at the City of Washington, the 13th day of August in the year 1894 and of the Independence of the United States the one hundred and nineteenth.

W. Q. Gresham.

NO. 15669.

INDIA.

Monetary Unit—Rupee of 16 Annas.

		s.	d.
Bronze—¼ anna, about =	0	0¼
" ½ " " "	0	0½
Silver— 2 annas " "	0	2
" 4 " " "	0	4
" 8 " " "	0	8
" 1 rupee, " "	1	4

Notes of the value of 5, 10, 20, 50, 100 rupees and upwards are in circulation. The rate of exchange varies considerably.

ITALY.

Monetary Unit—the Lira of 100 Centesimi. The money in general use is a paper currency in notes of—5, 10, 25, 50, 100, 500, 1,000 lire. Gold is invariably at a premium. The Lire (notes, gold, or silver) =1 Franc. (*See France.*)

SWITZERLAND.

Monetary Unit—the Franc of 100 Centimes.

		s.	d.
Bronze— 1 centime			
" 2 "			
Nickel— 5 " =	0	0½
" 10 " "	0	1
" 20 " "	0	2
Silver— 50 " "	0	4¾
" 1 franc "	0	9½
" 2 " "	1	7
" 5 " "	4	0
Gold — 20 " "	16	0

Notes of 50 francs, 100 francs, 500 francs, and 1,000 francs are issued by several Swiss banks under arrangements with the Government, and are available throughout Switzerland, and are the same value as gold.

FRANCE.

Monetary Unit—the Franc of 100 Centimes.

		s.	d.
Bronze—5 centimes =	0	0½
" 10 " "	0	1
Silver— 20 " "	0	2
" 50 " "	0	4¾
" 1 franc "	0	9
" 2 " "	1	7
" 5 " "	4	0
Gold — 5 " "	4	0
" 10 " "	8	0
" 20 " The "Napoleon" or "Louis"=	16	0

Notes are issued by the Bank of France for 50 francs, 100 francs, 500 francs, and 1,000 francs, and are the same value as gold.

UNITED STATES, AMERICA.

Monetary Unit—1 Dollar of 100 Cents.

		s.	d.
Copper—1 cent =	0	0½
" 2 " "	0	1
Nickel— 3 cents "	0	1½
" 5 " "	0	2½
Silver — 3 " "	0	1½
" 5 " "	0	2½
" 10 " (dime) "	0	5
" 25 " "	1	0½
" 50 " "	2	1
" 1 dollar "	4	2
Gold — 1 " "	4	2
" 2½ " "	10	5
" 3 " "	12	6
" 5 " "	20	10
" 10 " "	41	8
" 20 " "	83	4

Notes, Greenbacks, Gold Certificates, Silver Certificates, and National Bank Notes are issued in amounts of 1, 2, 5, 10, 20, 50, 100, 500, 1,000 dollars and upwards, and circulate at par with gold.

Time.

Time by the clock at the following places. When it is 12 o'clock, noon, at New York, it is

11:00	A. M.	in	Chicago, Ill.
9:00	"	"	San Francisco, Cal.
2:15	"	"	Yokohama, Japan.
12:23	"	"	Hong Kong, China.
2:10	"	"	Adelaide, Australia.
2:36	"	"	Melbourne, Australia.
3:00	"	"	Sydney, Australia.
4:00	P. M.	"	Ephesus, Asia Minor.
11:51	"	"	Singapore, India.
10:49	"	"	Calcutta, British India.
10:17	"	"	Madras, British India.
10:15	"	"	Colombo, Ceylon.
9:47	"	"	Bombay, British India.
7:56	"	"	Aden, Arabia.
7:05	"	"	Jerusalem, Palestine.
6:08	"	"	Brindisi, Italy.
4:56	"	"	Greenwich, England.

At home in the Northern Hemisphere the longest day is June 21st; the shortest, December 21st. In the Southern Hemisphere the longest day is December 21st, and the shortest, June 21st.

GETHSEMANE AND MOUNT OF OLIVES. GETHSEMANE IN ENCLOSURE CONTAINING TALL SPRUCE TREES.

(Taken from Photo.)

CHAPTER III.

LEAVING HOME.

FAREWELL—FEARS FOR SAFE RETURN—ACCOMPANIED TO CHICAGO
BY A FRIEND—CHICAGO MISSION—SALT LAKE—MOUNTAINS AND
DESERTS—OUR WESTERN METROPOLIS—CHINATOWN—
STARTING FOR THE LAND OF THE RISING SUN—
GOOD BYES—MUSIC—GOLDEN GATE.

HE day of our departure from home drew near without the least obstacle being in the way, and we took it for granted that the Lord was pleased with our purpose, since our prayer had been that if it was not in accordance with the Divine Will, He should hinder us in our contemplated undertaking.

On the 25th day of August, 1894, we bid adieu to our beloved family, wife and children, and many others who had met us at the railway station. Indeed it was like a man leaving his family and moving toward the battle field; especially after hearing some express themselves in words like these: "You will never return safely."

We boarded the train and were soon on our long tour, accompanied by our friend D. G. Musselman, as far as his home in Chicago, Ill. We stopped with him a short time, visiting some places of interest, among which was the Deaconess' Home in charge of Bro. J. Sprunger, and the Mennonite Mission in charge of Bro. S. F. Coffman of Elkhart, Indiana.

Leaving the city we stopped at several points in the West, including Salt Lake City, Utah, the great Mormon stronghold, where many sights are to be seen. The Temple and Tabernacle are in themselves wonders. The inhabitants appear very clever and sociable, and claim that polygamy has been abandoned. We also visited the tomb of Brigham Young, the celebrated Mormon prophet.

Traveling from there to the western coast we passed through mountains, tunnels, deserts, etc., that must indeed convince any one that this is a wonderful country, with its prairies and mountains, rivers and lakes, gas and coal, silver and gold, and in fact everything that is essential in making this a magnificent country and people.

Traveling across the Great American Desert was a very unpleasant part of our journey, on account of the sand and dust which found its way into the coach, though all the windows were closed. Going through California much is to be seen in the way of vineyards and fruit orchards of all kinds, until you reach the coast, where San Francisco, the great western shipping point of this country, is situated. It is amazing to see the immense warehouses, and the long trains and the large ships that come and go, loaded to their utmost capacity.

San Francisco is a great city. Although located thousands of miles from our eastern cities, yet it is apparently very similar to them. We spent some time at this place. Many religious meetings of all kinds were carried on here, yet we found many degraded places and a great deal of sin existing.

Chinatown is quite a sight, and all who visit San Francisco should go through Chinatown, accompanied by a guide. By the time a man becomes thoroughly interested, he almost forgets that he is yet so near home and in his own country; for everything is so very different from the other parts of the city. The docks, where the great ocean steamers are anchored, are very interesting. We found the ship Oceanica, of the Occidental & Oriental Line, at the dock, discharging her cargo and reloading for Japan and China.

On the 25th of September, 1894, passengers for the steamer began to arrive from all parts of our country. The weather was fine, and it was a time not soon to be forgotten. We soon met a number of passengers, some of whom were missionaries starting for the "Land of the Rising Sun" and the Orient. Among them, also, were a number that were making about the same kind of tour we had started to make. With many of them we formed acquaintances which, we trust, will never be forgotten. Just before the time for leaving, the crowd of people,—passengers and their friends who had accompanied them to see them off,—was an impressive sight. When the time came for sailing, the "good byes," the weeping, the cheering, and waving of handkerchiefs, was very affecting.

A brass band was on board and dispensed music, while the grand, ponderous ship swung around in the bay and began to move toward the Golden Gate. While listening to the solemn strains of a farewell hymn, grief and joy seemed to commingle. We heard a lady make the remark: "I wish that band would stop playing; it makes me feel so bad." As the Golden Gate hove in sight and the forts had been passed, a steam launch came up along-side the large steamer and took the band back to the city.

CHAPTER IV.

OUT ON THE DEEP.

SHIP ROLLS — SEASICKNESS — MISSIONARIES—TOURISTS — THE SHIP LIKE A COUNTRY TOWN—FARM YARD—HONOLULU—QUEEN'S PALACE—PRODUCTIONS — WATER MELONS — LEPROSY— LEPER DOCTOR—PART FOREVER—DOCTORS AS MISSIONARIES—NATIVES—OUT ON THE DEEP— SEA ROUGH—WAVES MOUNTAIN HIGH— CROSSING THE MERIDIAN—TORPEDO LINES–TURTLE SOUP– NATIVE BOATS.

SOON the ship was out on the deep, and began to have considerable motion and to rock and pitch so that the passengers soon felt the effects of it. We had a well-furnished room with four bunks. By the time we were fairly out and under way, night set in.

September 26th.—Had a good night's rest. The weather was fair but the sea rather rough; accommodations and meals were good, but we had no appetite, as by this time nearly all were seasick, the writer among the rest. Our Chinese steward was very good to us and did all he could to make us comfortable.

September 27th.—The sea was rough, and as a result, seasickness was in order. September 28th.—Ship rolling; passengers kept bunks; very sick, and without appetite. September 29th.—Pleasant day, sun shone clearly and the sea was more calm. Some passengers on deck. Seasickness about over and appetite returning. September 30th.—A beautiful morning and all on deck.

There are about fifteen or more passengers on board who are making the tour around the world, and quite a number of missionaries that are going into foreign fields, which makes a very pleasant company. O, what a world to move out in, where we can meet and associate with people of so

many different nationalities until our hearts swell with joy, sympathy and affection for each other!

The vessel seemed to carry a little of nearly everything, and reminded one of a little country town. Cattle, sheep, turkeys, geese, ducks, and chickens were carried along, as well as all kinds of vegetables, all for the accommodation and benefit of the passengers. For breakfast we had beef steak, fresh fish, eggs, pork and a variety of other eatables.

O, the wonders of God, in the night, upon the sea! In the evening the passengers on the upper deck joined in singing, "Nearer my God to Thee." To us it was indeed grand, in the darkness, on the sea, while the waters were raging and the billows rolling, with the stars shining upon us in their beauty, to sing of Him who made and controls the mighty deep. We felt to clap our hands with the waters, and wished that some of our many friends could participate with us on such an occasion. How they would have enjoyed it!

Sunday, October 1st.—Services were held on board the ship, conducted by Prof. Clark, one of our tourists from Rockford, Ill., U. S. A. October 2d.—A pleasant morning. We passed within sight of Molokai Island to which the lepers from the Sandwich Islands are banished.

We arrived at Honolulu on the specified time. This is the main city and sea port of the Sandwich Islands, which are eight in number. It is also the seat of government and location of the King's palace where the Queen resides. Many soldiers were seen and a warlike spirit was manifested on account of the political troubles on the island. These islands are sometimes called the "Paradise of the World."

The natives have a very dark color and do not appear to be much civilized. The islands have large sugar plantations, and the tropical fruits, such as pineapples, bananas, cocoanuts, etc., grow quite abundantly. Tea, rice and coffee are also raised. Their money is silver, and is equal in value with United States money. We took a walk into the city in the evening, and on hearing some singing found there was a mission meeting going on which we attended. The congregation consisted of a wonderfully mixed people. The meeting was conducted by an American and from what we could learn and comprehend, the workers seemed to be active and to understand each other in their different languages.

HONOLULU

(Original Photo.)

"Pass not unmarked the islands in that sea,
Where Nature claims the most celebrity,
Half hidden, stretching in a lengthened line
In front of China, which its guide shall be,
Japan abounds in mines of silver fine
And shall enlighten'd be by holy faith divine."

There are many Japanese and Chinese in this country. Many of the women carry their babies on their backs, while others with their children lie around on the sidewalks during the heat of the day, very improperly clad, according to our way of thinking. We also noticed that while eating watermelons in the grocery store, they dropped all the seeds and shells upon the floor, causing a terrible muss, and yet they considered it to be quite proper. Many poor people and cripples are to be seen. Leprosy prevails to a considerable extent, but all such, as fast as they are pronounced incurable, are banished to Molokai Island, where they must remain until death releases them. A short time previous there were twelve lepers, mostly young people, taken from Honolulu to the island. Parents and children, husbands and wives, were parted forever. Our friend, Mr. Rudolf Paweck, was an eye witness, and says, "It was a very sad sight to behold. While their friends wept, those condemned did not appear to mind it. This condition of mind is brought on by the disease." The government supports them, it is said.

We were told that a certain physician living on one of the healthy islands, was noticed, for a long time, to be wearing gloves. One day he came to the public authorities, and pulling off his glove, showed a small spot of leprosy on his hand, saying, "You see, I am doomed to die. I might hide this for a good while and keep off the Isle of lepers, but, as I am a physician, I choose to go now and be of some service to those who are further along in the disease. It would be selfish for me to stay here amid luxurious surroundings when I might soothe and help the wretched." He bade farewell to family and friends. The parting was agonizing, as they well knew that they could never see each other's face again. He was transported to the Isle of lepers and worked among the sick until prostrated for his own death, which finally came. That was sacrifice, radiant and magnificent, surpassed by none, save that of Him who Himself came from the health of heaven to the leprous isle of this earth, that He might heal our wounds, weep over our grief, die our deaths, and turn this isle of a leprous world into one great, blooming paradise of God.

The great mission work is carried on in different ways, and many claim that schools, where the children are brought and kept, are the most successful means. Missionary physicians find their way to them to help in case of need, giving relief and aid with good Christian advice and instruction. Dispensaries and infirmaries are to be found everywhere, under the control of the best doctors, some of them poorly paid, and others not paid at all. In one dispensary, within a year, one hundred and fifty thousand prescriptions were issued. The doctors, in many countries, do more missionary work, without charge, than all the others combined. May God bless the good missionary doctor.

October 3.—The ship just called at Honolulu, making a short stop of twenty-four hours. As the time came to leave, many Japanese and Chinese came on board. The gentleman above referred to, Mr. Rudolf Paweck, whom we found to be a friend, became our room-mate. We parted for the last time at Joppa, Turkey. Many people were at the port when the ship was about to leave. Natives came with their strings of flowers and bouquets to sell to the passengers, while the diving boys were in the water begging the passengers to throw money in that they might dive and get it. The twenty-four hours were spent by the passengers in viewing the city and surrounding country, but now they had all returned, and soon the ship weighed anchor and set sail for Yokohama, Japan.

EUROPEAN FUNERAL PROCESSION IN TURKEY.
(Original Photo.)

October 5.—Sea rough, and ship rocking, and at times almost lying on its side. Many are seasick, but we have not yet felt the effects very much.

October 6.—Sea very rough and winds high, affording wonderful sights. Waves, mountain high, striking each other and casting forth foam, looking like snow and ice mountains, were to be seen.

Sunday, October 7.—Ship rolling from one side to the other, keeping all the passengers in a continual swing. At 10 o'clock, P. M., the ship crossed the meridian, where one day is dropped. By traveling around the world, eastward, one day is gained, and as the meridian is crossed going westward the day is dropped; so we all retired on Sunday evening and awoke and arose on Tuesday morning, and yet we had slept but nine hours. The evening was spent in singing.

October 11.—The ship made good time, 319 miles in the last twenty-four hours. I carried a recommendation from a Chicago friend to a mission worker in China, and fortunately happened to meet the gentleman in charge of that work, on board the ship. We also met, among many others, the Rev. and Mrs. N. S. Hopkins and Dr. and Mrs. Garwood, the latter of Champaign, Ill., with whom we formed very acceptable acquaintances. We spent many pleasant hours together, both on the ship and in Japan, Egypt and Jerusalem, where we met for the last time.

October 15.—Arrived within about fifteen miles of Yokohama at 8, P. M., where we anchored and waited for the morning, as no ship is allowed to enter after a certain hour in the evening, on account of the torpedo lines and war trouble. A splendid supper was served, and among other things we had turtle soup, which was quite a rare dish for many of us. It seemed like a wedding feast, thanks to the generosity of the steam ship company. The next morning the ship drew near the port, and small boats came in large numbers to convey the poorer class to shore, while the other passengers were taken ashore by the steam launch. It was rainy and many of the natives were nearly naked, and so exposed to the rain and cold that they looked pitiful. We all found good quarters at the different hotels, and, for one, we felt grateful to God for our safe and successful voyage.

JAPANESE CONVEYANCE. (Original Photo.

CHAPTER V.

Yokohama and Kamakura.

Main Sea Port — Jinrikishas — Kamakura — Gods of War — Daibutsu — Dimensions of this Idol — Goddess of Mercy — "Where is your God?" — "I see it" — "Learn to know thyself."

APAN is a nice country with its tidy buildings. Yokohama is the place where most visitors first touch Japanese soil. It is the largest of the treaty ports and practically the port of Tokio, the seat of government. It is a matter of great interest to see the natives in their singular costumes. They are very polite in offering their services with their jinrikishas, two wheeled vehicles drawn by coolies, in which they will take you on short notice to any desired point.

The distance from Yokohama to Kamakura is about twenty-two miles, and is reached partly by train and then by coolies and their jinrikishas. The writer made this trip in company with several others and it was his first experience with the jinrikishas. The roads were miserable and at first it seemed like cruelty to have the natives draw us through the muddy streets, but we afterwards learned that it is considered by them a very honorable means of obtaining a livelihood. The roads were indeed so poor that at times all of us, five in number, were compelled to get out and walk. The chief attractions at Kamakura are the Temple of Hachiman, the Daibutsu or "Colossal bronze Buddha" and the great image of the goddess Kwannon.

The Temple of Hachiman contains the Gods of War, which are two in number. These idols are situated on either side of the main entrance to the temple, and present a frightful appearance. We noticed that they were spotted all over, and looked very filthy, as though fowls had been roosting over them. We were informed by our dragoman that this was on account of the war at that time being carried on with China. The Japanese, before going to war, come here to

JAPANESE TEMPLE.   (Original Photo.)

offer prayers to these idols. They write their prayers on paper, and then, after chewing them into a cud, throw them at the idol, aiming to make them stick, in which case they take it for granted that their God of War will answer their prayers. It reminds one of the mischievous school boy of our youthful days, chewing his paper wads and throwing them against the ceiling. We learned that the Japanese are highly delighted with their god, as the supposed means of their success in the war with China.

JAPAN.—DAIBUTSU.

The great Daibutsu or Great Buddha stands out prominently among Japanese works of art. Nothing else gives such an impression of majesty or so truly symbolizes the

DAIBUTSU. (Original Photo.)

central idea of Buddhism—the intellectual calm which comes of perfected knowledge and the subjugation of all passions. But to be fully appreciated, the Daibutsu must be visited many times, says Murry's Guide Book.

DIMENSIONS OF DAIBUTSU.

Height, - - - -	49 ft. 7 in.	Height of bump of wisdom, - - - - 9 in.
Circumference, - -	97 ft. 2 in.	Diameter of bump of wisdom, - - - - 2 ft. 4 in.
Length of face, - -	8 ft. 5 in.	
Width from ear to ear,	17 ft. 9 in.	Curls, (of which there are 830,) height, - 9 in.
Round white boss on forehead, - - -	1 ft. 3 in.	
Length of eye, - - -	3 ft. 11 in.	Diameter, - - - - 1 ft.
Length of eyebrows,	4 ft. 2 in.	Length from knee to knee, - - - - - 35 ft. 8 in.
Length of ear, - -	6 ft. 6 in.	
Length of nose, - -	3 ft. 9 in.	Circumference of the thumb, - - - - 3 ft.
Width of mouth, - -	3 ft. 2 in.	

The eyes are of pure gold and the silver balls weigh 30 lbs. Avoir. The image is formed of sheets of bronze casts, brazed together and finished on the outside with the chisel. The hollow interior of the image contains a small shrine, and a ladder leads up into the head. The writer ascended into the head of the image on this ladder and can truly say, the idols made by the hands of men have eyes, but they see not; they have ears, but they hear not; they have hands, but they cannot reach out and help the subjects who trust in them. Many come and go but none are benefited and yet it seems the natives remain zealous and very much in earnest in their mode of worship. We prayed with the dying missionary, who wore his life away in the interest of the natives in that country. His last prayer, as seen on his tombstone, was "God save the Japanese."

In the Temple of Kwannon stands the great image of the Goddess of Mercy, for which this temple is celebrated. It stands behind folding doors, which a small fee, to the attending priest, will suffice to open. The priest will first rap at the doors, pretending to awake the idol, and then the doors are opened; but the figure can only be indistinctly seen by the dim light of a few candles. It is a large image, gilded

TURKISH FESTAL DAY. *(Taken from Photo.)*

> Take Thou my hand and lead me—
> Choose Thou my way.
> Not as I will, O Father, teach me to say.
> What though the storms may gather,
> Thou knowest best;
> Safe in Thy keeping, Father, would I rest.

over, and is thirty feet and five inches high. Oh, how sad to think that these people are so ignorant of the real God.

An educated Japanese said to me, "I would like your religion, but I can't understand your God nor where He is." We had a long talk with him on the subject, explaining how a will or a testament made by a father previous to his death, is after his death read and brought into execution. We asked him "Who is speaking when the will is read." He said at once, "The father of the family," "So it is with God and His word," said I. "It is God speaking to us through His word or testament, as the deceased father, and we are to become obedient to Him." He then said, "I see it, I see it," and further said, "I will become a Christian. Oh, may the Lord lead many of those active young men to Himself through the Christian influence and efforts put forth by the so-called Christian world.

There are many sights that are very impressive. Men and women bow and worship, and bring their tithes and throw them into their cash box, while others are reading and watching the visitors very closely. We noticed a young woman walking around in one of the temples and clapping her hands as though she was very happy.

On entering one of the temples at Kyoto, into which you are admitted by paying a small fee, a curtain is lifted and you stand in front of a large mirror, where you see no one but yourself and the inscription on the mirror, "Man, learn to know thyself." O, what a lesson to be learned from that inscription. Instead of decorating this body and cultivating the pride of the heart, and the carnal inclinations of the natural man, "*Learn to know thyself.*"

CHAPTER VI.

Tokio.

A MISSIONARY'S STATEMENT—THE WAR SPIRIT—SHAVEN EYEBROWS AND BLACKENED TEETH—VISITS THROUGH TOKIO—JAPANESE DINNER WITH CHOPSTICKS—WOMEN BOUGHT AND SOLD—LEGALIZED PROSTITUTION—BATH ROOMS—CREMATORY—PRODUCTS—FUJIYAMA MANNER OF CONSTRUCTING BUILDINGS—CEMETERIES—IDOLS—WOMEN AS SLAVES.

T is stated by certain missionaries that their work is making slow progress, because a national feeling has grown up against it. The natives rather feel as though they could do their own mission work, and carry it on without foreign help; but all the missionaries are convinced that it would soon drift back into Buddhism. While the war with China was raging and a great war spirit was being shown by all the natives, the attendance at the missions, on an average, was very small. In a large meeting which the writer attended, the natives were holding a religious service in their own language, and indeed they manifested quite an earnestness, judging from their singing.

All Japanese leave their sandals at the door before they enter a place of worship, and before entering their homes. It is considered very impolite to step on their matresses with shoes on the feet.

JAPAN.—CUSTOMS IN TOKIO. 47

It was noticed that some of the women had their teeth blackened and eyebrows shaven. We were informed that these were married women, and that they do this to avoid the attraction of men. The single women do not have this distinction.

In company with Rev. Paul D. Berger of the American Presbyterian Mission, we took a trip to Tokio, the capital, and called at different missions, among others that of the Evangelical Association of America, where we found some

(Original Photo.)
JAPANESE DINNER. EATING MACARONI.

dear brethren, and indeed it seemed to me like home. Rev. G. E. Dienst is a dear Christian worker, and we believe he, with his dear wife and children, has the work at heart. In a later call we spent some time with them and were permitted to attend service with them in their church, although we could not understand anything in their language. We were also happy to meet with Rev. T. W. Foegeline, the Presiding Elder of that district. Our prayer is that God may bless them in their labors, as they have strong opposition to contend with, and besides this, they have left many friends in their native country and denied themselves the luxury of a home for the sake of Christ and the salvation of the poor heathen. We were permitted to spend one day with Rev. Dienst in and about the city, visiting points of interest.

Indeed the city is quite different from those in our country. There are many little shops and their keepers are very polite, as they sit on their mattresses and invite strangers in. We stopped together at a Japanese inn, but the accommodations were not fully as satisfactory to us as those of our American hotels. They have neither chairs nor tables, but sit on mattresses. We anxiously waited for something to eat. Rev. Dienst called again and again for our meal which we finally received. We had nothing but chopsticks with which to eat, and as we were not accustomed to their use, we had considerable trouble in eating. The best we could do was to lick our chopsticks. The natives at last took pity on us and brought us spoons with which to eat eggs. They did all in their power to make the meal pleasant and agreeable.

We visited the crematory where nineteen bodies were being cremated, and although it was horrible to look upon, yet it was much better than the mode we afterward saw employed in India.

The worst feature of Japanese social life is the business of houses of ill fame and prostitution, licensed and protected by the government. Certain portions of the city are set apart for this purpose. We were informed that 2,500 girls in one part of the city are licensed prostitutes, and that there are a number of such designated localities in the city.

Girls are sold by their parents, and men buy them and speculate on them, having places where they exhibit them

ST. ANNA'S CHURCH, JERUSALEM. (Original Photo.)

JAPAN.—MIYANOSHITA.

by the hundreds, as our merchants exhibit goods in their display windows. They are finely dressed and made to appear just as attractive as possible; then their owners go out on the streets and solicit for them. O, what a sad condition of affairs! We were informed that it is not considered so low and immoral by them as it is by us in America, and the fact that we put a higher estimate on female virtue, is, without doubt, due to the influence of Christianity.

(*Original Photo.*)
MIYANOSHITA, HOT SPRINGS AND BATH HOUSES.

Noticing a bath room as we passed along the streets in company with our guide and several Americans, we saw that the front of it was open to such an extent that all who traveled the streets could see that men and women were together in the same bath room. There were about ten or fifteen of both sexes in the room at the same time in a state of nudity, engaged in bathing and rubbing each other down. We were informed that such was the custom in that country and no one thinks evil of it. In approaching some of the hotels, especially in Miyanoshita, which is a very prominent place in Japan, women come and, for a small fee, offer to shampoo you, which consists of stripping the clothes from the bodies of their subjects, washing and rubbing them, and

JAPANESE JINRIKISHA AND TEA HOUSE. (*Original* *Photo.*)

applying friction to the extremities. This is considered proper, and is attended with no evil or impure thoughts or motives. Hence it requires presence of mind, purpose of heart and combined firmness to resist the evils with which one comes in contact. Japanese may have as many wives as they can support. These they can purchase for about 100 to 200 yen each, we were informed.

As the war was raging, many military movements could be observed. Cavalry, infantry and artillery, together with

JAPAN.—ITS PRODUCTS. 53

provision trains, were seen moving toward the battle fields. The country was in a general stir, and the natives were anxious to learn with which side the strangers were sympathizing. Children were parading the streets and shouting, while many pictures were exhibited giving illustrations and diagrams of battle fields. Many looked upon strangers with suspicion.

(*Original Photo.*)
JAPANESE MODE OF GREETING.

The Japanese are very polite and sociable in their communication with each other. When they meet they do not shake hands as we do, but bow very low two or three times, and in a most graceful manner, as shown in the illustration.

The country in general is rather mountainous, but in the valleys and on the plains the land is very productive. The principal products are tea, rice, wheat, buckwheat and some Indian corn, while vegetables grow in abundance. There are various kinds of fruit in Japan, but they are entirely of a different quality from either ours or those of the tropics. Women, as well as men, are seen out in the fields gathering rice, which is sometimes tied in tree-tops in order to have it out of the reach of water, that it may become dry and cured.

TEA PLANTATION. (*Taken from Photo.*)

Men and women carry almost everything on their heads in baskets. Even dirt and stone are carried in this way. It is stated that while their railroad was being constructed, the company introduced the wheelbarrow; but the natives would not use it, until urged upon; even then one would take hold of the handles while another took hold of the wheel, and in this way they carried the dirt out on the dump. Nothing is seen of our manner of cultivating the soil. The ground is mostly grubbed and spaded.

JAPAN.—FUJIYAMA.

From almost any point on the island, by looking up, one will be able to see Fujiyama, the great goddess of Japan. The peak is 12,365 feet above the sea level, and is covered with snow during the entire year. Some distance from Fujiyama are other smaller peaks, one of which has a smoky appearance, caused by the numerous hot springs. Some of these peaks are covered with grass, others with small timber, and a few with brush, all plainly visible to the eye in going

(Original Photo.)
JAPANESE DRAY.—FUJIYAMA IN THE DISTANCE.

from Miyanoshita toward Fuji. It being the fall of the year, the leaves were changing their color, and it was indeed a beautiful sight. Japan is claimed by many to be the most scenic and wonderfully picturesque country in the world. Many things there are too mysterious for man to understand.

The country and people are so different from our own. Different methods are employed in doing their work. In building houses, they frequently begin at the roof and then build downward. Noticing a two-story building in course of erection, we saw that the workmen first put up a scaffold, upon which they built the upper floors and the roof. That being completed, they began to work on the foundation. The native carpenters draw the plane and saw toward them; yet they are fine mechanics and their work is very nicely done when completed.

(*Original Photo.*)
STREET SCENE, SHOWING ENGLISH CHURCH, YOKOHAMA.

Their cemeteries present, to Americans, an unusual appearance, the graves being so close together. The Japanese bury their dead in an upright posture, in a box about two feet square and four feet long. Sometimes the poorer classes are buried in barrels. In the European and American cemeteries in Japan it is different. Monuments can be seen

JAPANESE IDOLS.

to mark the resting places of missionaries, consuls and seamen, with inscriptions stating the nationality of the deceased. Whenever you look into the cemeteries you may see that which is likely to move the heart with sympathy.

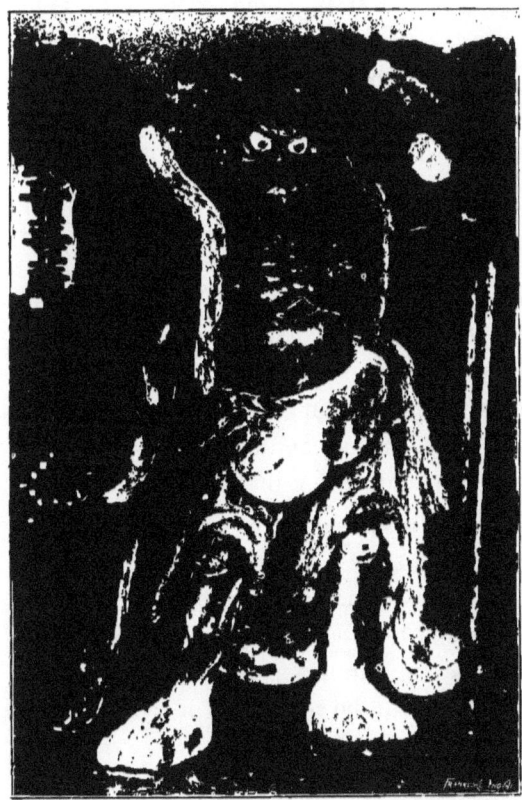
(*Original Photo.*)
JAPANESE IDOL.

How little do our own American people appreciate the blessings of living in such an enlightened Christian country where they have the advantages of early instructions; and, best of all, where the true and living God is acknowledged as the only God to be worshiped.

Along the way and at crossroads many little images are seen cut in stone and other material, many of them being no larger than a common-sized cat, including various kinds of animals, such as foxes, cattle and dogs. Instead of looking to such things made by the hands of men, as they do, we look up to Him who smiles upon us. O, blessed thought! How true we should be to Him and how we should love and obey Him as His children. O, how quickly these people should flee to Him!

This country is yet far from being brought to God. There are many temples, and the natives are very loyal to their gods and their mode of worship. This is a country that is visited by thousands of people from all parts of the world every year. The writer was able to learn many things by coming in contact with a number of these visitors.

The natives work hard. Poor women, some of them mothers, are out on the streets drawing carts so heavily loaded that we would consider it impossible for the women to move them. Some are half naked and are so poor that they follow strangers a long distance for the purpose of begging. Many poor, blind women are on the streets, singing their songs to attract attention, and offering their services in any way by which they may earn a little money.

Some women carry their little children on their backs, and in many cases they are like slaves, being compelled to do the hardest kind of work, such as coaling the large ocean steamers; but with all this they seem to be contented. How grateful we should feel in our own grand country! Our young people especially should be thankful for the privileges and blessings which they enjoy.

Many European people are living in Japan. The Clariden Hotel is a mission home where all ministers and missionaries are granted special rates of two yen per day.

(*Original Photo.*)
RUINS OF ST. JOHN'S CHURCH, EPHESUS.

"We are living, we are dwelling,
　In a grand and awful time;
In an age on ages telling—
　To be living is sublime.
Hark! the waking up of nations,
　Gog and Magog to the fray;
Hark! what soundeth? Is creation
　Groaning for her latter day?"

CHAPTER VII.

KOBE, NAGASAKI AND HONG KONG.

WIDOWED MOTHER AND CHILD—KOBE—INLAND SEA—NAGASAKI—
CITY OF THE DEAD—CHILD TAKEN FROM ITS MOTHER—
WAR VESSELS—SERVICES ON BOARD SHIP—
HONG KONG—SEAMEN'S MISSION—
STREET SIGHTS.

N Saturday, November 10th, we started by ship for Kobe and Nagasaki, boarding the ship Ancona, Peninsular & Oriental line. We found good quarters for the voyage. My attention was soon attracted to a woman who came aboard dressed in mourning, accompanied by a child, apparently about six years of age. Both the lady and child were pleasant and talkative, and we soon learned that the father, mother and child had come from India to Japan for a change of climate and for the father's health. While on the way the father, Mr. F. A. Nalor (an English officer in India), took a severe cold, which resulted in a more serious attack in Yokohama, from the effects of which he afterwards died, leaving the mother and child to return alone to their former home. The little girl took a fancy to the writer and asked her mother, "May I give Mr. Lambert a kiss? I have no pa to kiss anymore." The mother said, "O my child, don't talk so." The scene was touching. As we were on the same vessel for a

long distance, Mrs. Nalor repeatedly related to us her sad experience in Japan, which deeply aroused our sympathy for herself and child.

We arrived at Kobe, where we again met some of those with whom we had crossed the Pacific, and spent some time in visiting the mountains and temples along the seacoast.

Leaving Kobe we sailed through the Inland Sea, with its magnificent scenery, small islands and narrow straits, guided all along the way by its numerous light-houses. In the night it reminded us of sailing over the sea of time, and the dangers to which all are exposed, but, as the poet says, "There are lights along the shore." The great flash light is Jesus the Savior of the world, who lights the way and keeps us in the proper course, thus preventing ship-wreck.

Upon arrival at Nagasaki, November 16th, we found that it was a grand place. The bay is surrounded with beautiful mountain scenery. Many cemeteries are seen on all sides, giving it the appearance of a city of the dead. Here many Christians were massacred. Here again women were engaged in coaling the ships.

Before leaving Nagasaki we saw a small party on deck, consisting of a Chinaman, his Japanese wife and child, and his wife's mother. When the signal was given for all the passengers to get aboard, and for all those who were not passengers to go ashore, the Chinaman took charge of the child, while the two women, weeping, went on shore. We were afterwards informed that the Chinaman had, besides his Japanese wife in Nagasaki, a wife and family in Hong Kong, China, where he was engaged in business. It was his custom to take the children of his Japanese wife to his Chinese family in Hong Kong. What would our American mothers

SERVICES ON SHIPBOARD.

think of such treatment? The child, which was about eighteen months old, caused the father much trouble, day and night, during the voyage, although it was given the most watchful attention. We sighted several large war vessels during this voyage, looking after the interests of their respective governments.

(Original Photo.)
JAPANESE WORSHIP.

In the evening card-playing was introduced in which we were requested to take part but refused, and soon a religious service was in progress, consisting of talking and singing.

Sunday, November 19.—A pleasant day. We were requested to preach to the passengers and consented. Soon the dining room was prepared, and a pulpit, with the English flag covering it, was arranged. The Lord assisted us in recommending Him as the chief of all, and we had a good time.

Upon arriving at Hong Kong, we spent some time in visiting. The war was raging and there was no encouragement to go north or into the interior. Troops were expected and therefore not much time was spent at this point.

Hong Kong is an English colony. Many Europeans are doing business here. There are also many Chinamen here, but since the pestilence of 1894, some of the Chinese houses are not occupied, and even a few of the streets are closed. In the evening a steam launch went from one ship to another to take passengers to the Seamen's Mission, free of cost. A number of us availed ourselves of this privilege. It was not strictly religious, rather more of the nature of a concert, and we considered it rather degrading. It was a Christian mission simply in name and not in reality.

Throughout the city, women were seen sitting on the sides of the streets, sewing, knitting and washing. In fact all kinds of work is done on the streets. Tinners, blacksmiths, and shoemakers were seen sitting along the walks, working at their trades.

Many of the women can scarcely walk, their feet being cramped and no larger than those of a child; fortunately, however, the law at present prohibits deforming the feet as of old, yet it requires labor and time to reform them from their ancient customs.

We attended a heathen service, where the offering to the idol consisted of a pig, weighing eighty or a hundred pounds, and two fowls. These were roasted and placed in a standing position, with their mouths wide open toward a burning light. Near them were several dishes of eatables. One of the priests was engaged in reading and another in burning

CHINA.—HONG KONG.

incense, the two turning alternately to the idol and the offerings. Two attendants played small timbrels while another blew a small fife.

Looking into their meat markets as we passed along the streets, it was noticed that the carcasses of animals were roasted whole, and that the meat, when sold to customers, was ready to be eaten.

At Hong Kong all passengers for Singapore and Colombo were transferred to another ship.

LIGHT HOUSE.

CHAPTER VIII.

SINGAPORE AND COLOMBO.

SERVICES ON BOARD SHIP—SINGAPORE—SEA SHELLS—ALL KINDS OF WORK DONE ON THE STREETS—CHATS WITH PEOPLE OF DIFFERENT NATIONALITIES—POOR MEALS— MISSION SERVICE—PENANG—ISLAND OF SUMATRA—COLOMBO.

WE left for Singapore on the 23d of November. Sunday, November 25.—It was becoming very warm, as we were going southward. Services were held on board in the forenoon, and also in the evening. By request of the crew, we spoke to them in the evening and the time was spent quite pleasantly. A missionary lady also took part in the services. It is hoped some good impressions were made.

We arrived at Singapore November 27th and found a good home for $1.00 per day. This is a very warm country, only 80 miles from the equator. Nearly all here are dressed in white and have special hats to protect them from sunstroke. The inhabitants represent about all nationalities.

Many of the Indians are naked, with the exception of something about the loins. They seem to be very poor. The natives use the Japanese jinrikishas here. There are also many one-horse carriages used here, but the heaviest loads are drawn by bullocks. They look very much like our

SINGAPORE.- STREET SCENES.   67

Jersey cattle, with the exception of the humps on their necks and their very straight horns.

Many sea-shells of all kinds, shapes, sizes and colors are brought to this point by the natives, and offered for sale to strangers. It is almost impossible to walk along the sidewalks because of the many who are working and transacting all kinds of business; others carry loads of goods on their backs and we have even seen some carry hot stoves in this

(Original Photo.)
TWO SEATED JINRIKISHA SHOWING COOLIE WITH STRAW CAPE.

manner, setting them down at different places and baking pan cakes to sell. Others heat their flat irons on the sidewalks, and create a smoke which is very unpleasant. Time passes more quickly when one can meet with people of different nationalities, as is the case here, and have a chat with a

German, a Russian, an Irishman, a Scotchman, or an Englishman. Many soldiers and warships were here.

The meals in this country are not very appetizing to an American. The landlady asked us why we did not eat, and was told that we were not hungry; but the fact was, the meals were not good enough to make one hungry. To encourage us she said, "I do my own cooking and it is very good." As a general thing Chinamen are the cooks. She said,

AN ORIENTAL BURDEN BEARER. *(Taken from Photo.)*

"Do you like macaroni soup? Macaroni soup is very good, just wait till dinner and you will see. I will cook it myself." But during the time that the soup was being prepared, she was going in and out, attending to it so as to make it *very good*. She would come into the sitting room and sitting on the sofa in a half reclining position would call the dog to her, and, parting his hair, pick off the fleas, lice, nits, etc., that were on his body, and throw them on the floor, and then was off to the kitchen to see after the soup. Does the reader blame us for not eating *macaroni soup* under such circumstances? Such is life in the Orient at many places, for indeed, this is not the only locality where such things occur.

We visited here some of the missions, as well as the Methodist church, where we enjoyed a very good service. The minister had for his text Rom. 1:16, "I am not ashamed of the gospel of Christ," etc. He impressed upon his hearers the importance of not being ashamed of Jesus. Among other things he said, When we take each letter composing the name JESUS as the beginning of a word we make up the following sentence: "Just Exactly Suits Us Sinners;" as to how true this is, every Christian heart can respond.

We also attended services at the cathedral on Sunday, and although it is an immense building, yet only twenty-four persons were present. There is much to be seen and heard, yet sin and degradation prevail the world over. Surely the world was lost in darkness and sin, but Jesus came to seek and to save all. O, blessed thought!

December 12. The weather is very warm. We set sail for Colombo, Ceylon, on the steamer Ravanna. On board we met the American party, eight in number, under charge of Prof. Clark, with which we had at different times traveled. The ship's crew was a nice party, composed mostly of English people. We came up the strait of Malacca, which gave us a splendid view of the country. The ship anchored for a short time at Penang which gave our party the opportunity of riding out several miles through the celebrated cocoanut and banana groves. Many other tropical fruits are grown here, and the profuse vegetation afforded us splendid sightseeing. We noticed that notches had been cut by the natives on both sides of many of the trees to facilitate climbing them when gathering the fruit.

Leaving Penang we passed through the strait between the Malay Peninsula and the island of Sumatra, where it is said war has been raging for about twenty years, more or less, between the Dutch and the natives.

We were now sailing on the Indian Ocean. The sea was very calm and the weather warm. Nearly all the passengers

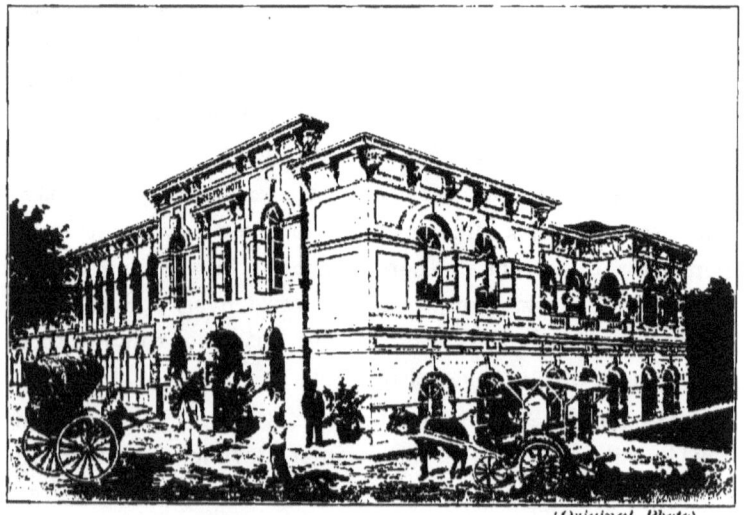

(*Original Photo*).
BRISTOL HOTEL, COLOMBO, CEYLON.

and crew were dressed in white clothing and large sun hats. We prepared our baggage to be forwarded, on the same ship, to Bombay, to await our arrival there, while we changed for Madras and Calcutta, India.

We arrived at Colombo, Ceylon, on the 18th of December. Here many large ocean steamers meet in the same way that trains meet in our large union depots. One arrived from London *en route* for China, while one was there from

CEYLON. COLOMBO. 71

China bound for London; one for Australia, and one to Australia; and one for Calcutta. Though thousands of miles to sail and in nearly all kinds of weather, these ships make their time as the schedule requires. A wonderful system of navigation is found on these long lines, and the greatest care and the best accommodations are given to passengers. Ceylon is noted for its cinnamon gardens.

The streets of Colombo are full of natives, with bullock-carts loaded with various kinds of merchandise, anxious to sell their goods.

A SCENE IN THE TROPICS.

CHAPTER IX.

Madras.

TRANSFERRED TO THE KHEDIVE — SAILING ON BAY OF BENGAL — POPULATION OF MADRAS — SEAT OF GOVERNMENT — COMPARED WITH OTHER NATIONS — NINETY TO NINETY-FIVE PER CENT. POOR PEOPLE — WOMEN CARRYING BRICK AND MORTAR — EAR, NOSE, AND NECK JEWELS — LOW WAGES — BUILDINGS — BUNGALS — HUTS — PENITENTIARY — AN AMERICAN IN PRISON — DANGERS OF OUR YOUNG PEOPLE.

ADRAS, India, was our next point. The passengers for this place were transferred to the "Khedive," while those bound for other points were taken to vessels sailing for the several ports they desired to visit.

Our ship left Colombo for Madras and Calcutta on the 21st of December. A number of missionaries were on board. We sailed north into the bay of Bengal and on the 24th of December arrived at Madras.

Madras is the largest city in Southern India, is situated on the coast, and is the seat of government of the Madras Presidency. This territory contains 138,000 square miles and is thickly populated. The native states of Cochin and Travancore occupy part of the south-western coast. The statistics show that Cochin has an area of 1,361 square miles, more than two-thirds of which is under cultivation, and contains a population of 600,728. The average population per square mile is 441; but in some parts it has as many as 1,430 per square mile. The population consists of 429,324 Hindoos, 136,361 Christians, 33,344 Mohammedans, and 1,249 Jews. Thus far the Christians comprise twenty-three per cent. of the whole population.

The state of Travancore is the most important native state in the government of Madras. It has an area of 6,722 square miles, about 4,000 square miles of which is cultivated,

MADRAS HARBOR AND PIER. *(Original Photo.)*

and has a population of nearly two and a half millions, which gives an average of 357 to a square mile. There are some places where the population per square mile is as dense as 1,318, 1,170, and 1,135. More than one-fifth of the population consists of Christians.

We Americans ought to be grateful to God for the country He has given us and for the blessings we enjoy. No wonder there are so many poor people (from ninety to ninety-five per cent.) in Southern India, and that they are so zealous in soliciting alms. Many poor, aged and crippled people are seen along the streets, crying and begging for alms. Imagine in our state and country an average of 357 or 441, or, as in some districts, 1,430 inhabitants per square mile; what would or could we do under such conditions? These statistics were taken from the official book called "Jubilee of the Queen Empress," and must, therefore, be accepted as correct. Some of our readers may say, " What is the population per square mile in the United States ? I will give a table showing the density of population of different countries, which will give us some idea of our noble country, a better than which there is none.

        India has from 357 to 441 per square mile.
        England has - - - 312 per square mile.
        Germany has - 237 per square mile.
        Belgium has - - - 540 per square mile.
        U. S. including Alaska, 17 per square mile.

This ought to encourage the fathers, mothers and children of this country, and make them loyal and patriotic, and above all, grateful and obedient to God. The United States is regarded by all the world as the grandest and greatest of all countries, and as a mighty nation.

The streets are full of people and bullock-carts; natives are poorly clad; women do hard work, such as carrying brick and mortar up on high buildings, while others go about the streets with baskets on their heads and pick up the droppings of the bullocks, which are dried and used for fuel. The natives keep and raise their little calves and bullocks on their front porches.

The women wear as much jewelry as they can afford, in their ears and noses and around their necks. Their ears are frequently torn by the rings coming in contact with some object while the owners are at work. The jewels are replaced by piercing new holes. Many of the native women carry the entire possessions of their families in jewels, and when a purchase is made, they pay the price of their purchase in jewelry.

Many follow you and are anxious to do you service in order to earn a few annas. Even a kind look and word is

MADRAS POST OFFICE.   (*Original Photo.*)

highly appreciated. The wages are very low, and the best mechanics and leading contractors receive only from one rupee to one rupee and two or four annas per day. The common laborers are paid proportionately and there is not much work to be had even at these wages.

BUILDINGS.

The buildings are mostly of brick, and a few buildings, such as the High Court and Post Office, with flash lights in the spires, make a very fine appearance. The churches are as fine as any, but they are without windows or glass, having in their place blind-doors, which are opened during services. They have large bungals in all the churches with which to fan the congregation during services, in very warm weather, the bungal being operated by a coolie who sits on the outside and pulls the rope which is attached to it. As a general thing churches and all buildings of any importance have a large plot of ground around them planted with trees and shrubs, with a large walk inclosing the whole premises. Many of the best private houses are the same, and are mostly one-story high, built of brick and plastered and often whitewashed. Many of them have a front projection, with heavy round pillars underneath, which make a fine appearance. Then there are other buildings of a poorer class, down to the huts in which the natives live, in their part of town. The roofs are principally made of clay-tile, as in all the Orient, while others are thatched.

THE PENITENTIARY.

Rev. Shaw and myself made a visit to the penitentiary in which, at this time, were about 800 convicts. We were taken to the gallows, the whipping post, and the dark dungeons, where a number of prisoners are kept. We were also shown the large tread mill, where many are put on to run the machinery. The officer that was with us referred us to an American that was among the convicts. Stepping up to him and giving him my hand I said, "Are you an American?" He answered, "Yes." I said, "What does this mean; you an American, so far from home and in such a place?" The young man, blushing, said, "When I was a boy I ran away from home and went to sea and finally landed in India. I

(Original Photo.)

was unfortunate and became crippled. Afterwards I violated the laws and now I must pay the penalty." I asked him where he was from and he told me "Cincinnati, O." I asked, "Is your father yet alive?" He answered, "As far as I know, my father and mother are alive. My father is a man of good standing in that city." I also asked him if his parents knew that he was here, and he told me, "Not unless the American consul has informed them, but I think not." He showed sorrow and said, "O, if I had only stayed at home I would not be in such a place." I expressed my sympathies for him and bade him good-bye. The officer then told me his name and also the charges against him. The name was Monbebars. There were two charges against him and he therefore had to remain two terms, one of six months, and the other of twelve months. He had already been there three months. O, what lessons the young men and women of this country should learn not to complain so soon of home, of father and mother, and imagine they know more than their parents.

Many of our young folks have good privileges and fine educations, and yet they are not careful enough, sometimes ignoring the advice of parents, thus doing them grievous wrong. The young people of our land often look upon their parents as old fogies in their views, and doings, and modes of religious worship, but ah, how true that the old parents and grandparents were much truer and better, and often more honest than many of the present day. Children and young people should remember the command: "Honor thy father and thy mother: that thy days may be long upon the land which the Lord thy God giveth thee," which is the first commandment with promise. Exodus 20:12.

CHAPTER X.

Mission Work.

MISSIONARIES — $15.00 PER YEAR — FURNISHES ALL — WHO WERE THE MEN OF GOD — THEOSOPHY — MISSIONS — CASTES — CHRISTMAS SONGS — MEETING OF MISSIONARIES — REV. HALICHAM BANNAGEE.

MISSIONARY must understand the language and dialect of the natives to the extent that he is able to teach them the fundamental principles of our religion. They say, "Where is your God? Show Him to us and we will believe." They must be taught that there is a God, and that He is a rewarder of those who diligently seek Him.

Many of the natives are very intelligent and hold with tenacity to their peculiar heathen views which must be supplanted by sound doctrines, if they are to be won for Christ. To do this requires grace, knowledge and wisdom, and many faithful workers have worn their lives away without seeing much apparent result. This should not discourage others from taking up the work where they have left off, especially since we know that it has taken hundreds of years for some other nations to become Christianized. It ought to be the prayer of all Christian people of this country that God would bless the mission work, and all those who labor therein so faithfully. We ought to contribute in that direction all we can and God will reward us for it.

LEND A HELPING HAND.

We were informed by Rev. Gurnsay, of Madras, that the chief and best method of converting the natives to our Christian religion, is to get the children under Christian influence, and to accomplish this end it requires more men and more means.

One institution is working on the plan of taking native children and keeping them under their influence until grown. There are many from heathen families that can be had by simply asking. A boy can be supported, clothed, fed, and

MADRAS CATAMARANS.

receive a good schooling for $15.00 per year. "O," said the poor missionary, "if the rich people in America only knew how much good they could do with a little money! If a man would agree to furnish $15.00 per year, he or the missionaries could select a bright young boy who would be kept and taught the gospel until he was qualified for a good Christian life, the child to be named after the man that furnishes the money for his education. For instance, if a child eight years old were taken and kept, for ten years, at a cost of $150.00, his benefactor would then have a boy, or rather a man, bearing his own name and working for God in a dark heathen country. Ought not such things attract the attention of our Christian people and should not every one ask: "What can I do both at home and in foreign lands for my fallen brethren?"

There are many from our country here, husbands, wives and children, laboring for the Lord. It appears that many live too high to reach the poor people, while others are right amongst them. As a certain missionary said: "O, I am married to this country and this people. Many look at these people as though they were ignorant, and incapable of being taught." Referring to Bible subjects and to many prominent Bible characters, he asked the question, "Who were they?" The answer came, "Asiatics; and what other nations now are, is largely due to what Asia gave them, long, long ago." How true this is.

One thing is threatening the success of the Christian work here and that is the doctrine of Theosophy. I heard Mrs. Besant, an American lady of great talent and influence, lecture among the Hindoos on that subject. She declared it to be the coming religion, comparing the eastern castes with the western classes, and made a strong impression on the natives.

It appears that the world is open for the gospel, and those poor people long to be led and helped, and when we see that they indeed are in need of help, in every way, it moves the heart with compassion. There are some that will fall at your feet, kiss your shoes, and beg for a little rice to satisfy

CHRISTMAS EVE IN MADRAS.

their hunger. The question comes, What can be done for such?

There are many mission societies in Madras, and great efforts are being put forth to convert the natives to Christianity.

The natives appear very clever and intelligent, many of them having but one view regarding religious worship. They are divided into castes and are nearly all known by their caste mark on the forehead. Most of them are poorly clad, and indeed many are almost naked. We had the privilege of attending some of their religious meetings, and they appear very earnest in their different forms of worship.

COOLIE GIRL. (*Original Photo.*)

On Christmas eve a number of Hindoo boys, in small companies, marched through the town singing songs. Next morning, about three or four o'clock, we heard music, and upon inquiry, were told that it was the custom of the Christian people to go through the streets of that large city on Christmas night, singing merry Christmas songs, announcing that a Savior is born. We listened, and listened, and it lifted our thoughts heavenward. Our thoughts then reverted to the Christian customs of the people in our own land; how indifferent many of them are! Here the Christian people are very earnest and enthusiastic, and are using their lives for God and His cause. We were informed that on Christmas night nearly all the churches call their singers out to sing in memory of the angels.

We attended a number of the services of the different churches here which were very good. The Salvation Army is also doing much in this country, and it is claimed by many that the most effectual work done here is done by them.

It was a source of pleasure to meet a number of our country men and women in the mission field, among whom were Rev. King, Rev. Gurnsay, and Rev. J. W. West of Ohio; Miss Ida Skimmer from Oregon, and Miss Penny of Valparaiso, Ind. These noble Christian workers have left their homes and comforts for Jesus' sake. On one occasion, while I was eating supper, five persons, three gentlemen and two ladies, came in and took seats. They were busily engaged in conversation, and after the meal was eaten I excused myself and went to my room. After I had left they inquired of the landlord who I was and to what nationality I belonged. When they learned that I was an American, they sent for me and I soon found that they were all Americans: Rev. Newcomer and wife, from Shelbyville, Ind., Rev. Frank and wife, from Lafayette, Ind., and Rev. Fuller, of Boston, Mass. I also met Rev. Shaw and family, who were on their way back to America. Such meetings with Christian people, in a foreign land, are very highly appreciated; and those dear missionaries will never be forgotten.

We were permitted to listen to a native minister by the name of Rev. Halicham Bannagee. There was a large attendance at this meeting. His subject was taken from Isaiah, "*I saw the Lord.*" It was an able and an interesting discourse, and it is hoped that the good seed so earnestly sown will grow until all his hearers may see the Lord.

(*Original Photo.*)
WOMEN CLEANING HEADS.

Many of the American and European missionaries are dressed in native costumes. It is said men wear their hair long to gain the confidence of the natives. O, how simple and Christ-like it looks to see them stoop down and sit together with these people in humility, having all things in common.

It is no small position to be a missionary in these dark countries. In our own enlightened, Christian country, if one can sing, pray and talk to the people, he may be able to do a great deal of good, because there are but very few people that do not at least theoretically believe in one God and in Jesus Christ as the Savior of the world; but in heathen countries it is different.

"NINETY TO NINETY-FIVE PER CENT. ARE POOR PEOPLE."

  Have pity on them, for their life
   Is full of grief and care;
  You do not know one-half the woes
   The very poor must bear;
  You do not see the silent tears
   By many a mother shed,
  As childhood offers up the prayer—
   "Give us our daily bread."

(Taken from Photo.)
THE FIELD OF BLOOD, OR VALLEY OF HINNOM.

> No action, whether foul or fair,
> Is ever done, but it leaves somewhere
> A record, written by fingers ghostly
> As a blessing or a curse; and mostly
> In the greater weakness or greater strength
> Of the acts which follow it; till at length
> The wrongs of ages are redressed,
> And the justice of God made manifest.
> —Longfellow.

CHAPTER XI.

MADRAS TO CALCUTTA.

MEETING THE AMERICAN PARTY — SERVICES ON BOARD — HUGLI RIVER — THE IMMENSE WASH OF THE HUGLI — SAGAR ISLAND — DANGEROUS PASSAGE — JUNGLES — MET MANY SHIPS AND BOATS — CALCUTTA.

SUNDAY, January 6, 1895, we left Madras for Calcutta, taking passage on the ship Mirzapore, and again met the party of Americans on board. Services were held on the ship, at which time some singing was done which was very encouraging to all. The sea was quite calm while sailing up the bay of Bengal. Our vessel was one of the largest steamers on these waters, smaller boats being usually used for coast trips to and from points on the bay.

On January 8 we entered the channel of the Hugli river, which is one of the outlets of the Ganges, and others of the Hindoo, so-called sacred rivers. We are now 120 miles from Calcutta. As we proceed up the river the water becomes very muddy. This is a very dangerous channel to pass on account of the immense quantities of sediment being continually deposited by the river, and on this account skillful pilots are required to steer clear of the many obstructions. It is estimated that it would require about 1,500 large ships every day to carry the sand and earth that the Hugli takes to the sea. Hence, the land is gradually drifting seaward. Ships once went forty miles above Calcutta, where now there is no passage. The first land to be seen is a low strip forming the southern boundary of Sagar island. The portion near the sea consists of thick jungles and marshes, where tigers and other wild beasts are numerous.

Once a year on this island a great bathing festival is held, called Ganga Sagar, to commemorate the supposed descent of the Ganges from heaven to restore to life the 60,000 sons of King Sagar. Here, too, mothers, in fulfillment

THE HUGLI RIVER.

of vows, used to offer their young children to the Ganges to be devoured by the crocodiles, until the practice was stopped by the British government. The mouth of the Hugli river is so wide that land cannot be seen on both sides at the same time, but the channel gradually becomes narrower as we proceed up stream. About forty miles from Calcutta is the James and Mary, a dangerous shoal, caused by the sand brought down by the Damodar and Rupnarayan rivers. If a ship touches the bottom at this place, she is immediately

APPROACHING CALCUTTA.

pushed over by the strong current. In the space of half an hour even large ships have been known to almost disappear, numbers of them having been lost.

The soil gradually becomes richer; trees, rice-fields, palm and bamboo groves become common. At length the port is reached. The long tiers of shipping, the fort rising from the great Maidan, and the domes, steeples, and noble public buildings of Calcutta beyond, gradually unfold their beauty. The traveler really feels that he is approaching the city of palaces.

CHAPTER XII.

CALCUTTA.

CITY OF PALACES—"A GLOBE TROTTER"—BATHING IN THE SACRED RIVER—MISSION SERVICE—BURNING GNATT—INFANT WEDDINGS—WIDOWHOOD—TOMBSTONE OF AN AMERICAN, AND A BROTHER'S WORDS.

HIS is a large city, containing 840,130 inhabitants. Hugli, across the river, united to Calcutta by a floating bridge, contains 130,000 inhabitants. Many visitors are seen in this city at the hotels in the evening. We were introduced to an American "Globe Trotter," as they are frequently called, whose name was Charles Randell, from New York. The young man started on the 26th of January, 1894, to make a tour around the world on foot, in two years, for a wager of $20,000.00. He has had wonderful experiences, and was then carrying with him compliments and government seals of every country through which he had come. He intended to leave Calcutta in a short time and, if successful, expected to reach New York by October, 1895. Mr. Randell is a strong, robust young man, twenty-four years of age, and has had some thrilling experiences in some of the dangerous places through which he passed. It seems strange that a young man would venture out on such a tour entirely

unprotected, risking his life at every step. We felt sorry to see him, thus recklessly, further expose himself. We also met another American, a gentleman from Scranton, Penna.

On the 11th of January, a company of us went down to the banks of the Hugli, where the natives worship the river, regarding it as very sacred. They bathe, pray, slap the

HIGH COURT, CALCUTTA.

water, throwing it over their heads, facing the sun, and, with folded hands, pray aloud. There are hundreds and hundreds of them, men, women and children. Some immerse their children and then pray, while others scatter flowers upon the waters. They seem very devoted, and leave no ceremony in their peculiar worship, unperformed.

The weather is very warm, and during the day people go out but little; in the evening, however, the city is all astir.

CREMATORY.

In company with two other gentlemen, we visited the "Burning Gnatt," where the bodies of the dead are burned. Six bodies were there at that time, and we passed one on the street. The body of the deceased is wrapped in a sheet, and carried on a kind of bier. A little ditch is made in the earth or ashes, sticks are laid over this first crosswise and then lengthwise, and in this manner the funeral pile, about four feet long, is built up until a few feet high. The corpse is then laid on the pile and more fuel put on both sides, and over it, the legs being bent under the body at the knees. The face is left uncovered. The administering priest and the wife of the husband prepare some food, usually rice mixed with vegetables, which is then put into and upon the mouth of the dead man, by his wife, who next takes a handful of thatch, lights it with fire, carries it around the corpse three times, and then holding it for a moment to the mouth of the dead body, applies the flames to the funeral pile which is soon ablaze. The foreman of the crematory, speaking English, said to us, "How glad that woman would be to be burned with her husband, but the law forbids it now; formerly this was done." There were five or six bodies burned during the time we were here.

A woman was seen walking back and forth, wringing her hands and crying, and seemed to be in deep agony. We inquired, "What does that mean?" They told us, "The body at her side is that of her husband." O, how sad! In this way they are burned by the thousand. Every day such scenes as we have described can be seen. After the body

(Original Photo.) Tomb of Absalom. St. James. Zacharias.
THE VALLEY AND TOMBS OF JEHOSHAPHAT.

is burned the ashes are thrown into the river Hugli which flows along at the side of the gnatt. The widows, of which there are twenty-one million, are never allowed to marry again. The English laws are about to change that also, and set them free.

INFANT WEDDINGS.

Many infant weddings, of which we witnessed several, take place in India. Parents contract for their children, and after they are married, keep them in charge until they attain a certain age, when they move away by themselves. If the husband should die in the meantime, the widow, though but a child, can never be married again; perhaps she may never have known her husband. It is required that widows shall lay aside all their ornaments, withdraw from society in general and live a separate and isolated life, which makes widowhood, judging from our standpoint, a very sad and lamentable life. The English government has already abolished the cruel custom of burning the widow with the dead body of her husband, and it is now making efforts to liberate her from this outcast and secluded life, and allow her to marry again just as widows in civilized countries do. There is nothing to be compared to a Christian life, a Christian death, and a Christian burial.

The air, we noticed, was full of crows, hawks and vultures, coming down in the streets of the city. No one molested them, as they are considered sacred by the Hindoos.

INSCRIPTION ON A TOMBSTONE.

Walking through the city we passed a marble yard, where tombstones were being made. In front of this yard was a slab lying in sand, at which the workmen were still employed. They place them in sand to prevent them from being broken. The inscription was as follows:—

"Emma Osborn Ambrose, born in Sharon, Mich., U. S. A., 2d of January, 1841; born again at the age of nine. Appointed to mission service, from Nebraska, July 9, 1879. Died here in the Bghai Kaven mission service, July 20, 1893.

HINDOO FESTIVAL. (*Original Photo.*)

Her parents, Ruel and Rebekah, surviving; brothers, Geo. W., of Omaha, Neb., and J. Clement, of Chicago, Ill. A brother's words: "Were parents and brothers standing by, they all would say, 'She was the best of our name.' Light after darkness."

Would to God this might be said of all that are dead and gone. "Though she is dead she yet speaketh."

THE SABBATH DAY.

Sunday, January 20, was a Sabbath day; this day, however, is not observed in the Orient as it is in our country.

RELIGION OF NEPAL.

Churches are not so well attended and places of amusement are preferred. Many of the business houses and shops are open. Theaters and the like are carried on to their utmost extent. You see traces all around that you are not in a Christian land. You see many bow to the sun, and others to the raging sea, offering their prayers in the evening, when the sun sets.

Buddhism is the religion of Nepal. Some of them have prayer wheels, which they turn with their hands or a string. Some are placed in streams and are kept constantly revolving by running water. Flags are also erected, upon which their six holy syllables are embroidered. Whenever they are blown by the wind, it counts as a repetition. The prayer mill, driven by the wind, is another device. True prayer is the heart's desire, and should be addressed to the one true and living God; all else is worthless. We are taught to pray without ceasing, not with a water-wheel or a wind-mill, but to have our affections on God and our hearts breathing to Him in prayer, making our wants known; and He who alone can hear the silent prayer, and the groanings of the honest heart, will hear and answer our petitions.

PRAYER MILL.

CHAPTER XIII.

BENARES.

RAILROAD ACCOMMODATIONS—A NICE COUNTRY—TEMPLES AND MOSQUES—BLOODY SACRIFICES—MONKEY TEMPLE—ANIMAL WORSHIP—PILGRIMS—THE TREACHEROUS LIE—A HINDOO SAYING—"SONS OF THE GANGES"—DISTANCES AND FARES—DISGRACEFUL CARVINGS—DANCING GIRLS.

N the 22d of January, at 20:59, we left Calcutta. Railroad time is not computed here as it is in America, the hours running from one to twenty-four, beginning at midnight. According to our way of counting time, 20:59 would be 8:59 P. M. The cars here are arranged in compartments, and at night only six passengers are allowed in each compartment, which gives plenty of room for all of them to lie down and sleep quite comfortably. Bunks, which are hinged to the sides of the compartments, are let down, and as they are not upholstered, those who want to be comfortable must carry blankets, pillows, etc., of their own; these are also needed at many of the hotels in this country. There are good hotel and restaurant accommodations along the railroad lines.

We passed through a nice country, growing with wheat, barley, and various agricultural products. Numerous palm groves, and mango trees, bearing a very palatable fruit, were

BENARES.—THE SACRED CITY.

seen; but there were very few buildings among them. We crossed the Ganges river, which is very wide, and in wet weather almost floods the whole surrounding country.

We arrived at Benares, the most sacred city of the Hindoos, the next day at noon. Its soil, its wells, its streams, its temples, its inhabitants, and everything in and around it are, by the Hindoos, considered sacred, or holy. Benares stands on the Ganges, and stretches about four miles

BURNING GHATT.

along the northern banks. The river, more than a third of a mile in breadth, sweeps around like a bay. Temples, mosques, palaces, and buildings of every description rise above a cliff one hundred feet high, from the summit of which a multitude of stone ghats, of great diversity, descend to the bed of the river. Hindoos, at one time, thought that the Ganges and some of the other rivers would not allow themselves to be bridged; but now there is a fine railroad bridge across the Ganges. The explanation now accepted by the ignorant, is that the British Government accomplished it through human sacrifices.

The streets of Benares are mostly crooked, and some are so narrow as not to admit carriages. Many of the houses are built of stone, some of them six stories high. In a few instances the upper stories of two buildings on opposite sides of the street are connected in such a way as to form rooms which are used as living apartments. There are shops here of every kind, and for every trade.

MONKEY TEMPLE.

Benares is noted for its enchased brass vessels, its cloths, finely embroidered with gold and silver, and its innumerable small shrines. There are in Benares about 1,500 Hindoo temples and nearly 200 mosques. In the front of the Durga temple, at the southern extremity of the city, bloody sacrifices are offered every Tuesday. A lamb is the offering. The temples, and yards surrounding them, are full of monkeys, which are fed as an act of merit. By giving a little money to the attendants you will receive a small quantity of grain, and when that is thrown down into the court yard the monkeys come from all directions, tumbling over each other fighting for their share. On entering this temple the shoes must be taken off, after which the priest comes and hangs a string of flowers around your neck, while so many of the natives follow and cause such a commotion that one is inclined to remain but a short time.

Another temple was visited, in which cows were wandering about, and it looked a little like our American barnyards. The cattle would, doubtless, have been far happier had they been in green fields. Animal worship is one of the most degrading features of Hindooism. Many places along the Ganges are considered so sacred by the Hindoos that the mere act of visiting them is supposed to possess the virtue of washing away their sins. They believe that at these places five rivers meet, but to an American, or any other civilized person, or even the natives themselves, only one is visible.

Pilgrims, separately or in crowds, are constantly seen entering or departing from Benares throughout the whole year, and especially on great festival occasions. They come from all parts of India, and many carry away with them, in small bottles, the sacred water of the Ganges. The bottles are placed in baskets, hanging from a pole, which they bear upon their shoulders. It is claimed by some that the sanctity of Benares extends from the Ganges to the Panch-kosi road. Whoever dies within this limit, or area, whether Hindoo, Mussulman, or Christian, whether pure in heart and life, or an outcast and a murderer, is sure of heaven. Hence the usurer, who has spent all his life in oppressing the poor, or he who is guilty of the foulest crimes, at the approach of death comes to Benares, and is comforted with the treacherous lie that his sins are forgiven and his soul is saved.

Intelligent Hindoos know that such hopes are false. There is a saying amongst them to this effect, "He who has guilt on his conscience will not become clean, though he wash himself until he dies, with all the waters of the Ganges, and smear himself with mountains of mud." It is stated that many of the business men of Benares bathe daily in the Ganges, and then go home to tell lies and defraud their customers. A number of the Brahmans are called "Sons of the Ganges."

DANCING GIRL. *(Original Photo.)*

Benares is 476 miles from Calcutta by rail. The fare, third-class, is six rupees. It is 945 miles from Bombay, and the fare is 12 rupees and 15 annas. From Madras the distance is 1,550 miles, and the fare is 23 rupees and 13 annas. The population of Benares is 222,500. In many of

(Taken from Photo.)
UPPER KIDRON AND MOUNT CALVARY, AS SEEN IN THE FOREGROUND.

When on Calvary I rest,
God, in flesh made manifest,
Shines in my Redeemer's face,
Full of beauty, truth, and grace.

Here I would forever stay,
Weep and gaze my soul away;
Thou art Heaven on earth to me,
Lovely, mournful Calvary.

—James Montgomery.

the temples, the most disgraceful carvings and sculptures imaginable are shown. They are life size, of both sexes, and are considered sacred, while in America they would be considered obscene, and most damnable in their sinfulness.

Next to the sacrificers, the most important persons about the temples are the dancing girls, who call themselves servants of the gods. Their profession is to be open to the embraces of persons of all castes. They are bred to this life, selected from all castes, and are frequently of respectable birth. It is a very common thing to hear of women with the belief that, to consecrate their children to the temple service will tend to their happy delivery. They make a vow, with the consent of their husbands, to devote the child, if a girl, to the service of the Pagoda, the vow being made before the child is born. In so doing they imagine that they are performing a meritorious as well as a religious duty, the infamous life to which the daughter is thus destined bringing no disgrace upon the family. According to the census in the Madras Presidency, the number of these dancing girls was 11,573. Such a condition of affairs is indeed lamentable. Oh! reader, imagine, if you can, the licensed shamelessness of this consecrated profligacy, carried on under the sanction of so-called religion, and in the full blaze of publicity, while statesmen and those at the head of a nation, with all its wise men of letters, look on unconcerned, not uttering one word of disapprobation, and not raising one finger to remove it!

CHAPTER XIV.

ALLAHABAD.

JUNCTION OF SACRED RIVERS—THOUSANDS OF PILGRIMS—BANNERS AND FLAGS FLOATING—UNDERGROUND TEMPLE—SUICIDE—BRAHMANS DROWNING — PRAYAG — INDIA PRODUCTIONS AND ANIMALS — ENGLISH OFFICERS—FORTS—SOLDIERS.

FROM Benares, we went to Allahabad, which is the capital of the North-west provinces. It is situated at the junction of the Ganges and the Jumna rivers. It is a very ancient city, and one of the principal places where the Hindoos gather to worship. The native town consists of a network of narrow streets, intersected by a few main roads. The English quarter is handsomely laid out, with broad streets, planted with trees and bordered by running streams on either side.

Thousands of pilgrims were gathered here, as is always the case the first of the year, from all parts of India; some came by train, some with their native bullock carts, others on pony carts, some on camels, and some on elephants.

The river banks were lined with people, and flags and banners were floating for miles. Thousands and thousands were here bathing and bottling the water of the Ganges. There was music in every direction; monks with long hair were sitting around with their faces smeared with clay and paint, some of them sitting on spikes driven through planks.

AN UNDERGROUND TEMPLE.

Seen from the river, the fort presents a striking appearance, crowning the point where the Ganges and the Jumna unite. Near Asoka's Pillar, steps lead down to an underground Hindoo temple. This building, dedicated to Siva, passes as the place where the river Saraswati unites with the Ganges and the Jumna. The damp walls of the chambers afford sufficient proof of its existence for the satisfaction of devotees.

SACRED TREE.

Passing through the narrow, damp passage with a guide and light, and in the presence of our friend, we came to the stump of a banyan tree, said to be fifteen centuries old, and still alive; it is here an object of worship. A light burns before it, and beside it sits a Brahman to receive the offerings. A cloth is so arranged that the tree cannot be properly seen. In reality it is merely part of a forked tree with its bark on, stuck into the ground, and it is renewed secretly by the priests when it threatens to decay. A gentleman tried the bark with his finger nail, and found it quite dry and brittle.

The temple also contains the image of a man named Makunba, a famous saint who committed suicide because he had been guilty of the great sin of having accidentally swallowed the hair of a cow, by drinking milk without first straining it.

The English officer, at the fort through which all must go to enter this underground temple, said, on inquiry, that

BRAHMANS DROWNING THEMSELVES.

every one who went in was recorded, and that on one day 30,000 had passed through, all with lights in their hands, and that only a small portion of those present outside, on the banks of the river, went in, because it required a small fee which they had not to give.

In many places soldiers and officers were present to keep order, as in the rush through the gates some tread others down, so as to get into the places of worship first.

Prayag is considered one of the most efficacious places in India for bathing. At Mela, early in the year, the point

MOUNT ZION AND THE MOUNT OF OLIVES FROM THE BETHLEHEM ROAD. *(Original Photo.)*

near the junction is crowded by thousands of pilgrims. It was the custom, until stopped by the British government, for some to drown themselves at this junction, in the supposed belief of thus securing heavenly homes. The victim went out to the middle of the stream with fellow Brahmans in a boat. One hand was tied firmly to a large earthen vessel; the other hand held a small cup. He was assisted into the water by those in the boat, the air in the empty vessel serving to keep him afloat. He then, with the cup, commenced slowly to fill the pot with water. As each cupful was added, the vessel gradually sank, until the balance was turned, when it rapidly filled, and by its weight dragged the deluded creature beneath the waters. So far from being a work of merit, it is a sin to destroy one's self.

The population of Allahabad is about 177,000.

On January 26th we started for Bombay by the way of Jubulpore. At this season of the year they were in the midst of the barley harvest. The principal crops are corn, barley, wheat, linseed, curry, and indigo. We saw several deer and large wild birds, but no wild tigers. It is said, however, that they are numerous in the jungles. We arrived at Bombay on Sunday morning.

The interior of India is full of interest to the traveler. Its soil is very productive, though poorly cultivated. It has large rivers, populous cities and beautiful scenery. The country is under British rule, and is well fortified. There are many very strong fortifications, and a large military force is maintained at an immense expense.

CHAPTER XV.

Bombay.

POPULATION — STREETS — BUILDINGS — MISSIONS — HOSPITAL FOR AGED BULLOCKS—ANT FEEDING—CHILD WIDOWS—ELEPHANTA CAVES.

TTENDING services at the Scotch church occupied our first evening in Bombay. The subject of the discourse was, "Jesus the Savior indeed." Bombay is the largest city and is situated on the finest harbor in India. The population is approximately 840,000. Hindooism is the prevailing religion; about one fifth of the inhabitants are Mohammedans; and besides these there are a number of Parsees, Jews and Christians.

The city itself consists mostly of well-built houses and broad streets, with some grand public buildings. It is claimed that Bombay was greatly enriched by the great demand for cotton during the Civil War in the United States. The fast increasing wealth and business of the city led to the erection of several magnificent buildings, among which are the Government Offices, the University Building and the G. I. P. Central railway station, said to be the finest building of its kind in the world.

One of the institutions in Bombay, which we visited, is a Pinjeapole, or hospital for old bullocks, dogs, cats, horses, sheep, goats, deer, monkeys, pigeons, chickens, ducks,

BOMBAY.—HOSPITAL FOR ANIMALS.

geese and all kinds of domestic animals, many of them in a lamentable condition, and all left here to die a natural death. While there are many diseased and crippled, some are lying among them dead, and are not buried till the following night. The dogs and cats were fighting, and many of the animals were in such a condition as to almost break one's heart to see them, although they are well taken care of. The institution and all animals kept here are considered sacred, and the

.VIEW OF BOMBAY HARBOR.

care which the keepers give them is regarded as a religious duty.

Many of our American people, who make high claims to civilization and Christianity, show far less kindness to their dumb brutes than is shown by these heathen people, upon whom they look down with the utmost contempt. Behold, what a contrast! Among our so-called Christian people a humane officer is needed to teach them their duty towards the domestic animals; among these heathen the care of a poor brute becomes a religious duty. The wise man teaches us, "The righteous showeth mercy towards his beast."

I was informed that it costs the society, to maintain this institution, between four and five thousand rupees per month. This is all under the control of a religious sect called the Jains, and is considered by them a work of great merit. Some of them, mostly those of the poorer classes, feed pigeons and scatter sugar near ant hills, looking upon this as "good works" from a religious standpoint, and doing what they can so that they may not be without something to render them acceptable before their god. Others feed the ox and the more exalted animals, but they do not look down upon and discard their poorer or less fortunate neighbors because they are not able to do as much as others, or to dress as finely as they. In this respect some of our American people would suffer in a comparison with the Jains.

The pity and sympathy of many of these people is altogether confined to the brute creation, going so far as trying to prevent the slaughter of sheep for food; while on the subject of female infanticide they are silent.

Principal Wordsworth, acknowledged to be one of the warmest friends of India, and from his position having the best means of ascertaining the truth, makes the following severe remarks regarding the action of some educated Hindoos:—

"I need hardly say, that I consider the existence of the Hindoo child-widow one of the darkest blots that ever defaced the civilization of any people, and it is the direct and necessary consequence of the system of infant marriage.

HINDOO CHILD WIDOWS. 117

Some years ago I should have expected that these sentiments would have an echo in the bosom of every Hindoo who had received an English education, and particularly among those persons who were attempting to appropriate the political methods and ideas of Englishmen. I have no such delusion now. I find some of them employing all the resources of theological sophistry and cant, not simply to palliate, but to vindicate what is plainly one of the most cruel, blighting, and selfish forms of human superstition and tyranny. I find others maneuvering to arrest every sincere effort at reform, sophisticating between right and wrong, defaming the character and motives of reformers, and laboring to establish by arguments as ridiculous as they are insulting, that English domestic society offers a warning rather than an example to Hindoos. I find them

(*Original Photo.*)
CHILD IN JEWELS.

vindicating early marriage as the only safeguard against universal sexual license, a confession of moral incompetence which I should have thought that any people, with a grain of selfrespect, would have shrunk from advancing." Hindoos believe strongly in the spirit of reaction. It is said to have its centre in Poona, the chief stronghold of Brahman orthodoxy. "On the other hand, Bombay has a few zealous reformers, and it is hoped that the reactionary movement will soon pass away."

THE CAVE TEMPLES OF INDIA.

The cave temples of India are among its greatest marvels. No other country in the world possesses such a magnificent group of rock-cut monuments. The period during which the people of India were given to making these excavations, is supposed to have begun about 250 B. C., and to have ended about 800 A. D. More than nineteen of the cave temples are found in the Bombay Presidency. I will give some account of a celebrated cave on the island of Elephanta, about six miles from Bombay, by boat, which I, with others, was permitted to visit. It was so called by the Portuguese, from a stone elephant which stood near the old landing place. The greatest cave is in the western hill of the island, and at an elevation of about 250 feet above the sea-level. It is hewn out of a hard, compact rock, which has also been cut away on either side, leaving an open, spacious front supported by two massive pillars and two half pillars. This forms three openings under a thick and steep rock. It is overhung by brushwood and wild shrubs. The whole excavation consists of three principal parts, the great temple itself, which is in the center, and two smaller compartments, one on each side.

The great temple is about 130 feet long, and as broad. It rests on twenty-six pillars, eight of them now broken, and sixteen half pillars. It varies in height from fifteen to nineteen feet. On entering the temple, one of the first objects which attracts notice, is a large figure of the *Trimurti*, nineteen feet in height. On each side stand gigantic door keepers about twelve feet in height. In approaching the *Trimurti*, the shrine or garbha of the temple is passed to the right. It is entered by doors on the four sides, with a gigantic doorkeeper at each door. The chamber is perfectly plain on the inside, and about nineteen feet square. In the center stands an altar or *vedi*, about ten feet square and three feet high. In the center of this is placed the *linga*, cut from a block of a harder grain than that in which the cave is excavated.

The compartment to the east of the *Trimurti* contains numerous gigantic figures, grouped about a gigantic *Ardhanari*, or Siva, represented as a half-male and half-female divinity. The figure is nearly seventeen feet high. It is seen from the description, which is given by competent and reliable men, that the temple belonged to the Siva sect.

On Sunday, February 3, 1895, we attended services conducted under the auspices of the Church of Scotland. The subject in the morning was, "The Transfiguration of Christ." Communion services were held in the evening. These services were conducted in a manner very similar to those in the Protestant churches of our large cities.

There are a number of mission schools and mission workers in Bombay. The Salvation Army is well represented and is very successful, as their members will venture into places where other Christian workers will not go.

CHAPTER XVI.

PARSEES.

PRINCIPAL MERCHANTS WORSHIP THE FOUR ELEMENTS—CHILD-TRAINING—MARRIAGE—MARRIAGEABLE AGE—MARRIAGE FUND—FUNERAL—PREPARING THE DEAD—"TOWERS OF SILENCE."

N proportion to their numbers, the Parsees are probably the richest class in India. They are descendants of the ancient Persians, who came to India many years ago to avoid Mohammedan persecution. Much of the mercantile business of the East is in their hands. Unfettered by caste like Hindoos, they are free to travel wherever they please. They are also distinguished for the attention they pay to education. In religion, they are followers of Zoroaster or Zarathustra. Their sacred book, which is to them as the Bible is to us, is called the Avesta. Theoretically they claim to be monotheists, but they adore the four elements—fire, air, earth and water. Like the Hindoos, they attach great purifying power to the urine of the cow, called "Nirang." It is brought to their houses every morning. A small quantity of it is applied to the face, hands and feet. In greater purifications, some of the liquid is drank.

A fire is kept ever burning in their temple. The learned Bishop Meurin, writing about the similarity between

(*Original Photo.*)
GATES OF THE CHURCH OF THE HOLY SEPULCHRE.

Not bleeding bird, nor bleeding beast,
Nor hyssop branch, nor earthly priest,
Nor running brook, nor flood, nor sea,
Can wash the dismal stain away.

Jesus, Thy blood, Thy blood alone,
Hath power sufficient to atone;
Thy blood can make us white as snow;
No other tide can cleanse us so.

the Parsee fire temple and the Christian sanctuary, says: "On this landing let us rest for a while. We have before us the sanctuary of the Parsee fire temple and the sanctuary of the Christian church. In both we see a perpetual flame indicating the presence of God; there the omnipotence of God the Creator, here the sacramental presence of God the Redeemer. I am unable to express in words the deep and vehement feelings which move my heart when I kneel in the sanctuary of my chapel and think of the Parsee fire temple a few yards off, in which a fire is ever burning like the flame in our sanctuary, and in our hearts."

The Bible so frequently refers to fire out of which God spoke, and by which He so often proved Himself, and which is so essential in the Christian work—the fire of the Holy Ghost.

The Parsees do not bury their dead, but expose them in towers to be devoured by vultures. In the Avesta, the earth complains that she is polluted by the burial of the dead. The bodies are laid in what are called "Towers of Silence." Each tower usually has several vultures sitting motionless around the top, with their heads pointed inward. When a corpse is brought the vultures swoop down, and in a few minutes fly back satiated, and take up their former position.

We will give here a selection from their code of morals, taken from a pamphlet, setting forth the principles of their religion, which was given us, along with a permit to visit the "Towers of Silence," by the secretary of their society.

Five questions are asked and answered:

Ques. "Who is the most fortunate man in the world?"
Ans. "He who is the most innocent."
Ques. "Who is the most innocent man in the world?"

Ans. "He who walks in the path of God and shuns that of the devil."

Ques. "Which is the path of God, and which that of the devil?"

Ans. "Virtue is the path of God, and vice that of the devil."

Ques. "What constitutes virtue, and what vice?"

Ans. "Good thoughts, good words, and good deeds constitute virtue; and bad thoughts, bad words and bad deeds constitute vice."

Ques. "What constitutes good thoughts, good words and good deeds?"

Ans. "Honesty, charity and truthfulness."

All must acknowledge that these are very good rules from a strictly moral standpoint; but there is no living Christ in them. The Parsees look to the God of nature. Oh, if they could only grasp and believe in the living God and His Son Jesus!

In the evening, as we were walking along the beach, we were surprised to see the Parsees, both men and women, making their way toward the sea, and here on the shore of the ocean, as the sun was sinking, they performed some of their religious rites. The sun was setting, and the water in the vast expanse of the Indian ocean was outstretched before them. There was no music save the solemn moan of the waves as they broke into foam upon the beach; but where shall we find an instrument making grander music? O, could we in our service but close our eyes and see the greatness of God in all His works, on both land and sea, we would become more and more as a Christian people should be—more loyal to God and more consecrated to His service!

ROCK OF THE APOSTLES. (Original Photo.)

PARSEE CHILD-TRAINING.

Obedience to parents is a religious virtue with the Zoroastrian religion. Disobedient children are considered great sinners. This virtue of obedience to parents was such a common characteristic with the ancient Zoroastrians that, as Herodotus says, "The legitimacy of a child accused of a misdeed toward the parent was looked at with great suspicion." The parents were the rulers of the house—the father the king, the mother the queen; so that the children, as subjects, were bound to be obedient to their rulers.

This obedience to parents at home, and to teachers at school, was a training for future obedience to the rules and manners of society at large, and to the constitutional forms for the government of their country. Children who are disobedient to their parents cannot be expected to be good members of society and good, loyal subjects to their rulers. For this reason the religious books greatly emphasize this virtue. One of the blessings that a priest prays for in a house, when he performs the Afingan ceremony, is the obedience of the children to the head of the family. He prays, "May obedience overcome disobedience in this house; may peace overcome dissensions, may charity overcome want of charity, may courtesy overcome pride, may truth overcome falsehood."

These writings agree well with the teachings of our gospel. Many of the children and the young people of Christian nations may learn good lessons from the teachings of a heathen people.

PARSEE VIEWS ON MARRIAGE.

Marriage is an institution which is greatly encouraged by the Parsee religion, on the grounds that a married life is more likely to be happy than an unmarried one; that a married person is more likely to withstand physical and mental afflictions than an unmarried one, and that a married man is more likely to lead a religious and virtuous life than an unmarried one. The following words are given in their writings: "I say these words to you, marrying brides, and to you, bridegrooms. Impress them in your minds: May you two enjoy the life of good minds by following the laws of religion. Let each one of you clothe the other with righteousness, because then assuredly there will be a happy life for you."

An unmarried person is represented to feel as unhappy as a fertile piece of ground that is carelessly allowed to lie uncultivated by its owner. The fertile piece of ground, when cultivated, not only adds to the beauty of the spot, but gives nourishment and food to many others round about. So a married couple not only add to their own beauty, grace and happiness, but by their righteousness and good conduct are in a position to spread the blessings of help and happiness among their neighbors. Marriage being thus considered a good institution, and being recommended by their religious scriptures, it is accepted as a very meritorious act for a Parsee to help his co-religionists to lead married lives.

Several rich Parsees have, with this charitable view, founded endowment funds, from which young, deserving

brides are given small sums, on the occasion of their marriage, for the preliminary expenses of starting in married life. Fifteen years is the minimum marriageable age spoken of by the Parsee books. Parents have a voice of sanction or approval in the selection of wives and husbands. Marriages with others than Parsees are not recommended, as they are likely to bring about quarrels and dissensions, owing to a difference of manners, customs and habits.

THE "TOWERS OF SILENCE."

We were permitted to stand on the opposite side of the street from a house in which a Parsee funeral service was being held. The Parsees are a very exclusive sect, and this was as close as we were allowed to approach. None but their own people are admitted or allowed to see the corpse. It appears, from the traditions of several ancient nations, that the dog played a prominent part in their burial services. They are still used by the Parsees. At this time the dog, led by a man, was taken into the house, and shortly afterward led out again. His particular part seems to be in seeing the dead body "four-eyed." A spotted dog, with a spot directly over each eye, is supposed by these people to possess the peculiar characteristic of instinctively designating to them whether or not the person is dead—staring steadily at him if life is extinct, and not looking at him at all if he is not altogether lifeless. Some attribute this "sag-deed" to some magnetic influence in the eyes of the dog; others to the fact that the dog is, of all animals, the most faithful to his master; others consider a dog to be symbolic of the destruction of moral passions, and as death puts an end to all moral passions, so the presence of a dog near the dead body emphasized that idea.

The corpse is wrapped in a winding sheet and carried by six men on a kind of bier rudely constructed of sticks and poles. The mourners and friends must all follow two by two, and are dressed in white.

The "Towers of Silence," which practically constitute the Parsee cemetery, are situated a mile or two from the

"TOWERS OF SILENCE" AND VULTURES. (Parsee method of disposing of the dead.)

main part of the city. They are situated on a hill, in a park or enclosure containing thirty or forty acres. The grounds are very nicely kept. There are five of these towers; one for family use, said to be over 200 years old, one for self-murderers, and three for general use. The rich and poor, great and small, are all alike brought to this place. No one but the attendants is allowed to enter these towers, as they are considered very defiling.

There is another tower in the park which was built for the express purpose of making a model so that the Prince of Wales could see how they were built, he not being allowed to enter the others. We had a permit to go through the park, and visited this tower, which is an exact counterpart of the others. It consists of a wall about twenty-five feet high, perhaps twenty or thirty feet in diameter, with a small door, which serves as an entrance. On the inside, in the center, is a well. Directly over the well is a crate upon which the bodies are exposed to the vultures sitting on the wall, waiting for their prey. The well is drained by other deeper wells near it, and the water and earth are disinfected with charcoal. There are other buildings in the park for the accommodation of the mourners and friends.

When the funeral party arrives, the dead body is placed on a stone near one of the towers; then two men take the corpse and carry it into the tower, placing it upon the crate. After the clothing has been removed, the men leave the tower, and the vultures are allowed to satisfy their cravings. There are from 300 to 400 of these vultures on the grounds, and in about one hour the fleshy parts of the body will be consumed by them, after which the skeleton is dropped into the well.

The towers and the dead are considered very defiling, this being the reason why no one is allowed to enter. The two attendants, who are set apart for this work, remain permanently on the grounds, and do not come in contact at all with the outside world.

How grateful we should feel that we are born in a Christian land, with Christian privileges, and under Christian influences.

(*Original Photo*)
CHURCH OF THE LORD'S PRAYER ON MOUNT OLIVET.
INTERIOR OF THE PASSAGE.

Oh, 'tis sweet to bring to Jesus ev'ry little care,
Trials and temptations, which we cannot bear.
Ev'ry sin which doth beset us, He will take away,
If in faith believing, thus we humbly pray:

"Our Father which art in heaven, Hallowed be Thy name. Thy kingdom come. Thy will be done in earth, as it is in heaven. Give us this day our daily bread. And forgive us our trespasses as we forgive those who trespass against us. And lead us not into temptation, but deliver us from evil: For thine is the kingdom, and the power, and the glory, for ever. Amen."

CHAPTER XVII.

BOMBAY TO EGYPT.

FAREWELL TO INDIA — WAR VESSELS — REV. AND MRS. HAZEN — ARABIAN SEA—ADEN—RED SEA IN SIGHT—BIBLE LANDS — CROSSING OF THE ISRAELITES—MOUNT SINAI—SUEZ —THE CANAL—SHORT CUT AROUND THE GLOBE — BITTER LAKE — CROCODILE LAKE AND ISMALIA.

E set sail on the 9th of February, going aboard the grand ship, Shannon, of the P. & O. line, on which we found very comfortable quarters for the voyage. Many came aboard, mostly Englishmen and Americans. Immense crowds gathered to see their friends off, as there is a close connection and good feeling between India and England, and other parts of Europe. Copious tears are shed on these occasions when husbands and wives and children part.

As we leave the harbor, the numerous warships anchored in and around Bombay present a magnificent appearance. Soon our ship was out on the deep, making her way across the Arabian Sea.

On Sunday, February 10th, very formal services were held on board by the captain. During the day we had the pleasure of meeting Rev. Hazen and wife, missionaries, on their way to visit their former home in America.

This particular Sunday evening was very pleasant. The sea was calm and the moon and stars were shining brightly upon the waters, giving us a splendid view of the sea by moonlight.

This beautiful sight brought the writer to realize how grandly and wonderfully God had arranged all these things, so that the sea, the moon and the stars obey His omnipotent will. The Parsees have great confidence in the moon and stars; why then should we fear, when we trust in Him who controls them? Why should the Christian fear when he has Christ in the heart?

Dear reader, it is not when we are at home, on land, where no dangers are seen, that we are safe ; but real safety is in God, even though we are in the midst of a great storm. He says, "I will go with thee." The Psalmist says, "A thousand shall fall at thy side, and ten thousand at thy right hand ; but it shall not come nigh thee...... Because thou hast made the Lord, which is my refuge, even the Most High, thy habitation; there shall no evil befall thee, neither shall any plague come nigh thy dwelling ; for he shall give his angels charge over thee to keep thee in all thy ways." Ps. 91 : 7—11.

As we were now drawing near Aden, all those who had written letters prepared to mail them. At this point we entered the Red Sea and soon were in the Bible lands. The weather was fine, and we were now in sight of land. The country looked very barren and sandy, while on the east we saw Arabia and on the west Africa.

We passed the wreck of a French steamer. Nothing but the mast was visible above the water. Large military sta-

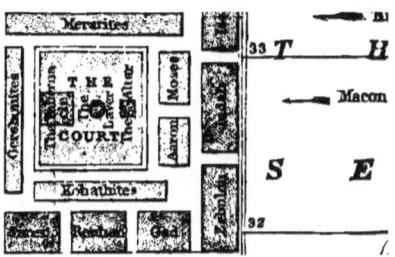

tions and forts were passed as we entered the Red Sea. Many mountain peaks were seen in the distance.

On the 16th of February, we had a very pleasant day, and the sea was like glass, almost without a ripple. How I longed for my friends and family to be with me.

The passage of the children of Israel through the Red Sea was bearing much upon my mind, and as we were drawing toward the locality, mountains were seen, and references were made to several places as being the ones referred to where the children of Israel passed through. The country looks very barren, and there is apparently no means of support for man or beast, but when there was a vast multitude of the children of Israel to pass through and take up their wanderings through the wilderness, God supported His own, by sending them manna from heaven.

It is claimed by some that Mt. Sinai can be seen from the ship on a clear day, while others dispute it. But one thing is true: as we sailed along the gulf, the country looked very inspiring to a Christian, on account of the thoughts connected with God's visits to Moses and Israel during their sojourn here of forty years. My heart throbbed within me as we were nearing these Bible lands. How I enjoyed it and felt grateful to God for the blessing conferred upon me in permitting me to visit these most interesting points in all the world,—The Bible lands.

The Red Sea is an arm of the sea extending from the Indian Ocean towards the north-west, between Arabia and Africa, to a distance of fourteen hundred miles. It is entered at the southern extremity through a strait only eighteen miles in width. At the widest place it is two hundred and twenty-one miles in width. Toward the north end it gradually contracts, and at length divides into two arms, the gulf of Akaba and the gulf of Suez, formerly called Heroopolitic gulf.

The water is of a beautiful, blue color, changing near the surface, where there are shoals or reefs, to a pale green. No satisfactory reason for the modern name (Red Sea) has yet been given.

CHILDREN OF ISRAEL CROSSING THE RED SEA.

The weather was very warm, and sailors say that the passage through the Red Sea is the warmest and most sultry of any part of the entire voyage around the world.

Suez was now in view, and we crossed at the place where historians claim the passage of the children of Israel was made. It is but a few miles from where the ship enters the Suez canal.

During the last half day of our passage here, the sea became very rough, caused by a strong south wind, and it was necessary for the ship to cast anchor about half a mile from Suez, and wait for the storm to subside and for morning before entering the Suez canal.

Suez is not much of a town. Numerous ships were passed and many were lying at anchor. The surrounding country is very sandy and barren. The sea was calm as we entered the canal at a very slow rate of speed. The Suez canal is a wonderful piece of work, and one of the greatest undertakings, if not in reality the greatest, in the world. It was completed in 1869, connecting the Red Sea with the Mediterranean. It was built at a cost of $130,000,000. The canal is about 100 miles long, 250 feet wide, and of sufficient depth to allow the largest ships to pass through without difficulty, thus saving in a voyage from Europe and America to India or China, from five to seven thousand miles in distance, and about one month in time.

The great mercantile importance of the canal is apparent from the following data. The distance from London to Bombay via the Cape of Good Hope, is 12,548 English miles; and via the Suez canal, 7,028 miles. The saving thus effected is forty-four per cent. of the distance. From Hamburg to Bombay, by the cape, it is 12,903 miles; by the canal 7,383 miles, a saving of forty-three per cent. From Triest to Bombay, by the cape, 13,229 miles; by the canal 4,816 miles, saving sixty-three per cent. From London to Hong Kong, by the cape, 15,229 miles; by the canal 11,112 miles, saving twenty-eight per cent. From Odessa to Hong Kong, by the cape, 16,629 miles; by the canal 8,735 miles, saving forty-seven per cent. From Marseilles to Bombay, by the cape, 12,144 miles; by the canal 5,022 miles, saving fifty-nine per cent. From Constantinople to Zanzibar, by the cape, 10,271 miles; by the canal 4,365 miles, saving fifty-seven per cent. From Rotterdam to the Sunda strait, by the cape, 13,252 miles; by the canal 9,779 miles, saving twenty-six per cent. The passage of the canal, which is open to vessels of all nations, has been practicable both by day and by night since the introduction of the electric light.

SUEZ CANAL.

In 1890, 3,425 vessels of an aggregate burden of 9,749,129 tons passed through the canal.

The nationalities of the vessels traversing the canal in 1890 were as follows:

		Aggregate tons.
British - - - -	2,522 vessels,	5,331,094
German - - - -	275 vessels,	490,586
French - - - - -	169 vessels,	365,903
Dutch - - - - -	144 vessels,	284,511
Italian - - - - -	87 vessels,	143,720
Austrian - - - -	55 vessels,	118,047
Other nationalities -	137 vessels,	192,233

The number of passengers on board these vessels was about 156,000.

The dues amount to $2.00 per ton with an extra payment at present of 60 cts. per ton, $2.00 for each passenger, and $2.00 to $2.40 for pilotage according to the tonnage of the vessel.

Many camels are seen starting out from Suez on their tours. Numerous natives, on the banks, follow the ship, crying for "Backshesh," a word used by the natives when begging for money or a gift, while the ship goes at the rate of about four miles per hour. Ships are not allowed to run faster than this rate of speed so as to avoid injury to the embankments caused by the motion of the water. The canal passes through Bitter lake, which Bruasch identifies as the Marah of the Bible where the waters were made sweet by casting a tree into them, when the children of Israel, under Moses, journeyed from Egypt to Canaan. Ex. 15:23. Before we entered Lake Timsah, we passed the foot of the Gebel Maryan, which an Arabian legend points out as the place where Miriam, when smitten with leprosy, for her disapproval of the marriage of Moses with the Ethiopian woman, spent seven days outside of the camp of the Israelites. Num. 12.

The canal enters Lake Timsah, or the crocodile lake, on the north bank of which lies the town of Ismalia. The lake is now about six miles in area, and of a beautiful blue color. Before the construction of the canal it was a mere pond of brackish water, and full of reeds. On the 18th of November, 1862, the waters of the Mediterranean were let into this basin, which is traversed by two artificial channels for the passage of large vessels. While the channels were being constructed, this town was the central point of the work, and the residence of numerous officials and traders, so that its traffic soon became very considerable, and it has even been extolled by modern poets as a wonder of the desert, owing to the fact that the mail steamers between Cairo and the great Asiatic and Australian ports are beginning to desert the former route, via Alexandria, in favor of that via Ismalia.

The climate is pleasant and the air dry, notwithstanding the proximity of the water. The ground, which has been reclaimed from the desert by means of irrigation, has been planted with tasteful gardens.

KARNAK, EGYPT.

CHAPTER XVIII.

THE LAND OF THE PHARAOHS.

MIXED POPULATION — STREETS CROWDED — WATER CARRIERS— TURBANS—ORNAMENTS—VEILING OF WOMEN (SINGLE, MARRIED)—CHILD CARRYING—WATER FOUNTAIN — MOSLEM'S PRAYER.

NOW we are in the land of the Pharaohs, the land in which the mighty works of God were wrought by the hands of Moses, His servant.

Cairo is the largest city in Egypt, and also the seat of government. It is reached by train from Ismalia, a distance of ninety-seven miles. Nowhere do we see such a mixed population of about 400,000, consisting of Germans, Italians, Greeks, French, English, Austrians, Africans, Bedouins, Syrians, Persians, Indians, and others, while there is a host of visitors constantly moving, coming and going. Their object is mostly to visit the ancient Egyptian ruins and the many places of interest connected with the Bible. Many also come to this country from Europe and America to spend the cold winter months, as the climate is very mild and uniform, hence well calculated for invalids.

Oriental life seems to feel the atmosphere of the newer quarters uncongenial, and it must therefore be sought for in the old Arabian quarters, which are still mostly inaccessible for carriages, notwithstanding the many new streets that have been of late years constructed in Cairo. Most of the streets in the old part of the town are still unpaved, and they are often excessively dirty. The lanes separating the rows of houses in the Arabian quarters are so narrow that there is hardly room for two riders to pass, and the projecting balconies of the harems with their gratings often nearly meet. The busy traffic in these streets presents an interminable, raveled and twisted string of men, women and animals; of walkers, riders, and carriages of every description. Add to this the cracking of the drivers' whips, the jingling of money at the tables of the changers, established at almost every corner of the street, the rattling of the brazen vessels of the water-carriers, the moaning of the camels, braying of donkeys and barking of dogs, and you have a perfect pandemonium.

Europeans, gentlemen and even ladies, may ride with perfect safety through the midst of all this confusion, and they will often have opportunities of observing most picturesque and amusing scenes. The denseness of the crowd seems sometimes to preclude the possibility of further progress, but the hammar, or donkey-boy, is pretty sure to elbow the passage through without much difficulty. Lovers of the picturesque will find such rides very enjoyable. It is not, however, until the traveler has learned to distinguish the various individuals who throng the streets, and understands their different pursuits, that he can thoroughly appreciate his walks or rides. We will therefore give a brief description of some of the leading characteristics of the different members of the community.

From a very early period it has been customary for the Arabs to distinguish their different sects, families, and dynasties by the color of their turbans. Green is the prophet's color. Green turbans, therefore, are the badge of the Sherifs, or descendants of the prophet, and they are also frequently worn by Mecca pilgrims. But the green turban is not much respected in Cairo, where it too often serves as an excuse for laziness; many of the prophet's descendants now wear white instead. The Ulama, or clergy and scholars, usually wear a very wide and broad, evenly-folded turban of light color. The orthodox length of a

(*Original Photo.*)
ORIENTAL WOMEN VEILED.

believer's turban is seven times that of his head, being equivalent to the whole length of his body, in order that the turban may afterwards be used as the wearer's winding sheet, and that this circumstance may familiarize him with the thought of death. The dress and turbans of the Copts, Jews and other non-moslem citizens are generally of a dark color, those of the Copts being blue and those of the Jews being yellow, in accordance with the decree issued in the 14th century. Blue is also the color indicative of mourning.

The women of the lower and rustic classes wear nothing but a blue gown and a veil. Their ornaments consist of silver or copper bracelets, earrings and anklerings, while their chins, arms and chests are often tattooed with blue marks. In Upper Egypt noserings are also frequently seen. The women of the upper classes are never so handsomely dressed in the streets as at home. When equipped for riding or walking, they wear a light-colored silk cloak with very wide sleeves over their home attire. They also don the veil, which consists of a long strip of muslin, covering the whole of the face, except the eyes, and reaching nearly to the feet.

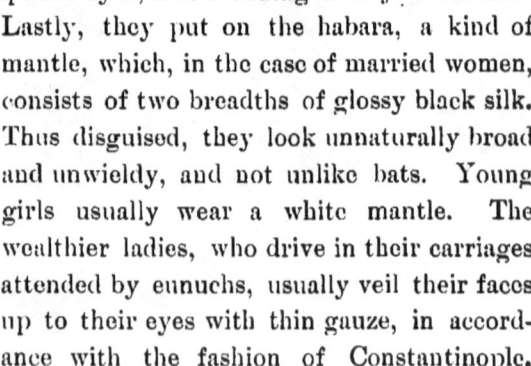

Lastly, they put on the habara, a kind of mantle, which, in the case of married women, consists of two breadths of glossy black silk. Thus disguised, they look unnaturally broad and unwieldy, and not unlike bats. Young girls usually wear a white mantle. The wealthier ladies, who drive in their carriages attended by eunuchs, usually veil their faces up to their eyes with thin gauze, in accordance with the fashion of Constantinople. The figure of Egyptian women in early life is generally upright and graceful. They color their eyelashes and eyelids dark, and their finger and toenails with henna, which gives them a brownish-yellow tint. Among other customs we may also mention the peculiar mode in which a woman carries her child—either astride her shoulder or resting on her hip. With regard to circumcision, weddings and funerals, the ceremonies are similar in all the Egyptian towns.

EGYPTIAN WATER CARRIERS.

Amid this busy throng of men and animals resound the various cries of street venders and other persons who transact their business in the open air, and the warning shouts of runners, coachmen, donkey attendants and camel drivers. Donkeys and camels are very numerous, and each one has an attendant. One of the most popular characters to be met with in the streets of Cairo, as in most of the other Oriental towns, is the *sakka*, or water-carrier, with his goatskin of water, carried by himself or by a donkey. This individual still carries on his trade, although the water works supply every house in the city, as well as every public place, with water. Many of the sakkas sell water to the people in the streets. These carry their supply of water either in a skin or in a large earthen vessel, on their backs. They offer drinks in a brazen saucer or cup to those passing by, for which they receive a small copper coin, but often times no payment at all is given.

It is stated that on the occasions of festivals, and particularly on the birthdays of nobles and saints, persons who desire to do a pious work, frequently hire one of the sakkas to dispense water gratuitously. The sakka then shouts in a singing tone, "*Sebil Allah ya atshan ya moyeh,*" thus inviting all thirsty persons to drink without money or price, while he occasionally turns to his employer, who generally stands near him, with the words, "God forgive thy sins," or "God have mercy on thy parents," to which the persons who have partaken of the water reply, "Amin," or Amen; or, "God have mercy on them and us." After numerous blessings of a similar kind have been exchanged, the sakka hands the last cup of water to his employer with the words, "The remainder for the liberal man."

In Egypt, as in the Holy Lands, a supply of good water is a fortune. In Alexandria the water is not so good, and a wealthy man opened a fountain of good water free to all passers by, with this inscription thereon: "Ho, every one that thirsteth, come ye to the water, and he that hath no money, come ye, buy and drink without money and without price." *

Places of interest are numerous, and as you go from one place to another you hear the voice of the *muezzins*, or priests, from the minarets or spires of the mosque. The repetition of prayers five times daily forms one of the chief occupations of faithful Moslems. The person praying must remove his shoes or sandals, and turn his face toward Mecca, as the Jews and some of the Christian sects turn toward Jerusalem or toward the East. They may be seen in their shops, on the streets, or wherever you go, engaged in prayer, quite frequently. They have many different positions and maneuvers to go through before their prayers are completed; and as one dragoman said, being one of their number, that if ever they were disturbed, or saw anyone laughing at them, they must commence again, as that was not good. How much we Christian people could learn of those who are far

* Isaiah 55:1.

(Original Photo.)
MOHAMMEDANS PRAYING.

Would you fear to have your windows open
    Three times each day,
If sinners saw that you were kneeling
    Three times to pray?

Would you offer up a bold petition,
    If well you knew
That awful den of roaring lions
    Awaited you?

The lesson taught is not to offer
    A world-wide prayer:
'Tis duty first, and then the promise
    Of heavenly care.

beneath us in light, knowledge and information regarding the one true God! Their hours of prayer are: (1) A little after sunset; (2) about one and one-half hours after sunset; (3) daybreak; (4) midday; (5) afternoon, about one and one-half hours before sunset.

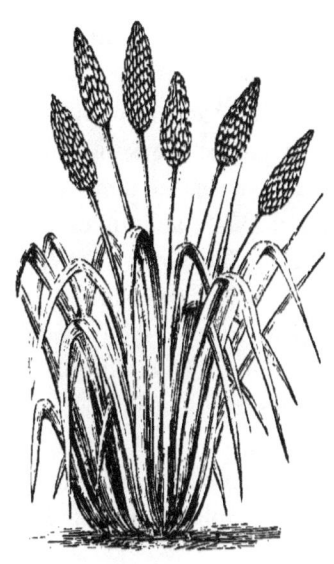

CHAPTER XIX.

Dervishes and the Tombs.

DANCING, AND HOWLING DERVISHES AND MODE OF WORSHIP—
CITIDEL—TOMBS OF THE MAMELUKES—KHALIFS—MOSQUE
OF SULTAN HASAN—TOMBS OF THE KHEDIVES—ISLAND
OF ROIDA—COPTIC CHURCH—HOLY FAMILY
SHELTERED—JOSEPH'S WELL—
AMERICAN MISSION.

FRIDAY is the usual day when the Howling and Dancing Dervishes are engaged in their peculiar and fanatical mode of religious worship. The dancing dervishes perform their Zikr, as they call it, within a circular space about thirty feet in diameter and enclosed by a railing, while on the outside of the railing is a space for visitors to stand, and on the left above us is a gallery enclosed with lattice work in which the women are enclosed. With slow, measured steps the shekh comes forward, followed by a dervish, and takes his seat on a carpet opposite the entrance. The other dervishes next enter the circle one after another, in the order of their age, wearing long gowns and conical hats. They walk solemnly up to their superior, make him a profound obeisance, kiss the hem of his robe, and take up their positions to his left. From the gallery is presently heard a rude kind of music, consisting of a single prolonged tone of a stringed instrument accompanied by a flute and a voice rising and falling. Time is

EGYPT.—DANCING DERVISHES.

beaten by a tambourine with great rapidity and vigor. The singer recites a hymn expressing the most ardent love of God. As soon as the singing ceases, the dervishes rise and walk in procession three times around the circle, headed by the shekh, each of them, including the shekh himself, making a low bow, in passing the spot from which the shekh has just risen. Then they resume their seats and the shekh with closed eyes, and in a deep, solemn voice, begins to murmur a prayer in which the word "Allah" alone is audible. When the prayer is over the dervishes divest themselves of their

gowns, under which they wear a long, loose, light colored skirt or kilt, reaching down to their ankles, and a more closely fitting vest. They then present themselves before the shekh, each in his turn, making him a profound obeisance, and begin to move slowly round in a circle. They turn on the left foot, propelling themselves by touching the waxed floor from time to time with the right. Most of them make about forty gyrations per minute, but some of them accomplish sixty and even more. The whole of the Zikr is performed by the dervishes noiselessly, with closed eyes, and outstretched arms, the palm of one hand being turned upwards and the other downwards, and their heads either thrown back or leaning on one side. During the dance soft strains of music are heard, while the beat of the tambourine gradually accelerates, and the skirts of the performers fly out in a wide circle like an opened umbrella. The tones of the flute become more and more shrill until a signal is given by the shekh when the music ceases, the dancers stop, cross their arms over their chests, and resume their seats. The dance is performed three times by all except the superior. The latter, however, walks several times noiselessly through the midst of the dancers, who, although their eyes are closed, touch neither him nor one another. The whole service occupies about one hour.

The howling or shouting dervishes perform their Zikr at Cairo, also on Friday, at another place. These dervishes take a standing position, swinging their heads backward and forward down to their knees, with their long hair swinging and switching, while every bow produces a groan, until they are almost exhausted, while some inferior music is heard, by which time is kept. At a certain notice all stop. Again they start, led by a leader, and so on. At other times they assume a kneeling or crouching position, with their heads and chests bent downwards. In this attitude they sometimes remain for hours, incessantly shouting the Moslem confession of faith. It need not be added that the American and Christian travelers will find these performances unpleasing and indeed painful.

Visits were made, in company with Rev. and Mrs. Hazen, from Boston, to the citadel, the tombs of the Mamelukes, tombs of the Khalifs, the mosque of Sultan Hasan,

(*Original Photo.*)
RUINS OF THE TEMPLE OF DIANA, EPHESUS.

"Away from the ruin!— Oh, hurry ye on,
While the sword of the angel yet slumbers undrawn!
Away from the doom'd and deserted of God—
Away, for the spoiler is rushing abroad!"

The warning was spoken—the righteous had gone,
And proud ones of Sodom were feasting alone;
All gay was the banquet--the revel was long,
With the pouring of wine and the breathing of song.

built 777 years ago by himself, and who, when it was completed, had the two hands of the architect cut off, so that he could not make another like it or better. The salary of the architect during the construction was £300 per day.

The tombs of the Khedives of Egypt are enclosed in a large mosque, costly, grandly, and durably built, and the monuments and tombs are very richly finished with carvings and gilding. The floors are all covered with the

PALM TREES, EGYPT.

finest of Brussels carpets. The tombs are twenty-four in number and all belong to the Royal family of Egypt.

On Sunday, February 24th, in company with our friends we attended the American mission service and Sunday school which is apparently in a very prosperous condition, where many warmhearted men and women are engaged in teaching and instructing the lower classes in the ways of

Christ and the Bible. It is a grand sight to see, in the different parts of the world, the children brought together and so nicely cared for by the Christian people of this and other nations. May the blessings of the Most High attend all the proper efforts that are put forth for the advancement of His cause and kingdom.

The Island of Roida is one of the places which nearly every one would like to visit, as one of the noted places of the Bible. In a small boat we crossed the branch of the Nile, which landed us on the island. Traditions locate this as the place where Moses was taken by his mother and put into an ark of bulrushes, laying it in the flags by the river brink, and the daughter of Pharaoh came down to bathe and when she saw the ark amongst the flags, she had it brought to her. When she had opened it she saw the child and beheld that the babe wept; she had compassion on it, and said, "This is one of the Hebrew children," and she called his name Moses, she said, "because I drew him out of the waters." Moses was appointed of God as a great deliverer to lead His people out of bondage, and in childhood the Lord had made provisions for his escape. A short distance from the crossing to the island is the Coptic church, underneath which a narrow flight of twelve steps descends to the crypt, a small vaulted chapel under the choir, consisting of nave and aisles. At the end of the nave is an altar in the form of an early Christian tomb-niche, which tradition indicates as the spot where the Virgin and child reposed. We have no reason to believe that all these traditions are correct, or can be relied upon, but this we all know, that the Holy Family fled from Herod in the land of Judea for the saving of the child's life because Herod sought to destroy it, and, as the Lord had instructed,

THE FLIGHT TO EGYPT.

they came to Egypt; so we have no reason to doubt that they were here, and were also sheltered and cared for. What thoughts and inspirations fill the heart and mind by coming to these places of sacred interest.

The so-called well of Joseph is a square shaft, sunk into the limestone rock to a depth of 280 feet, containing somewhat brackish water, which is brought to the surface by means of the sakiyehs, or Egyptian water wheels, one above the other, worked by oxen passing up and down a winding way cut around the well, in the solid rocks, with frequent openings to look out and down into the well. Since the completion of the new waterworks, however, the well has lost its former importance. When the citadel was constructed here in the twelfth century, the builders discovered an ancient shaft filled with sand, which was caused to be reopened and named after Joseph, Yusuf's or Joseph's well. This circumstance gives rise to the traditions which were chiefly current among the Jews, that this was the well into which the Joseph of the Scriptures was put by his brethren, and the story is still faithfully repeated by the dragomen. Others claim the well to have been constructed by Joseph previous to the great famine in Egypt, at which time Joseph was appointed to oversee and govern the country.

CHAPTER XX.

THE PYRAMIDS, AND UP THE NILE.

PYRAMIDS—SPHINX—MEMPHIS—UP THE NILE—WATER WHEELS—WORKING IN THE FIELDS—NECROPOLIS—RAMSES II.—SAKKARA—APIS TOMBS—SACRED BULLS—PASSAGE TO THE TOMBS—MONSTER COFFINS—MARIETTE—LASTING IMPRESSIONS.

HE Pyramids are the oldest and most wonderful monuments of human industry yet discovered. The Pyramids of Egypt form one of five groups of pyramids within the precincts of the Necropolis of the ancient city of Memphis. The exact time of their construction, as historians give it, is during the seventh century, B. C., and may have extended till about the time of the Pharaohs. Even at that time the kings, as well as their subjects, seem to have preferred rock tombs to mausolea above ground. The Great Pyramid is called by the Egyptians "Khufu Khut," or the glorious throne of Khufu. The length of each side is now 750 feet; the present perpendicular height is 451 feet; the height of each sloping side is now 568 feet; the stupendous structure covers an area of nearly thirteen acres. The ascent of the Pyramids, though fatiguing, is perfectly safe. There are a number of Bedouins in attendance there at all times, who, for a small fee, assist those who wish to ascend. Some make the ascent by the assistance of three men, one at either side

EGYPT.—THE PYRAMIDS.

pulling by the hands, and one at the back pushing. It is an experience that will not soon be forgotten. My friends, Rev. and Mrs. Hazen, did not undertake the laborious task of ascent. The sun shone very warmly, and the work of climbing was tiresome, as the steps are from two to three feet high. On the top there is a space of about twenty feet where a man can rest. The view from this elevated position is grand and striking, and fully repays one for the fatigue in gaining it. There is, possibly, no other place in the world from which life and death, fatality and desolation, are seen in so close connection and in such marked contrast.

PYRAMID AND SPHINX.

Looking west, and away from the Nile, we see glaring tracts of sand and many colorless monuments. On bare plateaus of rock stand the other Pyramids and the Sphinx, the latter rearing its head from the sand like some monster suffocated by the dust. To the south those of Sakkara will be seen, of which an account will be given hereafter. The descent of the Great Pyramid is more rapidly accomplished than the ascent, but is hardly less fatiguing. A visit to the interior of the Great Pyramid is comparatively uninteresting to the ordinary visitor. The explorer has to crawl and clamber through low and narrow passages, which, at places, especially near the entrance, are not above three and one-half feet high and four feet wide. The stones on the floor are often extremely slippery, and the confined air smells strongly of bats.

The Sphinx, which, next to the Pyramids themselves, is the most famous monument in this vast burial-ground, is hewn out of the natural rock, and, with some aid from artificial masonry, has been moulded into the shape of a recumbent lion, with the head of a man. The body was left in a rough form, but the head was originally most carefully executed. The entire height of this wonderful monument, from the crown of the head to the base upon which the fore legs of the lion rest, is said to be sixty-six feet. Not long ago the head, neck, and a small portion of the back were alone visible, but at this time the whole front part of the figure rises clear of the sand. The ear, according to Mariette, is four and a half feet, the nose five feet seven inches, the mouth seven feet seven inches in length, and the extreme breadth of the face is thirteen feet eight inches. If a person stands on the upper part of the ear he cannot stretch his hand as far as the crown of the head, and the space between these points must have been greater when the head decoration, which, as well as the greater part of the beard, is now broken off, was still intact. There is a hollow in the head, into which one of the Arabs, if desired, will climb. The face was deplorably mutilated at a comparatively recent period by a fanatic, shekh, and afterward by the barbarous Mamelukes, who used it as a target. It would appear, from Abdellatt's accounts, that it was in perfect preservation in his time. The face is very pleasing, and is of a graceful and beautiful type; one might almost say that it smiles winningly.

We also visited the ancient Memphis of the Bible, and the Necropolis in which the Egyptian dead were buried,[1] including Sakkara and the Pyramids; also the caves, vaults, and tombs almost beyond description.

In company with other Americans, we took a small boat at Cairo and started up the river Nile, of which the Bible speaks so much, leaving the Island of Roida on our left, and going on toward Upper Egypt, a wide tract of level land on both sides of the river, which is overflowed in the wet season of the year. The river still divides and encircles a tract of land, forming islands. On the banks of the river many water wheels are seen, to which oxen, having their eyes tied shut with a cloth, are attached. It is claimed that the oxen, being thus blinded, need no one to drive or urge them. The water is drawn up and emptied into a ditch on the bank of the river, which carries it into the country for irrigation purposes. Many are seen drawing water by hand and pouring

[1] Hosea 9:6.

it into ditches, while in other places canals have been dug for the purpose of carrying water into the country. The natives, working in the fields with their long Egyptian costumes, present a very interesting appearance. There are many palm groves to be seen.

After going a distance of about twenty miles we leave the boat, and find there are plenty of donkeys and drivers in

EGYPTIAN WELL NEAR CAIRO.

readiness to convey the visitors to places of interest. A short distance from the river Nile we entered a shady palm grove strewn with blocks of granite, broken pottery and fragments of brick. This is the ancient site of Memphis, which is now very interesting from a historical point of view only. Were it not for the vast Necropolis to the west of the ancient city, no one would imagine that one of the most famous and populous capitals of antiquity had once stood here.

THE JEWS' WAILING PLACE, JERUSALEM, (ON FRIDAY). (*Original Photo.*)

The Egyptians, from the earliest period down to the Roman imperial epoch, built their edifices, with the exception of palaces and temples, of large sun-dried brick, made from Nile mud; but even the public buildings of Memphis have entirely disappeared, as the stones were carried off in former centuries to build other edifices on the right bank of the Nile. The narrow streets of this city are said to have been half a day's journey in length, even down to the twelfth century.

After a few minutes' walk further on we come to the Colossal Statues of Ramses II. The first of these, discovered a short time ago, is made of granite, and lies on its back on a slight eminence, so that in order to see the face it is necessary to climb to a position on the breast. Further on we reach the hut which conceals the Second Colossus, which historians claim was erected by Ramses II. after his victories over the people of the East.

There are a number of holes and hollows near these statues, in which we observed remains of foundations, the most important of which is supposed to be the foundation of a temple of Ptah (Vulcan).

The Necropolis, or grave-yard, of Sakkara contains sepulchral monuments of every kind, from the pyramid to the rock-hewn cavern, dating both from the ancient and the latter empire. Ancient writers have recorded that the pyramids at Memphis were eleven in number, of which many are no longer visible, while others may yet stand for many centuries.

Amongst other sights are the Apis Tombs, of which we will give a short description and illustrations. In the subterranean part of the Egyptian Serapeum are the Apis Tombs, hewn in the rock, where the Apis bulls were interred. The worship of Apis, or the sacred bulls, belongs to the religion of the ancient Egyptians. The sacred animals and the mixed forms, which generally consist of human bodies with the heads of animals, frequently recur as companions of the gods, or are used as emblems of the deities themselves. In each case those animals were selected whose inherent dispositions and habits corresponded to the power or phenomenon of nature personified in the god. Specimens of these animals were kept in and near the temple, and the finest of them were embalmed after death, and revered in the form of mummies, with the belief that, like the soul of a man, the spirit of the deceased bull also was united with Osiris and became the *Osiris Apis*. The carcass was solemnly interred in a special vault.

Among other animals was the cow, represented as the patient mother and nurse; the goddess of love, the bride of Ptah, was represented with the head of a fierce lion or a cat; the crocodile was sacred to Sebek, the god who caused

the water of the Nile to rise; and the hawk, which soars toward heaven like the sun, was dedicated to Ra. The symbol of Ptah was the black Apis bull, whose great power of generation seemed analagous to the never-ceasing creative energy of the black soil of Egypt. While there are many tombs to which we might refer, we will call the attention of the reader to but one of the many. The passages to the Apis Tombs, which are now open to visitors, have an aggregate length of 380 yards, and are about ten feet in width and seventeen and one-half feet in height. Passing through the gateway we enter a chamber of considerable dimensions, with niches of various sizes in the bare limestone walls bearing inscriptions which have yielded much valuable information. Visitors light their candles here. The guide now proceeds toward the right. After taking a few steps we observe at our feet a huge block of black granite, which once formed the lid of a sarcophagus (or coffin, as we would call it). A little further beyond this we reach an enormous granite sarcophagus which so nearly fills the passage that there is just room to pass it on the right side. This passage is flanked with the side chambers, about twenty-six feet in height, the pavements and vaulted ceilings of which are constructed of excellent Mokattain stone. Twenty-four of the chambers still contain the huge sarcophagi, in which the Apis mummies were deposited. Each of these monster coffins consists of a single block of black or red polished granite, or of limestone, and averages thirteen feet in length, seven feet in width and eleven feet in height, and no less than sixty-five tons in weight. The covers, five of which are composed of separate pieces of stone cemented together, have, in several instances, been pushed to one side, and on the top of some of them the Arabs, for some unexplained reason, have built rude masses of masonry. All the sarcophagi, when discovered by Mariette, had been emptied of their contents, with the exception of two, which still contained a number of trinkets. Much more could be added to the subject, but we will give the words of the fortunate man who first excavated them.

"I confess," says Mariette, "that when I penetrated for the first time, on the 12th of November, 1851, into the Apis vaults, I was so profoundly struck with astonishment that the feeling is still fresh in my mind, although five years have elapsed since then. Owing to some chance, which it is difficult to account for, a chamber which had been walled up in the thirtieth year of the reign of Ramses II. had escaped the notice of the plunderers of the vaults, and I was so fortunate

INTERIOR OF THE APIS TOMBS. PRINCIPAL PASSAGE.

as to find it untouched. Although 3,700 years had elapsed since it was closed, everything in the chamber seemed to be precisely in its original condition. The finger-marks of the Egyptians, who had inserted the last stone in the wall built to conceal the doorway, were still recognizable on the lime. There were also the marks of naked feet imprinted on the sand which lay in one corner of the tomb chamber. Everything was in its original condition in this tomb, where the embalmed remains of the bull had lain undisturbed for thirty-seven centuries. Many travelers would think it terrible to live here alone in the desert for a number of years, but such discoveries as that of the chamber of Ramses II. produced impressions compared with which everything else sinks into insignificance, and which one constantly desires to renew."

CHAPTER XXI.

MUSEUM OF GIZEH AND HELIOPOLIS.

MUSEUM —EGYPTIAN COLLECTIONS—COFFINS—MUMMIES-DIFFERENT NECROPOLES—ANCIENT JEWELRY — ORNAMENTS — OBELISK OF HELIOPOLIS—VIRGIN AND CHILD HID — PALM TREES — LAND OF GOSHEN—CANALS—RAILROAD CUT.

THE museum of Gizeh is about three miles from the principal part of the city, and is one of the most remarkable places to visit in all Egypt, as the museum of Egyptian antiquities is the most valuable collection of the kind in existence. Its value is much enhanced by the fact that the place where the various objects were discovered is in nearly every case precisely known.

All kinds of coffins and mummies and other antiquities are seen here, of which we will describe only a few. Here are the coffins and mummies of five kings dated 1591 B. C., and others of even an earlier date; and statues dated 3000 B. C. To the surprise of all, these coffins and statues appear quite new, and are in a well preserved condition, the mummies, which are dry and hard, showing their features remarkably well. It is a wonderful place in which to spend hours or even days, in viewing the remains of ancient kings.

In the middle of room V. is a sarcophagus, in red granite, of Prince Hubaif of Memphis, (2840 B. C.) while others date back to 3800 B. C. These relics were taken out of the great excavations made in Egypt, from the tombs and caves of the different necropoles.

The jewels of Queen Aah-hotep, mother of Aahmes I., (1600 B. C.) found with the mummies of the queen at Drah Abu'l Negga (Thebes) in 1860 A. D., consist of bracelets of gold, double-hinged bracelets, necklace of gold, gold chains, gold boats, boats and crews of silver, dagger and sheath of gold, golden breastplate, mirror, anklets, armlets and many other valuable things. We saw also the ornaments of the Princess Hathor dated 2000 B. C., as well as thousands of other objects of interest.

O, what thoughts and wonders these things awaken in the mind of man! While traveling in that ancient country so much may be seen of which the new world knows nothing; and, indeed, when we compare the new and old worlds, they are to each other as a young child to an aged man of great experience.

Many things from Bible times may be seen, and many questions, to which the Scriptures frequently refer, can be settled in the mind and heart of man.

HELIOPOLIS, OR THE CITY OF ON.

I, in company with others, took the train and made a visit to Heliopolis, or the city of On. In Gen. 41:45 we are informed that Pharaoh gave Joseph to wife Asenath, the daughter of Poti-pherah, priest of On. Here we visited the Obelisk of Heliopolis, also the tree of the Virgin, and the well where Joseph, Mary and the child stopped. The tree, a sycamore, is not the original one, but one planted in its place in the year 1672. It measures about ten feet by three feet, is irregular in shape and considerably decayed; yet the branches are green and seem to thrive. At this place, according to tradition, the Virgin and child once rested under its shade during the flight from Herod, and there is another tradition to the effect that the persecuted Mary concealed herself with the child in a hollow of the trunk and that a spider so completely covered the opening with its web as to screen her effectually from observation. The garden is watered by means of a reservoir fed by springs.

We will now call the reader's attention to the land of Goshen, to which the Bible refers so frequently, and in which the children of Israel dwelt, after Joseph finally became ruler of Egypt, having previously been sold by his brethren to the merchantmen for twenty pieces of silver.

And they "brought Joseph into Egypt," but Joseph grew up and found favor with God, and was endowed with wisdom so that he could interpret the dreams of the Butler and Baker, and also the dreams of Pharaoh, whereupon he found great favor in the sight of the king. "and Pharaoh said unto Joseph, Forasmuch as God hath shewed thee all this, there is none so discreet and wise as thou art: thou shalt be over my house and according unto thy word shall all my people be ruled: only in the throne will I be greater than thou. And Pharaoh said unto Joseph, See, I have set thee over all the land of Egypt."[1] And Joseph went out, "and he gathered up all the food of the seven years, which were in the land of Egypt, and laid up the food in the cities: the food of the field, which was round about every city, laid he up in the same."[2]

"And the famine was over all the face of the earth:" and Joseph opened all the storehouses. and sold, because the

---
[1] Gen. 41:39—41.   [2] Gen. 41:48.

famine was so sore in all lands. "And Joseph's ten brethren went down to buy corn in Egypt," for the famine was in the land of Canaan, and Joseph made himself known to his brethren and kissed them and wept upon them, and after that his brethren talked with him.

And it pleased Pharaoh, and Pharaoh said unto Joseph, "Say unto thy brethren, Take your father and your households, and come unto me: and I will give you the good of the land of Egypt."[1] And the sons of Israel took Jacob, their father, and their children, and their wives; and they took cattle and their goods which they had gotten in the land of Canaan, and came into Egypt, Jacob and all his seed with him.[2] And Pharaoh spoke to Joseph saying, "The land of Egypt is before thee, in the best of the land make thy father and thy brethren to dwell; in the land of Goshen let them dwell."[3]

So the land of Goshen is the land in which the brethren and their posterity dwelt. "And thou shalt dwell in the land of Goshen, and thou shalt be near unto me, thou, and thy children, and thy children's children, and thy flocks, and thy herds, and all that thou hast;"[4] but in a later passage the sacred records mention the cities in Goshen in which the Israelites were compelled to work at the tasks imposed on them by Pharaoh. "Therefore they did set over them taskmasters to afflict them with their burdens, and they built for Pharaoh treasure cities, Pithom and Raamses."[5]

The land of Goshen is located north-east of Cairo, and about eighty miles from Cairo are the ruins which mark the site of the Pithom of the Bible, where the Jews served in hard bondage.

[1] Gen. 45: 15—18. [2] Gen. 46: 5—6. [3] Gen. 47: 6. [4] Gen. 45: 10. [5] Ex. 1: 11.

The country is very fertile and well cultivated, and is intersected by many irrigating canals. There are also many wells and water-wheels to be seen. It is sad to think the children of Israel were once enslaved in this beautiful country; but by the strong hand of God they were delivered, and we can much more rejoice that the way to liberty is now open for all who are in spiritual captivity, and that we can go and possess the land promised by God.

The palm groves and the green crops are growing here, while just beyond is the barren sandy desert, where the sand drifts like snow in our country. The railroad company has a force of men constantly at work keeping the cuts open, which would otherwise be drifted full of sand in a comparatively short time.

We are now near the seaport, and we look back upon the land of Egypt once more, and then bid adieu, passing on toward the Promised Land.

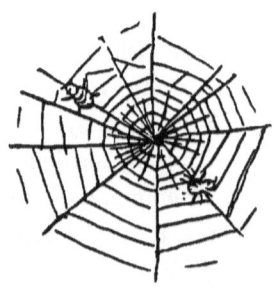

CHAPTER XXII.

PORT SAID, EGYPT, TO JOPPA, PALESTINE.

HISTORY—SAILING FOR JOPPA—LAND IN VIEW—JOPPA SEA PORT—PASSPORT—HOTELS—HOUSE OF SIMON, THE TANNER—PLAIN OF SHARON—FLOWERS AND PRODUCTIONS—RAILROAD—STATIONS—ORANGE GROVES—JERUSALEM CONFUSION.

PORT SAID is a town of about 37,000 inhabitants, and its origin is due to the Suez Canal. The new railroad and the increase of navigation through the canal make it a prosperous town. At this place the ship calls, on her way to Joppa and other Mediterranean points.

On the 7th day of March we were sailing toward the Holy Land. The sea was very calm; the moon and stars were shining very brightly while we were moving along on the great sea, so often referred to in the Bible. On the south of us land was seen, and along that coast was the old Egyptian and Damascus road.

The first sight of the Holy Land was Joppa, where so many interesting Bible lessons occurred. The ships anchor about one-half mile out in the sea from Joppa, on account of the very shallow and rocky harbor. The scenery is beautiful from the ship, the town lying in front of us on a hill.

The launch boats were all around the ship to convey the passengers to the shore, while the water was raging and the small boats pitching and rolling so that it seemed almost impossible to land. A reef of sharp, jagged rocks, over which the surf breaks fiercely, runs parallel with the shore. A narrow opening admits boats to the harbor inside. The calling and chatting of the natives in their boats, while their agents come and go for their passengers, make it very lively. The advice to all is, "Give yourselves into the hands of the boatmen," while they stand below, on the little boats, which are rocking, swinging and tossing in such an uneasy manner that it takes help for one to get into them; but one after another was caught hold of by the boatmen until all were safely aboard their little crafts, and in a short time we were all on the shore.

Calls were made for passports, and the custom officers were at work inspecting the baggage and giving permits. Soon we were all landed at the Jerusalem Hotel, about thirty-five in number, mostly Americans.

A rich, fertile plain stretches for twelve miles inland, and then a range of hills bound the view. Joppa was always the seaport of Jerusalem, and it was here that Hiram, King of Tyre, sent the wood to King Solomon that was cut out of Lebanon, for the building of the temple,[1] and from here it was taken to Jerusalem. From Joppa Jonah also went into a ship, and paid his fare, and fled from the presence of the Lord;[2] but the Lord invariably follows those that would flee from Him. As the sea became very boisterous, and fear came upon all, they began to cast forth the wares, that were in the ship, into the sea, to lighten it of its burden. But Jonah was fast asleep. So the master came and said unto him, "What meanest thou, O sleeper? Arise, call upon thy

---

[1] 2 Chron. 2:16.   [2] Jonah 1:3.

SEAPORT OF JOPPA, PALESTINE.
(Original Photo.)

God." And they said one to the other, "Come and let us cast lots, that we may know for whose cause this evil is upon us." So they cast lots, and the lot fell upon Jonah. And Jonah humbly acknowledged and said unto them, "I am an Hebrew, and I fear the Lord, the God of heaven, which hath

JONAH AND THE WHALE.

made the sea and the dry land." And they were exceedingly afraid, and said unto him, "What shall we do unto thee, that the sea may be calm unto us?" And Jonah said, "Take me up and cast me forth into the sea, so shall the sea be calm unto you." Nevertheless, the men rowed hard to bring the ship to the land, but they could not. So they took up Jonah and cast him forth into the sea, and the sea ceased from her raging. But we find the Lord had prepared a great fish to swallow Jonah; and Jonah prayed unto the Lord, and the Lord heard him, [1] as He always will, and the Lord spake unto the fish, and it vomited Jonah out upon the dry land. [2] What a lesson this ought to teach everyone—not to flee from what the Lord requires of us, but humbly to yield obedience! He, as a wise parent, will not require more of us than we are able to perform.

At Joppa the widows stood weeping, and showing the coats and garments which Dorcas had made while she was yet with them. [3] "And they called for Peter, who put them all forth, and kneeled down and prayed, and turning him to the body said unto her, Arise. And she opened her eyes; and when she saw Peter, she sat up." This is a very good example. If we are in distress or in sickness, the apostle says, "Is any sick among you, let him call for the elders of the church; and let them pray over him, anointing him with oil in the name of the Lord: and the prayer of faith shall save the sick, and the Lord shall raise him up; and if he have committed sins, they shall be forgiven him." [4]

On the shore stood the house of Simon the tanner, to which we made a visit. Here Peter was taught by a vision that Jewish exclusiveness must come to an end, and that henceforth he should call nothing common or unclean. [5]

Here Napoleon Bonaparte infamously shot four thousand Turkish troops, who had surrendered as prisoners of war.

The population of Joppa is about eight thousand, but indications point to an increase. The plain of Sharon lies

[1] Jonah 2:1. [2] Jonah 2:10. [3] Acts 9:36–43. [4] James 5:14–15. [5] Acts 10:1–18.

RUINED CHURCH AT LYDDA.

along the coast north of Joppa. It is famed for its fertility and beauty. Its fields bear rich harvests. Groves of oranges, lemons, olives and palms are interspersed with many vineyards, and in spring, in many places, it is covered with a profusion of flowers. Indeed, the blossoms and the flowers of various kinds send forth a perfume which is very invigorating, in connection with the pleasant climate and the sea breeze. In Solomon's Song of songs we find the expression, "I am the rose of Sharon,"[1] in which the rose is used as a symbol to express the highest ideal of grace and beauty. Now "Sharon is like a wilderness."[2] A few years ago there were only a few wretched hamlets of mud huts on the entire plain. But it will not be so always; once more "Sharon shall be a fold for flocks."[3]

RAILWAY TO JERUSALEM.

This railway, fifty-four miles in length, was opened in 1862. We heard it proclaimed in Jerusalem that it was the fulfilling of the prophecy in Isa. 35:8. "And an highway shall be there, and a way, and it shall be called The way of holiness." This we consider an erroneous idea. The prophet has reference to the blessings of the gospel and the entire deliverance from sin, through the cleansing power of His precious blood. There are five stations between Joppa and Jerusalem. Crossing the plain of Sharon, the first station is Lod, the Lydda of the New Testament, situated among the palms. Here the Apostle Peter healed Eneas of the palsy.[4] The next station is Ramleh, where there are not less than twelve square miles of orange groves.

The Jerusalem station is two thousand four hundred and thirty-five feet above the sea level. Hence the railroad rises

[1] Song of Solomon 2:1.   [2] Isa. 33.   [3] Isa. 65:10.   [4] Acts 9:33-35.

rapidly as it approaches the holy city. It is constructed on the narrow gauge plan, and the journey occupies about three hours. At this season the trains are packed to their utmost capacity, as there are many visitors, tourists and pilgrims from all countries, especially pilgrims from Europe, who come by the thousands. Many go afoot from Joppa to Jerusalem, others on donkeys and in carriages; we went on a special train. We went up toward the holy city, around curves and through mountains, until at last we caught the first glimpse of the city. Oh, what impressions crowd the mind, making one feel as though he should bow to everyone, and pull off his shoes before entering! As the train came up slowly around the curve, with the leper hospital and the German colony in view, we arrived at the station, where the first of the Jerusalem life is seen. We did not feel well at the time, being weary, and could scarcely realize that we were in the "Land of Christ." The crowding and soliciting of the natives and hackmen is very confusing. When an individual first arrives, seeing the country and towns, hills and valleys, orange and olive groves, vines and fig trees, and alleys, walls, houses and temples, donkeys, camels, carriages with two horses attached to them and loaded to their utmost with anxious visitors and pilgrims, natives driving like madmen, and a hard-looking class of people howling, screaming and talking, without knowing what is said, crowding the sidewalks with donkeys and everything else imaginable, and then thinking of it as the most holy city, the hills and streets, in which our beloved Savior lived, walked and died, the memory of which is so dear to every Christian child, it makes an impression that is beyond the power of language to describe.

JAFFA GATE. (*Original Photo.*)

O when, thou city of my God,
   Shall I thy courts ascend,
Where congregations ne'er break up,
   And Sabbaths never end?

When shall these eyes thy heav'n-built walls
   And pearly gates behold?
Thy bulwarks with salvation strong,
   And streets of shining gold?

A PLEASANT ACQUAINTANCE.

I was very fortunate in meeting Mr. John C. Mack, of Bristol, Conn., U. S. A., and to join him as a room-mate. Mr. Mack is a dear Christian man, and our pleasant visits, and the acquaintance which we formed, shall never, I trust, be forgotten. We found a good home in a hotel, with a family in the German colony, which was very satisfactory; charges, five francs per day, equal to one dollar of United States money.

The weather was cool and quite rainy, and being weary and worn, I did not expose myself to the wet and cold weather, as the changes are great going from India to Egypt and Palestine. Sunday, March 10th, the weather was cool and wet; Mr. J. C. Mack and myself, for the first time, entered the Jaffa gate.

CHAPTER XXIII.

Jerusalem and its History.

VISITOR'S FIRST IMPRESSION—INTEREST GROWS—JERUSALEM NOT A PLACE OF AMUSEMENT—KING DAVID'S REIGN—CHARACTER OF THE CITY—ANCIENT WALLS—MOUNT ZION—SOLOMON'S REIGN—THE CITY BEAUTIFIED—JERUSALEM DESTROYED AND REBUILT.

JERUSALEM, to most travelers, is a place of overwhelming interest; but at first sight many will be sadly disappointed in this dirty modern town, with its crooked and badly paved lanes. It would seem, at first, as though little were left of the ancient city of Zion and Moriah, the farfamed capital of the Jewish empire. It is only by patiently penetrating beneath the modern crust of rubbish and rottenness, which shrouds the sacred places from view, that the visitor will at length realize to himself a picture of the Jerusalem of antiquity, and this will be the more vivid in proportion to the amount of previously acquired historical information which he is able to bring to bear upon his researches. The longer and the oftener he sojourns in Jerusalem, the greater will be the interest with which its ruins will inspire him, though he will be obliged to confess that the degraded aspect of the modern city, and its material and moral decline, form but a melancholy termination to the stupendous scenes once enacted here.

The combination of wild superstition with the merest formalism which everywhere forces itself upon our notice, and the fanaticism and jealous exclusiveness of the numerous religious communities of Jerusalem, form the chief modern characteristics of the city, the holy city, once the fountain-head from which the knowledge of the true God was wont to be vouchsafed to mankind, and which has exercised the suprem-est influence on religious thought throughout the world. Jerusalem is therefore not a town for amusement, for every thing in it has a religious tinge, and from a religious point of view the impressions the visitor receives here are anything but pleasant. The native Christians of all sects are by no means equal to their task; the bitter war which rages amongst them is carried on with very foul weapons, and the contempt with which the orthodox Jews and Mohammedans look down on the Christians is only too well deserved.

When they conquered the country the Israelites found the Jebusites settled among the mountains of this district, Jebus, afterward the site of Jerusalem, being their capital. From the natural strength of its position the town was believed to be impregnable. We are informed very briefly that this Jebus was at length captured by King David.[1] The inhabitants, trusting to the strength of their city, derided the Israelites; but David took the city and established himself in the "Stronghold of Zion."

What then was the precise situation of this holy Mt. Zion? In order to answer this question we must first examine the topographical character of the city. The city was surrounded by deep valleys. Towards the east lay the valley of the Kidron, afterwards called the valley of Jehoshaphat,

[1] 2 Sam. 5 : 6—10.

and on the west and south sides, the valley of Hinnom. These two principal valleys enclosed a plateau, the north side of which bore the name of Bezetha, or place of Olives; and olive groves are still to be found in that locality.

On the south half of this plateau lay the city of Jerusalem, which was divided into different quarters by natural depressions of the soil. The chief of these natural boundaries was a small valley coming from the north, running at first south by south-east, and then due south, and separating two hills, of which that to the west now rises 105 feet above the precipitous east hill. This valley was called the Tyropœon (cheese-makers' valley or better, valley of dung).

On the south terrace of the east hill, where, to the south-east of the present Haram, lay the Ophel quarters, as well as on the other hill to the west of the Tyropœon, extended the ancient Jerusalem as far as the brink of the valley. The city-wall crossed the Tyropœon at its mouth far below. On the south side of the west hill (where there are now no houses) there was as early as David's time that part of the town which Josephus calls the Upper City. North-east of this quarter, opposite the hill of the temple, probably lay the bastion *Millo* ("Filling up").

Such are the undisputed facts. The questions which now arise are: what were the names of these hills, and what was the site of the ancient buildings?

In the first place, the site of the ancient temple must certainly have been on the east hill. The name Moriah for this hill of the temple occurs exceptionally in Gen. 22:2, and then in 2 Chron. 3:1, as a specifically religious appellation.

There are numerous passages in the Bible which prove that down to a late period the hill of the temple was included

MOSQUE OF OMAR, OR SOLOMON'S TEMPLE AS IT IS AT THE PRESENT TIME. (*Original Photo.*)

in the more popular name of Zion. This accounts for the frequent mention of the glory of Zion in the poetical books, for it was there that the temple stood. On the other hand, Zion is frequently used as synonymous with the city of David,[1] and is even poetically applied to Jerusalem itself, (Daughters of Zion).

Solomon began to beautify the city in a magnificent style, and above all, he erected on Mount Zion a beautiful palace and sanctuary. In order, however, to procure a level surface for the foundation of such an edifice, it was necessary to lay massive substructions. The temple of Solomon occupied the north part, the site of the upper terrace of the present day, on which the Dome of the Rock now stands.

The work begun by Solomon was continued by his successors, who constructed a more spacious precinct around the temple on ground which must have been artificially leveled for the purpose. The royal palace rose immediately.[2]

During his reign, Jerusalem first became the headquarters of the Israelites, and it was probably then that this new city in the north sprang up which he surrounded with fortifications. The glory of Jerusalem as the central point of the united empire was, however, of brief duration and it shortly afterwards became the capital of the southern kingdom of Judah only.

As early as Rehoboam's reign, the city was compelled to surrender to the Egyptian king Shishak, on which occasion the temple and palace were despoiled of part of their golden ornaments.

About one hundred years later, under King Jehoram, the temple was again plundered, the victors on this occasion

---

[1] 2 Sam. 5:7; 1 Kings 8:1.   [2] Ezek. 43:7, 8.

being Arabian and Philistine tribes.[1] Sixty years later, Jehoash, the king of the northern empire, having defeated Amaziah, king of Judah, effected a wide breach in the wall of Jerusalem and entered the city in triumph.[2] Uzziah, the son of Amaziah, re-established the prosperity of Jerusalem. During this period, however, Jerusalem was visited by a great earthquake.

Again the fortifications were repaired by Hezekiah,[3] to whom also was due the great merit of providing Jerusalem with water. The solid chalky limestone on which the city stands contains little water. The only spring at Jerusalem was the fountain of Gihon on the east slope of the temple hill.

[1] 2 Chron. 21:17.   [2] 2 Kings 14:13—14.   [3] 2 Chron. 32:5.

CHAPTER XXIV.

Jerusalem, from Hezekiah's Reign to the Present Time.

Jews carried into captivity — Solomon — Treasures stolen from Temple and carried to Babylon — Temple burned — Jews return — Destruction and bloodshed — Herod captured the city — The city enriched — Time of Christ — Was taken by the Persians — Fell to the Egyptians — Saladin captured the city — Kharezmians took it by storm — Under Turkish rule.

HEZEKIAH, on the whole, reigned prosperously, but the policy of his successors soon involved the city in ruin. In the reign of Jehoiachin, it was compelled to surrender, at discretion, to King Nebuchadnezzar.

Again the temple and the royal palace were pillaged, and a great number of the citizens, including King Jehoiachin, the nobles, 7,000 house owners, 1,000 craftsmen and their families, were carried away captive to the East.[1] Those who were left, having made a hopeless attempt under Zedekiah to revolt against their conquerors, Jerusalem now had to sustain a long and terrible siege (one year, five months and seven days). Pestilence and famine meanwhile ravaged the city. The Babylonians now carried off all treasures that still remained, the Temple of Solomon was burned to the

[1] 2 Kings 24 : 15.

ground, and Jerusalem reduced to the abject state of humiliation, so beautifully described by the author of the Lamentations, particularly in chapter 2. Jerusalem, however, was permitted to recover, to some extent, when the Jews returned from captivity, but it was not till the time of Nehemiah, the favored cup-bearer of the Persian king, Artaxerxes Longimanus, that the city was actually rebuilt.

But, alas! it was in the time of Antiochus Epiphanes that it again became a theatre of bloodshed. The inhabitants were slain, Jerusalem was destroyed, and a stronghold was established in the city by Antiochus for himself. Many struggles had to be undergone before this national restoration was consolidated, and frequently the Jews were compelled to capitulate by hunger alone; and in one struggle no less than 12,000 Jews are said to have perished.

Thirty-seven years before Christ, Herod, with the aid of the Romans, captured the city against a gallant defense. Under Roman rule Jerusalem became well fortified, and was rebuilt, so that with its numerous palaces and handsome edifices, the sumptuous temple with its colonnades, and the lofty city walls with their bastions, it must have presented a very striking appearance; and in picturing to ourselves the rebuilt city, we see numerous villas standing in beautiful gardens, some of which were probably very handsome buildings.

Such was the character of the city in the time of Christ. We learn from the New Testament that especially on the occasion of festivals the city was crowded with people. At the time of a certain festival it is said the Roman governor caused the counting of the paschal lambs, and found the vast total to be 270,000. From this we may infer that the number of partakers was no less than 2,700,000. Although these figures, like many of the other statements of Josephus, are probably much exaggerated, they at least tend to show that the great national festival was attended by vast crowds.

In 614, A. D., Jerusalem was taken by the Persians, and the churches destroyed, but it was soon afterward restored, chiefly with the aid of the Egyptians. In 969 Jerusalem fell into possession of the Egyptian Fatimites. Under their rule the Christians were sorely oppressed. Money was extorted from the pilgrims, and savage bands of Ortokides, or Turkish robbers, sometimes penetrated the churches of Jerusalem and maltreated the Christians during worship. In 1187 Saladin captured the city, treating the Christians, many of whom had before this fled to the surrounding villages, with great leniency. In 1244 the Kharezmians took the place by storm, and it soon fell under the supremacy of the Eyyubides. Since that period Jerusalem has been a Moslem city. In 1517 it fell into the hands of the Osmans.

In 1800 Napoleon planned the capture of Jerusalem, but gave up his intention. In 1825 the inhabitants revolted against the pasha on account of the severity of the taxation, and the city was, in consequence, bombarded by the Turks for a time; but a compromise of the disputes was effected. In 1831 Jerusalem submitted to Mohammed Ali Pasha, of Egypt, without much resistance; in 1834 a revolt of the Bedouins was quelled; and in 1840 Jerusalem again came into possession of the Sultan Abdul-Mejid, and is at the present time under Turkish rule.

CHAPTER XXV.

Solomon's Temple.

CITY WALLS—POOLS — HOUSES—STREETS — CLIMATE — ITS WATER SUPPLY — POPULATION — MOSQUE OF OMAR OR SOLOMON'S TEMPLE—MOUNT MORIAH—ROCK IN INTERIOR—FROM WHERE CHRIST DROVE THE CHANGERS—ABRAHAM AND MELCHIZEDEK SACRIFICING — WELL OF SOULS — GOLDEN NAILS — BLOWING THE TRUMPET—CALLING TO JUDGMENT—WIRE ROPE ACROSS THE VALLEY—VAULTS - STABLES OF SOLOMON.

ERUSALEM is enclosed by a wall thirty-six and a half feet in height, with thirty-four towers, forming an irregular quadrangle about two and a half miles in circumference. Seen from the Mount of Olives, Jerusalem presents a handsome appearance. The town possesses a few open spaces; the streets are illpaved and crooked, many of them being blind alleys, and are very dirty, especially after a rain.

In the walls there are eight gates, but one of them has been walled up: (1) Yafa gate; (2) The New gate, opened in 1889; (3) The Damascus gate; (4) Herod's gate; (5) St. Stephen's gate; (6) The Golden gate, which has long since been walled up; (7) Dung gate; (8) The gate of Zion.

As Jerusalem possesses no springs except the pool of Siloah (*Ain Silwan*) and Hammam esh-Shifa, or healing

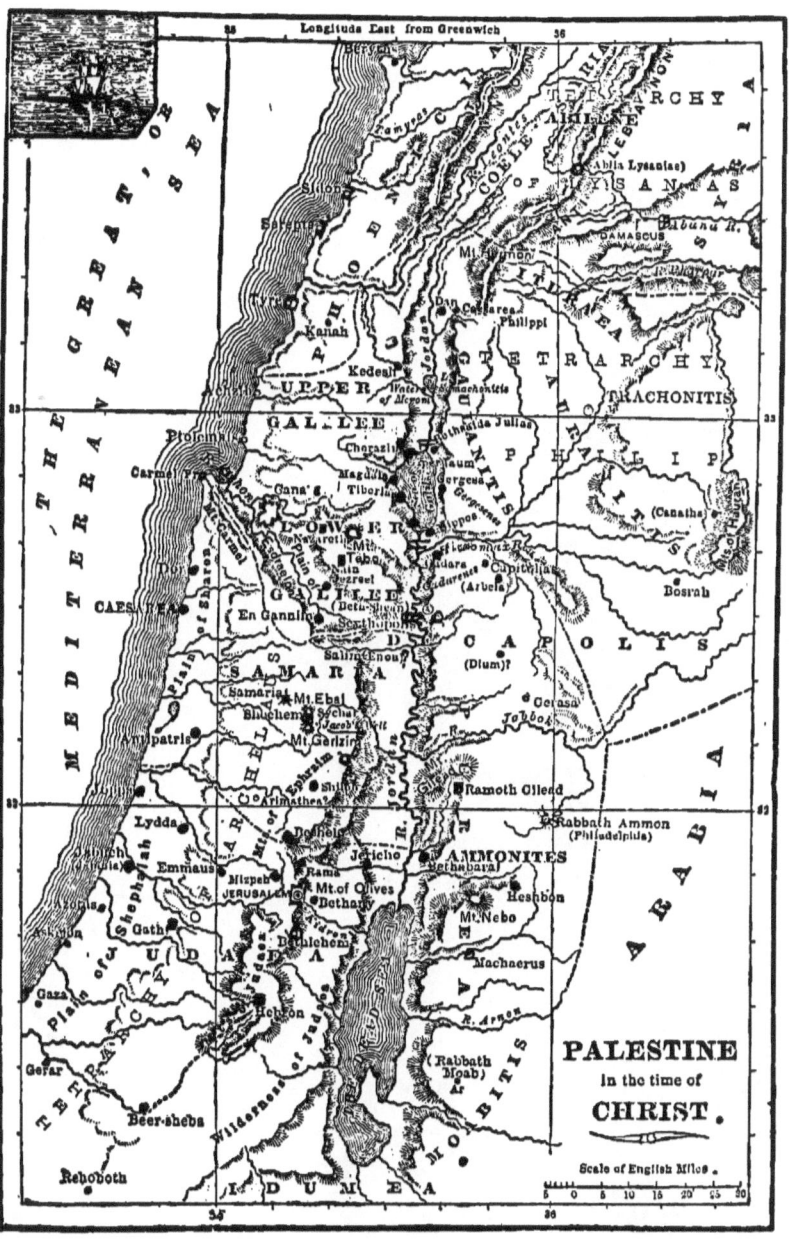

bath, supposed to have been the pool of Bethesda, the inhabitants obtain their supply of water from cisterns, the roofs of the houses and every available open space being made to contribute the rain that falls upon them. Owing to the scarcity of wood the houses are built entirely of stone. The court with cisterns forms the central point of each group of rooms. A genuine Jerusalem dwelling house consists of a number of separate apartments, each with an entrance and a dome shaped roof of its own. Some houses have flat roofs, but under these is always concealed a cupola. The cupolas do not spring from the tops of the walls, but a little within them, so that it is possible to walk round the outside of the cupolas. Pots and troughs for flowers are built into the roof and courts by the architects. In some of the houses there are no glass windows; nor are chimneys by any means universal, the charcoal smoke being in their absence allowed to escape by the doors and windows. The floors are composed of stone or hard cement.

The climate, on the whole, is healthy. The fresh sea breeze tempers the heat even during the hot months; at night there is frequently a considerable fall of temperature. The cistern water, too, is good and not in the least unhealthy when the cisterns are kept clean. The water in the cisterns certainly gets very low towards autumn and the poorer classes then have recourse to water from the pools. According to the usual estimate, the population numbers about 40,000, according to statistics of 1887 about 43,000. Of these about 7,560 are Moslems, 28,000 Jews, 2,000 Latins, 150 United Greeks, 50 United Armenians, 4,000 Orthodox Greeks, 510 Armenians, 100 Copts, 75 Ethiopians, 15 Syrians, and 300 Protestants. The different nationalities are distinguished by their costume. The number of Jews has greatly risen of late years in consequence of the persecution in Roumania and Russia. The immigration steadily increases, both of those who desire to be buried in the holy city and of those who intend to subsist on the charity of their European brethren,

from whom they receive their regular allowance, and for whom they pray at the holy places.

A VISIT TO SOLOMON'S TEMPLE.

The Haram esh-Sherif (Mosque of Omar) is one of the most profoundly interesting spots in the world. It was about this spot where David erected an altar.[1] It was to this place also that the Lord said to Abraham, "Take now

[1] 2 Sam. 24:25.

thy son, thine only son Isaac. whom thou lovest, and get thee into the land of Moriah."[1] It was here that Abraham prepared the altar and, when the Lord found him true and obedient, that the angel called unto him out of heaven, and said, "Abraham, Abraham," and he said "Here am I." The angel then said, "Lay not thine hand upon the lad, neither do thou anything unto him; for now I know that thou fearest God, seeing thou hast not withheld thy son, thine only son, from me." O what a thought to know that you stand where God so often manifested Himself on various occasions.

This is the place where David had determined to have the temple built for the Lord by his son Solomon, the king. For this purpose it was necessary to lay substructions on the slope of the hill, especially on the east (valley of Jehoshaphat), south (valley of Hinnom), and west (valley of Tyropœon) sides in order to procure a level surface.

A company of us, six in number, with our dragoman, entered an archway where on both sides were openings like those of many oriental shops. This archway looks very ancient, and the dragoman stated, "This is the place from whence Christ drove the buyers and sellers," saying "It is written, 'My Father's house shall be a house of prayer,' but ye have made it a den of thieves." The large space within the enclosure, covered with buildings, forms a somewhat irregular quadrangle. The west side measures 536 yards, the east side 518 yards, the north side 351 yards, and the south side 309 yards in length; the surface is not entirely level, the north-west corner being about ten feet higher than the north-east and the two south corners.

[1] Gen. 22:2.

We now proceed to the description of the Holy Rock as it is called. It is fifty-seven feet long, forty-three feet wide, and rises about six and a half feet above the surrounding pavement. According to Jewish tradition, Abraham and Melchizedek made sacrifices here, and it was regarded as the central point of the world. The ark of the covenant is said to have once stood here. The probability is that the great sacrificial altar stood here, and traces of a channel for carrying off the blood have been discovered on the rock. The place is shown where Zacharias was offering and also where he was slain.

The guide knocks on a round stone plate almost in the middle of the floor; there is evidently a hollow underneath. The Moslems maintain that beneath this rock is the well of souls, where the souls of the deceased assemble to pray twice weekly.

A number of noted places are referred to by Moslems. In front of the north entrance there is let into the ground or floor a slab of jasper into which Mohammed is said to have driven nineteen golden nails; a nail falls out at the end of every epoch, and when all are gone the end of the world will arrive. We were carefully led there by the accompanying Moslem, kneeling down and pointing with his finger to this spot, repeating foreign words and saying to us, "Now all those that pay bakhshish on this stone will then go to heaven and those who will not pay will not go to heaven;" also claiming that from this place the great trumpet of God will be blown for all to come to judgment.

Every step is of great interest to them at that place, and while they are the followers of Mohammed, they honor Christ as a prophet.

(Original Photo).
INTERIOR OF THE MOSQUE OF OMAR.
(Showing the traditional rock upon which Isaac was offered.)

I look upon the holy mount
    Where Israel's father stood
Long years ago, at God's command,
    To offer guiltless blood.

On this " Jehovah-Jireh" mount
    In later years arose
God's holy temple, Israel's joy
    And strength midst all her woes.

And in that temple, on that mount,
    Did Zacharias stand
To offer holy sacrifice
    At the divine command.

A little further on we find a stair ascending to the top of the wall, which affords an admirable view of the valley of Jehoshaphat with its tombs immediately below, and of the Mt. of Olives. We find here the stump of a column built in horizontally and protruding over the wall. A small building has been erected over the inner end, for prayer.

The Moslems say that all men will assemble in the valley of Jehoshaphat when the trumpet blast proclaims the last judgment. From this prostrate column a thin wire rope will then be stretched to the Mt. of Olives opposite. Christ will sit on the wall, and Mohammed on the Mount, as judges. All men must pass over the intervening space on the rope. The righteous, preserved from falling by their angels, will cross with lightning speed, while the wicked will be precipitated into the abyss of hell.

Descending thirty-two steps, we enter a small Moslem oratory, where a horizontal niche, surmounted by a dome borne by four small columns, is pointed out as the "Cradle of Christ," under which name it was also known in mediaeval times. In pre-Islamic times the Basilika Theotokos (of the Mother of God) or Maria Nova was here. This curious tradition seems to have been founded on an old custom of Hebrew women who came hither to await their confinement. According to the legend, this was the dwelling place of the aged Simeon, and the Virgin spent a few days here after the Presentation in the Temple.

From this point we descend into the spacious substructions, which the Arabs attribute to the agency of demons, but which in their present form are of no great antiquity. They consist of semicircular vaults about twenty-eight feet high, resting on one hundred square piers, chiefly composed of ancient drafted stones, and are an imitation of similar older substructions which once occupied the same spot. Tradition calls them Solomon's Stables, and there may be some true foundation for the name, for the palace of that monarch was probably somewhere in this neighborhood.

Many Jews sought refuge in the subterranean vaults during their struggle against the Romans, and there is other evidence that substructions of this kind existed at an early period in this corner and the stables of the Frank kings and of the Templars were here, and the rings to which they attached their horses still exist. The vaults extend ninety-one yards from east to west and sixty-six yards from north to south. There are altogether thirteen vaults of unequal length and breadth. Thus a few of the many items have been given. The arch work, the columns, and space underneath are almost beyond description. The illustration of Solomon's Stables will give the reader some idea of their appearance.

It is but a few years since it was death for a Christian to enter this great Mosque of Omar; but now any one can be admitted on payment of a small fee, the feet being covered with large slippers. The general appearance of the temple is fascinating, and a great deal of mosaic work is seen. Frequently the dragoman points to certain parts which are claimed to be from the original temple of Solomon. Here is given what was observed, and what traditions say, and truly the words of Christ are confirmed in our minds, where He says, as He went out of the temple, "Seest thou these great buildings? there shall not be left one stone upon another that shall not be thrown down." There are, however, on and around the mountain, traces left of the extent and grandeur of the buildings which once adorned its crest.

(Original Photo.)
STABLES OF SOLOMON.

CHAPTER XXVI.

Calvary and Tomb of Christ.

Jews' Wailing Place—Chanting—Immense Stones—Golgotha Grotto of Jeremiah—The Cross Conquered the World —Dearest Spot on Earth—Rent in the Rock— Consoling Angel.—Turkish Officials— Different Chapels—Decoration.

COMING around the outside wall and turning down a narrow lane leading to the left, we reach the wailing place of the Jews (see illus., p. 175), situated beyond the miserable dwellings of the Moghrebins. The celebrated wall which bears this name is fifty-two yards in length and fifty-six feet in height. The lowest nine courses of stone consist of huge blocks, some of which, however, are drafted. Above these are fifteen layers of smaller stones. Some of the blocks, many of which have suffered much from exposure, are of vast size, one in the north part of the wall being sixteen feet, and one in the south part thirteen feet in length. It is probable that the Jews, as early as the middle ages, were in the habit of gathering hither to bewail the downfall of Jerusalem.

This spot should be visited repeatedly, especially on a Friday after 4 o'clock, when a touching scene is presented by the figures leaning against the weather-beaten wall, kissing the stones, and weeping. The men, many of them barefoot, often sit here for hours, reading their Hebrew prayer-books. The Spanish Jews, whose appearance and bearing are often refined and independent, present a pleasing contrast to their squalid brethren from Poland.

On Friday, towards evening, the following lines are chanted:

1. Leader. For the palace that lies desolate,
   Response. We sit in solitude and mourn.
2. L. For the palace that is destroyed,
   R. We sit in solitude and mourn.
3. L. For the walls that are overthrown,
   R. We sit in solitude and mourn.
4. L. For our majesty that is departed,
   R. We sit in solitude and mourn.
5. L. For our great men who lie dead,
   R. We sit in solitude and mourn.
6. L. For the precious stones that are burned,
   R. We sit in solitude and mourn.
7. L. For the priests who have stumbled,
   R. We sit in solitude and mourn.
8. L. For our kings who have despised Him,
   R. We sit in solitude and mourn.

Another chant is as follows:

1. Leader. We pray Thee, have mercy on Zion!
   Response. Gather the children of Jerusalem.
2. L. Haste, haste, Redeemer of Zion!
   R. Speak to the heart of Jerusalem.
3. L. May beauty and majesty surround Zion!
   R. Ah! turn Thyself mercifully to Jerusalem.
4. L. May peace and joy abide with Zion;
   R. And the branch (of Jesse) spring up at Jerusalem.

CHURCH OF THE HOLY SEPULCHRE.

Leaving the place of wailing, we pass immense blocks of stone, one seven and one-half feet thick and eighteen feet long, now situated ten feet above the ground; another is twenty-six feet long, and still another twenty-seven and one-half feet long. This is very remarkable, although it is sometimes difficult to distinguish the joints from clefts caused by age.

THE CHURCH OF THE HOLY SEPULCHRE, AND GOLGOTHA.

The Bible says that Golgotha (see illus., p. 105) lay outside the city.[1] "Now when they were going, behold some of the watch came into the city, and showed unto the chief priests all the things that were done." Golgotha was an eminence, or perhaps only a small rocky elevation, called, on account of its peculiar shape, "skull." To the north and south of the place pointed out by tradition the ground drops gradually. The first point of controversy, among many, is whether the genuine Golgotha lay in this neighborhood or not. Several modern explorers look for Golgotha to the north of the city, near the grotto of Jeremiah. As there is much written on this subject, we can only present the arguments advanced by others in support of the authenticity of the sites.

No one can doubt for a moment that the early disciples and apostles were acquainted with the place of their Master's death and burial; and many of those who were with Him on His triumphal entry into the city but a short time before His crucifixion, must certainly have known the site of Golgotha.

There were many in Jerusalem at this time, and a few weeks after His death, at the remarkable event of the outpouring of the Holy Ghost, there were three thousand

[1] Matt. 28:11.

witnesses, and others daily, added to the church. There never was a time when there was not a Christian community in the city, and can any one suppose that during this period, when the religion of the Cross was conquering the world, and thousands from distant lands were visiting the holy city, the locality of Calvary and the tomb of Jesus could be forgotten? It is true that during the siege of Titus many of the Christians took flight beyond the Jordan, and others took refuge in the caves and rock tombs along the Kedron; there were, however, many aged, and sick, and poor, who remained in the city. Eusebius says that not more than half the population left, and most of those who left returned immediately after the siege was over. But can it be supposed that in this brief interval of less than five months, the place before all others dear to them would be lost sight of so easily?

There is not a spot on earth so dear to the Christian heart as Mount Calvary, where the Lord was crucified, surrounded by a howling mob. While there were a few of His beloved following Him to behold what was to take place, the others were scattered like sheep without a shepherd. O, the place where the Lamb of God was nailed to the rugged cross, which was raised up and dropped into its socket! Innocent as He was, yet He was placed between two thieves. The sun lost its light, the heavens darkened, the earth quaked, while He cried out with a loud voice, saying, "My God, my God, why hast Thou forsaken me?" The Father had not forsaken Him, but it was that the great plan of human redemption might be completed for you and me, my dear reader.

And Jesus, when He had cried again, gave up the ghost. And behold, the vail of the temple was rent in twain, the

THE CHURCH OF THE HOLY SEPULCHRE.

earth quaked, the rocks rent, and the graves were opened Many of those who had slept arose and came out of their graves,[1] and all acknowledged, saying, "Truly this was the Son of God."

Oh, my readers, that sacred spot (Mount Calvary) should be dear to you all, because there the plan of redemption was settled forever, when He cried, "It is finished!" All may come to Him and be saved.

This is the place where He was taken from the cross by Joseph and laid in his own tomb with the greatest respect and honor, as the one that would draw all the world to Himself; there were many dear ones from the city, and John, to whom the Lord committed the care of His mother, following Him.

By removing a slab, our attention was called to a rent in the rock underneath, which it is claimed was caused by the earthquake at the time of the crucifixion. We were also shown the spot and socket wherein the cross stood, together with a part of the stone that was rolled upon the tomb.

This is also designated as the place where the women came early in the morning to see the sepulchre. And behold there was a great earthquake, for the angel of the Lord descended from heaven and came and rolled away the stone from the door, and sat on it. And the angel so kindly and affectionately said unto the women, "Fear not ye: for I know that ye seek Jesus, which was crucified." And Mary stood without at the sepulchre, weeping; and as she wept she stooped down, longing to know where He was. She saw two angels, which said unto her, "Woman, why weepest thou?" Oh, how often does the angel come to you and me.

[1] Matt. 27.

in the hour of grief and distress, to comfort and console! She answered, "Because they have taken away my Lord."

Oh, what a heart of humility, of meekness and tenderness, is shown by this dear Christian woman, out of whom the Lord had cast seven devils![1] How true the words of the Lord, "To whom much is forgiven, the same loveth much."

It is an unpleasant fact that Moslem officials, appointed by the Turkish government, sit in the vestibule of the Church of the Holy Sepulchre, built on this site, for the purpose of keeping order, particularly on Easter occasions, among Christians (as they are called). Pilgrims come from all parts of the world, and yet the presence of such a guard is absolutely necessary, so completely does jealousy and fanaticism usurp the place of true religion in the minds of many of these visitors to the holy city.

The church is divided into many different chapels and departments, some of which are: 1, The Church of the Apostles, so-called, with the altar of Melchizedek; 2, Chapel of the Sacrifice of Isaac; 3, Chapel of St. James, where stands the tree in which the ram is said to have been entangled; 4, Chapel of St. Mary of Egypt; 5, Greek Chapel of St. James; 6, Chapel of Mary Magdalene; 7, Chapel of the Forty Martyrs; 8, Post of the Moslem Officials; 9, Stone of Anointment;[2] 10, Place from which the women witnessed the anointment; 11, Angels' Chapel; 12, Chapel of the Sepulchre; 13, Chapel of the Copts; 14, Chapel of the Syrians; 15, Chamber in the Rock; 16, Passage to the Coptic Monastery; 17, Passage to the Cistern; 18, Cistern; 19, Antechamber of next chapel; 20, Chapel of the Apparition; 21,

[1] Mark 16:9. [2] John 19:38-40.

CHURCH OF THE HOLY SEPULCHRE.

Latin Sacristy; 22, Catholicon; 23, Centre of the World; 24, First seat of the Patriarch of Jerusalem; 25, Second seat: 26, Aisle of the Church of the Crusaders; 27, Chapel (Prison of Christ); 28, Chapel of St. Longinus; 29, Chapel of Parting of the Raiment; 30, Chapel of the Derision; 31, Chapel of the Empress Helena; 32, Altar of the Penitent Thief; 33, Altar of the Empress; 34, Seat of the Empress; 35, Chapel of the Finding of the Cross; 36, Chapel of the Raising of the Cross; 37, Hole of the Cross; 38, Chapel of the Nailing to the Cross; 39, Chapel of the Agony; 40, Abysinian Chapel.

All these different departments being decorated with pictures and paintings, lights, lamps and curtains, make a very solemn impression; and while thousands visit this place and show it the greatest reverence by removing their shoes, and kissing the stones on which they walk, others roam around without showing any respect whatever. While we sincerely deplore the ignorance and fanaticism of these people, we also admire the zeal and honesty of many that come from distant lands, spending much time and money to make a pilgrimage to the holy city at least once in their lifetime.

CHAPTER XXVII.

Easter in Jerusalem.

EXCITING SCENES—EASTER FESTIVAL—GRAND MASS—GOOD FRIDAY—
HOLY FIRE—IMMENSE CROWDS—CHURCH ILLUMINATED—
FIGHTING AND ACCIDENTS—ROUGH MANNERED
OFFICIALS — WILDEST CONFUSION —
TURNING SOMERSAULTS.

E were permitted to spend about six weeks in and about Jerusalem, which time included Easter. Many painful sights were witnessed that were enacted by the so-called Christians as well as the Mohammedans while holding their great feasts. The worst of all is the scene of the holy fire for a description of which Baedeker is quoted:—

"During the Festival of Easter, the Church of the Sepulchre is crowded with pilgrims of every nationality, and there are enacted, both in the church and throughout the town, many disorderly scenes which produce a painful impression. The ecclesiastical ceremonies are very inferior in interest to those performed at Rome.

In former times, particularly during the regime of the Crusaders, the Latins used to represent the entry of Christ riding on an ass from Bethphage, but this was afterwards done in the interior of the church only. Palm and olive-branches were scattered about on the occasion, and to this day the Latins send to Gaza for palm branches, which are consecrated on Palm Sunday and distributed among the people. On Holy Thursday, the Latins celebrate a grand mass and walk in procession round the chapel of the Sepulchre, after which the 'washing of feet' takes place at the door of the Sepulchre. The Greeks also perform the washing of feet, but their festival does not always fall on the same day as that of the Latins. Good Friday is also celebrated by the Franciscans with a mystery play, the proceedings terminating with the nailing of a figure to a cross, and the Greeks still have a similar practice.

One of the most disgraceful spectacles is the so-called miracle of the Holy Fire, in which the Latins participated down to the sixteenth century, but which has since been managed by the Greeks alone. On this occasion the church is always crowded with spectators. Strangers are admitted to the galleries, which belong to the Latins. The Greeks declare the miracle to date from the apostolic age, and it is mentioned by the monk Bernhard as early as the ninth century. Khalif Hakim was told that the priest used to besmear the wire by which the lamp was suspended over the sepulchre with resinous oil, and to set it on fire from the roof. Large sums are paid to the priests by those who are allowed to be the first to light their tapers at the 'sacred flame sent from heaven. The wild and noisy scene begins on Good Friday. The crowd passes the night in the church in order to secure places, some of them attaching themselves by cords to the sepulchre, while others run round it in anything but a reverential manner.

On Easter Eve, about 2 p. m., a procession of the superior clergy moves round the Sepulchre, all lamps having been carefully extinguished in view of the crowd. Some members of the higher orders of the priesthood enter the chapel of the Sepulchre, while the priests pray and the people are in the utmost suspense. At length, the fire which has come down from heaven (?) is pushed through a window of the Sepulchre, and there now follows an indescribable tumult, every one endeavoring to be the first to get his taper lighted. In a few seconds, the whole church is illuminated. This, however, never happens without fighting, and accidents generally occur owing to the crush. The spectators do not appear to take warning from the terrible catastrophe of 1834. On that occasion, there were upwards of 6,000 persons in the church, when a riot suddenly broke out. The Turkish guards, thinking they were attacked, used their weapons against the pilgrims, and in the scuffle that followed about 300 pilgrims were suffocated or trampled to death. — Late on Easter Eve, a solemn service is performed; the pilgrims with torches shout Hallelujah, while the priests move round the Sepulchre singing hymns."

During these exciting ceremonies the guards and soldiers are on duty. When the pilgrims make a sudden rush in their excitement, no respect whatever is shown by the guards, who, having whips with long lashes, strike the crowd over the heads. One aged lady was seen to weep like a child because of the severe treatment she had received in this way.

Arrangements must be made with some of the guides or priests for admission, or the probability is that nothing can be seen or heard. We occupied a position in the gallery, and all the available space was occupied by a densely packed crowd.

During the time previous to the coming of the holy fire the wildest confusion prevailed; there was singing, shouting,

(*Original Photo.*)
INTERIOR OF THE COENACULUM, ENTERING THE UPPER ROOM.

> That doleful night before His death,
>   The Lamb, for sinners slain,
> Did, almost with His latest breath,
>   That solemn feast ordain.
> O tune our tongues, and set in frame
>   Each heart that pants for Thee,
> To sing, "Hosanna to the Lamb,
>   The Lamb that died for me."
> —J. Hart.

and yelling beyond description. The people stood very close together. During the most intense excitement six men climbed upon the shoulders of others and formed a circle by putting their arms around each other's necks; soon two others mounted the shoulders of the six; from this position they turned somersaults upon the heads of the crowd below. The people in return threw and pushed them promiscuously about upon the heads of others, all of them yelling, shouting and singing: Ha! O! Ho! Ho! Ho! Ha! O! Ho! Ho! Ho!

The noise and confusion as well as the danger was most alarming to those who had never before witnessed these scenes. The crowd was apparently completely exhausted, and the air was foul and heated. It would seem to the intelligent mind that such scenes and doings do not belong to the worship of the Most High God.

CHAPTER XXVIII.

Missions, and Jewish Passover.

MISSIONS—GERMAN AND ENGLISH SERVICES—JEWISH PASSOVER—
TWO MILLION SOULS—PASSOVER SERVICES IN EVERY HOUSE—
MESSIAH COMES — WINE AND UNLEAVENED BREAD —
GREEK FOOT-WASHING—LATIN FOOT-WASHING ST.
STEPHENS' GATE—POOL OF BETHESDA—VIA
DOLOROSA — ECCE HOMO ARCH — HOUSE
OF DIVES — BATHING THE
STONES WITH TEARS.

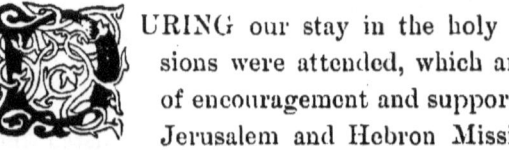URING our stay in the holy city several missions were attended, which are indeed worthy of encouragement and support. The one called Jerusalem and Hebron Mission is under the charge of Mr. and Mrs. Murry, Europeans. Mr. Murry is a dear Christian brother, and has his work at heart. He is ably supplemented by his wife, who, although blind— not able to see with her natural eyes—goes from place to place without much difficulty, and earnestly pleads for all to come to Christ. We spent some time with them in their home and mission.

We also attended a mission at Jerusalem, conducted by D. C. Joseph, who labors principally among the Jews. Mr. Joseph, being a converted Jew himself, takes great delight in laboring among his own people. It being our first visit here, we were requested to preach to the Jews, to which we

POOL OF SILOAM.

responded, preaching twice—once in the English and once in the German language, as they understood the German rather better than the English. The Jews, in their simple way of being open-hearted, stepped up to me and said, "*Danke inen fir euren guten rath. Danke fir den guten rath.*" May the Lord bless these dear young Jewish people in Jerusalem, is my prayer.

PASSOVER.

The time had come for the Jewish passover,[1] it being the 8th day of April, and the day after Christ made His triumphal entry into Jerusalem with 2,000,000 souls, according to Josephus.

This is a time of great importance in Jerusalem, and, on an invitation from a Jewish family, with others from the mission, one of whom was Mr. R. Poweck, we attended these services. Going down through the Jewish quarters we heard a peculiar noise, and on inquiry, found that in every house services were being held according to the instructions in the Bible.

They have books in the Hebrew language, out of which they read. The father of the family which had invited us to be present at their services could speak the English language quite well, and translated for us the most important parts, stating that the book gave the history of the great delivery of Israel from bondage, besides containing some prayers.

A table was set in the middle of the room, with three wine glasses thereon; these were filled, and one of them removed to the farther side of the table, with the statement that it belonged to Elias, who would come before the Messiah

[1] Exodus 12:18.

came. They also have unleavened bread—nothing but flour and water, with bitter herbs, and boiled eggs. Then reading in their books of God's dealings with them, and of His command to them to keep this Passover, they drink of the wine in the two glasses. Thus they read four times, and continue to drink wine. They had no lamb at this service, but meat to represent the lamb, and also the head of a fowl, to show that a sacrifice had been made. They then ate boiled vegetables, fish and soup, doing away with knives and forks, simply using their fingers. There was no prayer offered, and all seemed to be indifferent and uninterested. Previous to this feast their houses are cleansed, and all the clothing and dishes are either new or thoroughly cleansed.

There was something sad connected with this service, knowing that the Jews were the appointed people of God, but were left and forsaken, and thus they lament their sad condition. A Jew told me that they were forsaken by God, and that they never see a really peaceful day. I told him that was not the case, that God had done all; they left God and rejected His Son Jesus Christ, and they, with all others, must repent and come back to God. But they believe that God will yet send the Messiah and restore Jerusalem, and gather them into their own land.

GREEK FEET-WASHING.

April 11.—During the Easter festivals feet-washing is observed by the Greeks, and also by the Latins. This was a very interesting service to us. In front of the Church of the Holy Sepulchre there is a yard in which a platform was erected, on which sat the patriarch and the twelve chosen ones, to represent the twelve disciples, one of the twelve to represent Peter and one to represent Judas. The one who

(*Original Photo.*)

GREEK CEREMONY OF FEET WASHING.

takes the part of Judas usually betrays himself by his looks. After reading the Scripture lesson, the Greek partriarh, representing Christ, went a short distance with three of his pretended disciples, and knelt down, as though in prayer, under an olive tree, planted there for the occasion. After a few minutes he returned to the stage, and taking off his garment washed and afterward kissed the feet of those on the stage with him. The one representing Peter at first hesitated and then refused to submit to such an act on the part of his lord, but finally was persuaded to yield.

The vessel which was used in this ceremony was rich in its appearance; and the water, after being used, was put into small bottles that were handed in, and given out by those on the platform to their friends, for which favor they undoubtedly were well paid, as there was quite a struggle among those who wished to obtain some of it. The patriarch, with a bunch of hyssop, sprinkled the vast assemblage with the water that remained.

After the feet had been washed, the patriarch put on his robe and sat down and talked to those whose feet he had washed, as the Scripture teaches that Christ did.

In the afternoon the Latins held their feet-washing in the interior of the church. This seems to be a very popular service amongst these ancient Christians, but in these days of progression there are many Peters that hesitate, and even some that ridicule this ceremony; but Jesus says, "I have given you an example, and as I have done, so ye also ought to wash one another's feet."

The spirit of humility that Mary possessed did not need any urging as she sat at His feet washing them with the tears that fell from her eyes, and wiping them with the hair of her head. O, what a lesson of humility and an example for all Christians to imitate in the fear of the Lord! Jesus says, "If ye know these things, happy are ye if ye do them."

FROM THE PRISON TO CALVARY.

JERUSALEM   ARC DE L'ECCE HOMO, VIA DOLOROSA.

Must Jesus bear the cross alone,
And all the world go free?
No! there is a cross for every one,
And there is a cross for me.

Saint Stephen's gate is so called from the fact that it was near here that Stephen was stoned to death. On the outside of the gate, over the entrance, are two lions hewn in stone in half-relief. Within the gate a doorway immediately to the right leads to the church of St. Anne, descending to a crypt, which is almost entirely hewn in the rock and consists of two parts, the second of which resembles a cistern. This was formerly a sanctuary with altars, and is said by tradition to have been the dwelling of St. Anne, and the birthplace of the Virgin.

To the north-west of the church is the pool of Bethesda. In this pool there was virtue to heal when the water was stirred by the angel; and Jesus saw a man there which had an infirmity thirty and eight years. And He said unto him, for He knew that he had been in that condition for a long time, "Wilt thou be made whole?" Jesus then saith unto him, "Rise, take up thy bed and walk,"[1] and immediately the man was healed.

Passing the Chapel of the Scourging, and going a few steps further we are in front of the barracks, and here begins the *Via Dolorosa*, or the Street of Pain, the route by which Christ is said to have borne His cross to Golgotha. The present barracks occupying the site of the ancient castle of Antonia, are said to stand on the ground once occupied by the Pretorium, the residence of Pilate.

The Street of Pain, or the road traveled by Christ bearing the cross, is divided into fourteen different stations. The first is the chapel in the Turkish barracks already mentioned; second, where the cross was laid upon Christ, just below the steps ascending to the barracks. We next observe a large, handsome building on the right. This is the institution of the Sisters of Zion, and here an arch, called the Ecce Homo arch, or arch of Pilate, crosses the street, marking the spot where the Roman governor is said to have uttered the words: "Behold the man."[2]

Passing on we come near a broken column, forming the third station, near which Christ is said to have sunk under

[1] John 5: 2—9. [2] John 19:5.

the weight of the cross. Farther on we come to the traditional house of the poor man Lazarus,[1] beyond which, opposite this lane, is the fourth station, where Christ is said to have met His mother. Farther on we come to the "House of Dives," the rich man. The house is built of stone of various colors and possesses a small balcony. Here is the fifth station, where Simon of Cyrene took the cross from Christ. A stone built into the next house to the left has a depression in it said to have been caused by the hand of Christ. About one hundred steps farther on we come to the sixth station. To the left is the house and tomb of St. Veronica, who is said to have wiped the sweat from the Savior's brow at this spot, whereupon His image remained imprinted on her handkerchief.

Before passing through the vaulting or arch work, we see to the left a house against which Christ is said to have leaned, or near which He fell the second time, the seventh station. The eighth station is where Christ is said to have addressed the women who accompanied Him; the ninth is said to be where Christ sank again under the weight of the cross; the tenth is where Christ was disrobed; the eleventh, where He was nailed to the cross; the twelfth, that of the raising of the cross; the thirteenth, where He was taken down from the cross; the fourteenth, the Holy Sepulchre.

What a record this is of the journey from prison to Calvary, loaded with the sins of the world. Whatever our views and feelings may be in regard to these different places designated by the Greeks and Latins, we cannot altogether disregard them, drenched as they have been with the tears of multitudes for generations. Many, both rich and poor, bathe

[1] Luke 16:20.

these hallowed stones with their tears, and kiss them as they pass along, some on their hands and knees, thus symbolizing the humility, sufferings, and obstacles met by their blessed Master. Others go in groups accompanied by a priest, and at each station, on their knees, a short prayer is offered up. So while we are here, in this Christian land, let us not forget that it becomes us as Christians to follow the Master through the street of pain in our minds and hearts and become more obedient and subject to His divine will.

CHAPTER XXIX.

STREETS AND SHOPS.

STREETS—LANES—GRAIN MARKETS—BAZAARS—JEWISH QUARTERS—SHOPS—CASTLE OF DAVID—JAFFA GATE—VALLEY OF HINNOM—BURIAL GROUNDS—GIHON—OFFICIAL BUILDINGS—HOSPITALS—ZION'S GATE—COENACULUM—TOMBS OF KINGS, DAVID AND SOLOMON—OUTPOURING OF THE HOLY GHOST—WASHING OF THE APOSTLES' FEET—LAST SUPPER—HOUSE OF CAIAPHAS.

THE three principal streets of Jerusalem are called Christian street, David street, and Damascus street. On Christian street the shops are somewhat more in European style than on the other streets. David street, to the left, forms the corn market, as we see by the large heaps of grain and baskets of seed in every direction. Proceeding farther on will bring us to the Old Bazaar, consisting of three covered streets running north and south and intersected by several transverse lanes. The bazaars occupy the center of the town, but are very inferior, as Jerusalem possesses neither manufactories nor wholesale houses worthy of mention. The east bazaar street which leads towards the south to the Jewish quarters is a dirty street with brokers' stalls, shops for the sale of tinware manufactured by the Jews, and many Jewish shops where work is done in olive wood, all kinds of curious things being made to sell to the pilgrims in memory of Jerusalem and Mount Olivet; and indeed these manufacturers

are very anxious to sell their goods. Further on we reach the castle of David, tradition gives it that this monarch once had his palace here.

We are now just inside of the Jaffa gate, which is the main entrance into the city, and consequently always crowded, some coming and others going, elbowing their way through the crowd, while the mules and carriages hold the way. The space outside of the gate is generally enlivened by processions of arriving and departing pilgrims. The muleteers and horse owners, Arab saddlers and ferriers are generally posted outside the Jaffa gate.

On Fridays and Sundays the scene is especially lively, the Jaffa road being the favorite promenade of the natives. Many European shops have been built along each side of the road. A second road which turns to our left after leaving the Jaffa gate, will bring us to the Mamilla pool lying in the middle of a Moslem burial ground, which is situated near the end of the valley of Hinnom.

The pool is ninety-seven yards long and sixty-four yards wide, and is supposed by some to be the upper Gihon. It is partly hewn in the rock, but the sides are also lined with a wall. In the winter it is filled with rain water, but it is empty in the summer and autumn.

The Post Office, Custom House, Telegraph Offices, Hotels, Consulates, Hospitals, etc., are the principal sights in this part of the city. There are also mission schools and churches of various kinds. The Russian Palestine Society has erected immense buildings here consisting of an insane asylum, hospitals, mission-house and different departments for the accommodation of pilgrims.

Coming around the so-called Suburb of Zion we see the English and German Protestant burial grounds and Bishop Gobat's English school, where Arab orphans and other children are educated. Leaving there we come to the Coenaculum called by the Moslems Neby Daud (prophet David). Zion's Gate is on the north side. It formerly belonged to the Christians, but is now in possession of the Moslems.

The Chamber of the Last Supper, or Coenaculum, (see illus., p. 237) is shown here, and by paying a fee, you will be conducted by a Moslem, with a pack of howling boys following which makes it very unpleasant for one, to a room on the first floor, divided into two parts by two columns in the middle; it was formerly a part of a Christian church. Half pillars with quaint capitals are built into the walls. The ceiling consists of pointed vaulting of the fourteenth century.

Three windows look into the court, and under the center one is a niche for prayer. In the south-west corner of the room a staircase descends to a lower room, in the middle of which is shown the place where the table of the Lord is said to have stood. A stone in the north wall marks the Lord's seat. The visitor is led into another room where he sees a long, covered, modern coffin, styled the Sarcophagus of David, and said to be a copy of the genuine coffin of David, which, it is alleged, still exists in subterranean vaults below this spot.

The church on Zion is mentioned as early as the fourth century before the erection of the church of the Sepulchre. In the time of Helena a "Church of the Apostles" stood on the supposed scene of the Descent of the Holy Ghost, which was probably this spot. The "Column of scourging" was also supposed to be here. It was not until the seventh century that tradition combined the scene of the Last Supper with that of the Descent of the Holy Ghost. The scene of the Virgin's death was also at a later period transferred hither. In the time of the Franks, the church was called the "Church of Zion," or "Church of St. Mary."

The church of the Crusaders consisted of two stories. The lower had three apses, an altar on the spot where Mary

THE LAST SUPPER.

died, and another on the spot where Jesus appeared "in Galilee." The washing of the Apostles' feet was also said to have taken place here, while the upper story was considered the scene of the Last Supper. Connected with the church of Zion there was an Augustinian abbey. In 1333 the Franciscans established themselves here, and from them the building received its present form. Attached to the monastery was a large hospital, erected in 1354 by a Florentine lady, and committed to the care of the brethren. To this day the superior of the Franciscans is called the "Guardian of Mount Zion."

For centuries the Moslems did their utmost to gain possession of these buildings, and as early as 1479 they forbade pilgrims to visit the scene of the Descent of the Holy Ghost, as they themselves revered the tombs of David and Solomon on the same spot. In 1547 they at length succeeded in depriving the Franciscans of all their possessions, and for the next three centuries Christians had great difficulty in obtaining access to the place. The "Tomb of David" formed one of the holy places in the church of Zion so far back as the Crusaders' period, and it is possible that ancient tombs still exist beneath the building; what is now shown, however, is hardly worth visiting.

As David and his descendants were buried in "The city of David,"[1] the expression was once thought to mean Bethlehem, and their tombs were accordingly shown near that town from the third to the sixth century. The evangelists, however, who were doubtless aware of the site of David's tomb, appear to place it in Jerusalem,[2] where by this time Hyrcanus and Herod had robbed the tombs of all their precious contents. According to Nehemiah 3:16 and Ezekiel 43:7, we are justified in seeking for the tombs of the kings on the Temple mount, above the pool of Siloah.

The Scriptures are very explicit in their account of David coming up from Hebron and taking the strong Castle of Zion, and building the New City of David round about the old fortress of the Jebusites. Zion henceforth became his royal residence, and when Israel's great king closed his

---

[1] 1 Kings 2:10, etc.   [2] Acts 2:29.

17

(*Original Photo.*)
MOUNT ZION AND TOMB OF DAVID AND SOLOMON.

Behold the Mountain of the Lord,
　In latter days, shall rise
Above the mountains and the hills,
　And draw the wondering eyes.
The beam that shines on Zion's hill,
　Shall lighten every land;
The King who reigns in Zion's towers,
　Shall all the world command.

THE CITY OF DAVID.

eventful reign of forty years, it is written, he was buried in the City of David, and so it is said of Solomon his son, and of twelve of their successors to the throne, that they were all buried in the City of David on Mount Zion which is Jerusalem.

Approaching the town the edifice forming the corner is the Armenian monastery of Mount Zion or the House of Caiaphas, where tradition states that Christ was imprisoned; a stone is also shown with which the Holy Sepulchre is said to have been closed, and which pilgrims kiss. The spot where Peter denied Christ and the court where the cock crew[1] are here shown.

[1] Luke 22:61.

CHAPTER XXX.

A Walk to Gethsemane.

VALLEY OF KIDRON — BEGGARS — LEPERS—HOSPITAL — LIST OF LEPERS—STEPHEN STONED—VIRGIN'S TOMB—CAVERN OF AGONY—GETHSEMANE — SORROWFUL EVENT — AFFECTING SCENES IN THE GARDEN—MOUNT OF OLIVES—TREES AND SHRUBS.

N company with others we left St. Stephen's gate for a Sunday afternoon walk. Outside the gate we saw many graves on both sides of the road as we descended the mount to the valley of the Kidron. To the right of the gate is a pond, thirty-one yards long, twenty-five yards wide and thirteen feet deep. The pond is sometimes called Hezekiah's Pool, a name for which there is no authority.

Going down the hill until we strike the Bethany and Jericho road, and turning to our right, many beggars and lepers are seen, making an awful sight to look upon. They have their faces disfigured and their hands and fingers off; some have their toes and feet off, while many have their voices so affected by the terrible disease that it is almost impossible for them to make a loud noise as they call "Bakhshish, lepers, lepers," and follow you, showing their hands and begging for sympathy and for alms.

This state of affairs should not be, because there is a hospital for lepers, not far from the German colony, very pleasantly located, which gives them all aid and care; but as they must be kept clean while here and abide by the rules, they prefer to sit by the wayside begging. The foreman at the hospital said to me that visitors ought not to support or encourage them in their way because that would tend to keep them out of the hospital, as there are no laws to compel them to go there. The institution is maintained by the brethren of Herrnhut. We were very kindly shown through the hospital, took a sad look at the patients, and heard the nature of the disease explained.

The disease is not at all infectious, but the seclusion of the patients is necessary to prevent them from marrying, thus extending and perpetuating this dread disease.

Hideously repulsive leprous beggars are still met on the Yafa road, as many of them, particularly the Jews, have a great repugnance to being lodged in the hospital; but it is hoped that most of them will in time be thus secluded, as there is no other effectual mode of eradicating this generally incurable disease. The malady being hereditary, the children of leprous persons are almost always attacked with it in later life. Leprosy was a disease of somewhat frequent occurrence among the Israelites. There are now forty to fifty lepers in Jerusalem. The Biblical regulations regarding leprosy are of a very rigorous character.[1]

Leprosy is the consequence of a kind of decomposition of the blood. Several months before the outbreak of the disease, the patient feels languid and suffers from cold chills, shivering in the limbs, and attacks of fever. Reddish spots

[1] Levit. 13:14.

then make their appearance on the skin, and under them rise dark red lumps which are more or less movable. In the face particularly these lumps unite into groups resembling bunches of grapes. The mouth and lips swell, the eyes run, and the patient is frequently tormented by excessive itching over the whole body. The mucous membrane begins to be destroyed, and the nodules form internally also. The organs of speaking, seeing, and hearing become affected. At length the swellings burst, turn into dreadful, festering sores, and heal up again, only to break out at a different place. The fingers become bent, and some of the limbs begin to rot away.

This kind of leprosy, with its accompanying swellings, differs from the smooth leprosy, which produces painful, flat, inflamed patches on the skin, followed by sores. Other maladies are generally superinduced by leprosy, but the patient sometimes drags on his melancholy existence for twenty years or more. The patients in this hospital present a spectacle of human misery in one of its most frightful phases, and the visitor will not fail to sympathize with the benevolent efforts that are being made to alleviate their suffering to the utmost, and to prevent the farther spread of the scourge.

A list of names, ages, and dates of arrival will here be given, as received at the hospital on the 21st of March 1895.

Men.
1 Christians.

	Age.	Admitted.
1. Chalil, Greek Catholic,	41 years,	April 1874
2. Ode, Evangelical,	28 years,	December 1889
3. Jakub, Greek Catholic,	33 years,	March 1891

INMATES OF HOSPITAL.

		Age.	Admitted.
4.	Gabriel, Roman Catholic,	18 years,	May 1891
5.	Dieb, Evangelical,	35 years,	May 1893

2 Mohammedans.

		Age.	Admitted.
6.	Mohammed I.	38 years,	June 1890
7.	Said,	25 years,	May 1891
8.	Salem,	51 years,	May 1891
9.	Suleiman,	20 years,	September 1891
10.	Ismain,	25 years,	April 1893
11.	Mohammed II.,	33 years,	April 1893
12.	Mahmud,	24 years,	May 1893
13.	Achmed,	50 years,	June 1893
14.	Hassan,	30 years,	July 1893
15.	Abdul-Rhamin,	45 years,	October 1893
16.	Mohammed III.,	55 years,	November 1893

WOMEN.
1. Christians.

		Age.	Admitted.
1.	Smikna, Evangelical,	26 years,	June 1875
2.	Name, Greek Catholic,	42 years,	January 1887
3.	Haluwe, Greek Catholic,	40 years,	March 1890
4.	Habsa, Greek Catholic,	40 years,	March 1893

2. Mohammedans.

		Age.	Admitted.
5.	Fatme I.,	25 years,	November 1885
6.	Arsise	46 years,	April 1892
7.	Halime,	46 years,	June 1892
8.	Salha,	25 years,	October 1892
9.	Fatme II.,	25 years,	March 1893
10.	Nithme,	30 years,	June 1893
11.	Sabha,	35 years,	July 1893
12.	Fadige,	25 years,	July 1893

Just before turning to cross the Kidron, there is a rocky place where tradition locates the stoning to death of St. Stephen. O, what a man, being dead yet speaketh! And they stoned Stephen while he called upon God, saying, "Lord Jesus, receive my spirit." And he kneeled down and cried with a loud voice, "Lord, lay not this sin to their charge," and when he had said this, he fell asleep.

We now crossed the Kidron by a little bridge, but there was no water, the bed being perfectly dry. It is claimed that in wet weather there was water flowing. Tradition claims that there is an under current of water, while the rubbish of centuries has so closed up the valley that the water course is changed; and it looks quite reasonable, as further down the valley water is seen.

To the left of the road, beyond the bridge, is the chapel of the Tomb of the Virgin, where, according to the legend, she was interred by the apostles, and where she lay until her assumption. A flight of steps descends to the space in front of the church. The only part of the church above ground is a porch. In this church are the tombs of Joachim and Anna the parents of the Virgin; also the tomb of Joseph, and the tomb of the Virgin Mary the mother of Jesus. On our return, to the left, is a passage that leads to the so-called "Cavern of the Agony."

A few rods from the Tomb of the Virgin, on the opposite side of the road leading to the Mt. of Olives, is situated the Garden of "Gethsemane." The name signifies "oil-press." In 1847 a wall was erected around the garden (see illus. p. 23) by the Franciscans, to whom it now belongs. The entrance is on the side next to the Mt. of Olives. A rock immediately to the east of the door marks the spot where Peter, James and

John slept.[1] The rock, which is called the "Rock of the Apostles," (see illus. p. 127), covers a large space. Some four or five rods from this rock is the spot, outside of the garden wall, where tradition says Judas' betrayal of Jesus

TOMB OF THE VIRGIN. (*Original Photo.*)

with a kiss took place. On the inside of the walls are pictures of the fourteen stations, as given before. There is a neat fence around the the garden inside the outer wall and about six feet from it; between this and the outer wall vis-

[1] Mark 14:32.

itors are allowed to pass while looking at objects of interest in the garden. Inside of the garden are eight venerable olive trees, with trunks bursting open from age, some of them walled up with stone. The trees are said to date from the time of Christ.

The monk or priest who acts as guide presents the visitor with a boquet of roses, pinks and other flowers as a memento or in memory of the place, and expects a small sum of money for the maintenance of the garden. The olives yielded by the trees of the garden are sold at a high price, and rosaries are made from the olive stones.

All these places seem to be in harmony with the Scriptures. It is here that Jesus came and prayed when loaded down with sorrow, for he said, "My soul is exceeding sorrowful, even unto death." "Tarry ye here and watch with me."[1] How the Lord Jesus longed for some one to be with Him in His sorrow! And is it not true that man, when in the deepest sorrow and distress, longs for some one to be with him; but those called for that purpose, fell asleep, about a stone's cast away[2] from where their blessed Savior fell on His face and prayed, saying, "O my Father, if it be possible, let this cup pass from me, nevertheless not as I will, but as thou wilt."[3]

O, what a time that was in the garden! He cometh unto the disciples and findeth them asleep, and sayeth unto Peter, "What, could ye not watch with me one hour?" So, Jesus found that He was left alone with no one to watch with Him. Jesus sayeth unto them, "Watch and pray, that ye enter not into temptation: the spirit indeed is willing, but the flesh is weak."[4]

[1] Matt. 26:38.   [2] John 22:41.   [3] Matt. 26:39.   [4] Matt. 26:41.

THE GARDEN OF GETHSEMANE.

He went the second time and prayed, saying "O my Father if this cup may not pass away from me except I drink it, thy will be done," having reference to the cup of suffering. When He said, "O, my father if this cup may not pass away from me," He meant if it be not possible to redeem fallen man unless I drink this cup, unless I suffer for them; Thy will be done. So He went also the third time and prayed, but the cup was not removed and thus He became willing to die for all mankind.

There is a very interesting scene in the garden of Gethsemane — a life size picture showing Christ as broken down under the burden, and an angel coming down from heaven to comfort Him. This is inclosed under a round dome. Hours could be spent here in this noted place looking and meditating.

The large old olive trees in the midst of the garden, it is claimed by tradition, date from the time of Christ, and it seemed as though the trees almost expressed the agony and stood as monuments in memory of Christ in the garden. We wish all our readers could have been with us on that Sunday afternoon. It is certain that it would be one of the great things in their lives that would not be forgotten. This place was visited quite frequently during our six weeks stay in Jerusalem, and since we left the holy land, O, how vividly these places come up to our minds; and as we write our heart burns within us.

CHAPTER XXXI.

Mount of Olives and Surroundings.

CHURCH OF THE LORD'S PRAYER—ASCENSION—GREAT INGATHERING—RUSSIAN BUILDING—VALLEY OF JEHOSHAPHAT—RESURRECTION—ABSALOM'S TOMB—GROTTO OF ST. JAMES—VILLAGE OF SILOAH—POOL OF SILOAH—ST. MARY'S WELL.

URNING to our right, on the side of the mountain leading towards Bethany, we come to the place where tradition says the ascension of Christ into heaven took place.[1] "And He led them out as far as to Bethany, and He lifted up His hands and blessed them." Oh, what a place that is for the Christian heart! No wonder that many spend their last mite to visit these sacred places at least once in their lifetime. "And while they looked steadfastly toward heaven as He went up, behold two men stood by them in white apparel; which also said, Ye men of Galilee, why stand ye gazing up into heaven? this same Jesus, which is taken up from you into heaven, shall so come in like manner as ye have seen Him go into heaven."[2]

The disciples returned from the Mount of Olives and gathered together in that upper room waiting for the endowment of power and the Holy Ghost. And when the day of Pentecost was fully come, they were all with one accord in

[1] Luke 24:50.   [2] Acts 1:10, 11.

INTERIOR OF GETHSEMANE AS IT APPEARS AT THE PRESENT DAY.

(Original Photo.)

one place, when suddenly, very quickly, came a sound, and a rushing, and a mighty wind, which filled all the house; and the cloven tongues and the fire came, and every one was conscious because it sat on them, and the Holy Ghost filled them, and they spoke with other tongues. Oh, what a time, dear reader! Would you not like to have been there? But the Lord has promised the same to all at this day. There is

reason to rejoice that I am not exempted, but stand as a witness to the power of saving and of the Holy Ghost. Blessed be the dear name of the Lord!

The result of this wonderful outpouring was that three thousand souls were added to the church the same day. Thus we see that the gathering of souls into Christ's kingdom does not depend so much upon the efforts of man, but upon union, love, oneness of mind and spirit, and, above all these, the power of the Holy Ghost. When a soul has been influenced by the Holy Ghost the work is well done, and no earthly power can claim the credit. The efforts of the ablest preacher or most noted evangelist will avail nothing unless accompanied by the power of the Holy Spirit. May the Lord bless the Christian churches of this land, and gain to Himself great honors, is the prayer of your humble servant.

A beautiful church, called the "Church of the Lord's Prayer" (see illus., p. 138), is built on the spot where tradition locates the place at which Christ taught His disciples the "Lord's Prayer." It was built in 1868 by the Princess Latour d' Auvergne, relative of Napoleon III. Around the passageways are thirty slabs, upon which the Lord's Prayer is inscribed in as many different languages. The Latin building and the Russian building, standing on the Mount of Olives, are controlled by their respective societies. From this point we had a magnificent view of Jerusalem. The valley of the Kidron bounds Jerusalem on the east, and in the time of Christ the Kidron was called the winter brook.

The name, "Valley of Jehoshaphat," is of early origin, having already been applied to this valley by the venerable pilgrim of Bordeaux. The tradition that this gorge will be the scene of the last judgment, founded on a misinterpretation of a passage of Scripture in the book of Joel,[1] is probably of pre-Christian origin, and has been borrowed from the Jews by Christians and Moslems alike. The Moslems accordingly bury their dead on the east side of the Temple of Solomon, or the Mosque of Omar, while the Jews have their cemetery on the west side of the Mount of Olives. At the

[1] Joel 3:2.

(*Original Photo.*)
THE GOLDEN GATE, JERUSALEM.

Jerusalem, the golden,
  With milk and honey blest,
Beneath thy contemplation,
  Sinks heart and voice opprest:
I know not, O, I know not,
  What social joys are there;
What radiancy of glory,
  What light beyond compare.
            —Alexander Ewing.

resurrection, the sides of the valley are expected to move farther apart, in order to afford sufficient room for the great assembly.

There are different roads leading from the garden of Gethsemane to the Mount of Olives; there are also many different things to notice, but as it was raining at this time, and the water was washing down the sides of the Mount, we spent the time, as we walked along with our umbrella open, in picking up some beautifully colored pebbles to take along home with us. We now came to the place where Christ beheld the city, and wept over it.[1] The spot commands a beautiful view of the city.

The top of the Mount of Olives is reached from Gethsemane in about fifteen minutes. The principal trees are the olive, fig, and carob, and here and there a few apricot, almond, terebinth, and hawthorne trees, but not many of either kind. This is a very tiresome walk, as the roads are rough and in clear weather the sun is very hot. We made frequent visits to Mount Olivet.

To the west of Gethsemane a road branches off to the lower bridge, and the first object of interest we come to is Absalom's tomb. "Now Absalom in his lifetime had taken and reared up for himself a pillar, which is in the king's dale: for he said, I have no son to keep my name in remembrance: and he called the pillar after his own name: and it is called unto this day, Absalom's place."[2]

The tomb is cut into the solid rock; is six and one-half yards square and twenty feet high, and is detached on three sides, being separated from the rock by a passage eight feet wide by nine feet long. As the surrounding rock was not

[1] Luke 19:41.   [2] 2 Samuel 18:18.

high enough to admit of the whole monument being executed in a single block, a square superstructure of large stones was erected above the massive base. So far as it is visible above the rubbish, the monument is forty-seven feet high. Near by is the tomb of Jehoshaphat, and also the grotto of St. James, or tomb of St. James (see illus., p. 95). The grotto of St. James is considered holy by the Christians, from the tradition that St. James lay concealed there after the crucifixion, and that he ate no food until after the resurrection. Here may also be seen the Pyramid of Zacharias, executed under direction of the Christians, in memory of the Zacharias mentioned by Matthew.[1] The monument resembles Absalom's tomb, but is twenty-nine feet high.

In about four minutes we reach the village of Siloah. Near this village is the house for lepers, erected by the Turkish government, and the inmates are seen on every hand. No wonder that the Lord was moved with compassion when He saw so many cursed with sin and the dreadful disease of leprosy, and healed them as they came to Him. "And when the evening was come they brought unto Him many that were possessed with devils, and He cast them out, and healed all that were sick."

A short distance from here we come to the Pool of Siloah (see illus., p. 241), which is fifty-two feet long and eighteen feet wide. In consequence of the miracle recorded by John[2] the pool was deemed sacred. The wall of the pool has now fallen in, and the bottom is covered with rubbish. The water is generally more or less salty to the taste, perhaps from the decomposition of the soil through which it percolates; it is also polluted by the washerwomen and tanners.

[1] Matthew 23:35. [2] John 9:7.

A little further on is the place where tradition says that the prophet Isaiah was sawn asunder in the presence of King Manasseh. The tradition of this martyrdom is alluded to by some of the authors of church history. Thus, wherever you go, or whatever you see, there is some noted Bible occurrence connected therewith.

There are two important wells in the valley of the Kidron, which are called "St. Mary's Well" and the "Well of Job," which lies 345 feet below Gethsemane. The first is so called because tradition claims that the Virgin once washed the swaddling clothes of her son at this place, and the second is so called from the tradition that the Holy Fire was concealed in this well during the captivity, until recovered by Nehemiah. Probably we are here standing on the brink of the well of En Rogel (or Fuller's spring), mentioned in Joshua 15:7, as the boundary between the tribes of Judah and Benjamin. Here, too, Adonijah prepared a feast for his friends on the occasion of his attempted usurpation of the throne of David.[1]

The valley of Hinnom is bounded on the south by the Hill of the Tombs, or Hill of the Field of Blood (see illus., p. 87). The valley separates the hill from Zion, and the name of the valley occurs in the description of the boundaries between Judah and Benjamin.[2]

It was in this valley that the children were anciently sacrificed to Moloch.[3] The spot was called Topheth, or place of fire. These sacrifices took place just outside of the present city walls. Jeremiah vigorously opposed these revolting practices, and Josiah caused the place to be defiled that it might never again be the scene of such sacrifices.

[1] 1 Kings 1:9. [2] Joshua 15:8. [3] 2 Kings 23:10.

CHAPTER XXXII.

A Visit to Bethlehem.

"HILL OF EVIL COUNSEL"—TREE ON WHICH JUDAS HANGED HIM-
SELF—BOUNDARY LINE—WELL OF MAGI—RACHEL'S TOMB—
BETHLEHEM—NAOMI—RUTH—BOAZ—DAVID ANOINTED—
CHURCH OF THE NATIVITY — MANGER—"MILK
GROTTO"—DAVID'S WELL—SHEPHERD'S
FIELD—CAVE OF ADULLAM.

EAVING the Jaffa gate, we turn to our left into the valley of Hinnom. Crossing the stone bridge and leaving the station and the German colony to our right, the ascent of the "Hill of Evil Counsel" is made. Tradition states that here Caiaphas, at his country house, consulted with the Jews how to take Jesus, and from this the hill received the name "Evil Counsel."

Passing on, our attention was called to the tree upon which Judas hanged himself. All of its branches extend toward the east. The tree is certainly very old, but it is very doubtful whether this is the original tree. The plain extends hence toward the south, and is identical with the Valley Rephaim, through which the boundary between Judah and Benjamin ran.[1]

The Philistines were frequently encamped here, and it was here that they were defeated by David.[2] Further on,

[1] Joshua 15:8. [2] 2 Samuel 5:18.

the spot is shown where it is said the house of Simeon stood.[1] The place is occupied by a small church. A little further on, to the left of the road, is a cistern, the "Well of the Magi," where, it is said according to tradition, the guiding star was again seen.[2] We observe to our right a house of the Catholic

(*Original Photo.*)
ST. STEPHEN'S GATE, JERUSALEM.

Maltese Order, where is shown the "Field of Pease," so called from the legend that Jesus once asked a man what he was sowing, to which the reply was, "Stone." The field thereupon produced pease, or stone, some of which are still to be found on the spot.

About a ten minutes' walk from here we see to the right of the road an insignificant building, styled the "Tomb of

[1] Luke 2:25. [2] Matt. 2:9.

Rachel." Rachel was the beloved wife of Jacob. On his death bed he said, "When there was but a little way to come unto Ephrath, Rachel died by me and I buried her there, in the way of Ephrath; the same is Bethlehem."[1] This spot is revered alike by Jews, Christians and Mohammedans.

In about fifteen minutes more we reach Bethlehem, which is next to Jerusalem in interest, in all Palestine. Around it clusters a number of sacred memories. It lies about six miles south of Jerusalem, on the crest of a limestone ridge. Although so near Jerusalem it is hidden by an intervening height; but through the valleys, stretching eastward to the Dead Sea, fine views are gained of the mountains of Moab. The sides of the ridge are terraced, and sweep around it in graceful curves like natural stairs. They are covered with rows of olive trees, intermixed with the fig and the vine.

In Bible history, Bethlehem is noted as the city of Naomi, to which she returned from Moab, with Ruth, her daughter-in-law. Here Boaz married Ruth and founded the family of Jesse, from which David sprang. The book of Ruth, in the Old Testament, contains an interesting account of these events.

At Bethlehem young David kept his father's flocks. In protecting them he acquired the skill in the use of the sling and stone which was displayed in his battle with the giant Goliath. Here David was anointed king of Israel by the prophet Samuel.[2] From him Bethlehem was called the city of David.

But Bethlehem is especially distinguished as the birthplace of Jesus Christ, the Saviour of the world. It was

[1] Gen. 48:7.   [2] 1 Sam. 16:13.

(*Original Photo.*)
CAVE OF THE NATIVITY: THE MANGER.

Hail the blest morn when the great Mediator,
   Down from the regions of glory descends.
Shepherds, go worship the Babe in the manger;
   Lo! for His guard the bright angels attend.

Cold on His cradle the dew-drops are shining,
   Low lies His bed with the beasts of the stall;
Angels adore Him, in slumber reclining,
   Maker, and Monarch, and Savior of all.

thus foretold centuries before it took place, by the prophet Micah: "Thou, Bethlehem Ephratah, though thou be little among the thousands of Judah, yet out of thee shall He come forth unto me that is to be ruler in Israel; whose goings forth have been from of old, from everlasting."[1]

One night, when some shepherds were watching their flocks near Bethlehem, suddenly a bright light shone around them, and an angel said to them: "Fear not: for, behold, I bring you good tidings of great joy, which shall be to all people. For unto you is born this day in the city of David a Saviour, which is Christ the Lord." Then a great company of angels sang, "Glory to God in the highest, and on earth peace, good will toward men." The shepherds went in haste to Bethlehem to see the child. They found Him lying in a manger, with Mary His mother.[2]

To Bethlehem also came wise men who had seen in the East a star which denoted the birth of a great King. They worshiped the child and presented to Him gold and sweet smelling spices.[3]

In the Church of the Nativity is shown the spot where the Savior was born, and the manger in which He was laid. As we were escorted by the attendants from one department to another, attention was called to a place in one chapel where, it is stated, Joseph was warned and commanded by the angel to flee into Egypt. Traditions locate many other occurrences in the life of the Holy Family, but reference is here especially made to the chapel of the "Milk Grotto," where, according to tradition, they once sought shelter or concealment, and that a drop of the Virgin's milk fell on the floor of the Grotto. For many centuries both Christians

[1] Micah 5:2.   [2] Luke 2:9—17.   [3] Matt. 2:1—12.

and Moslems have entertained a superstitious belief that the rock of this cavern has the property of increasing the milk of women and even of animals, and to this day round cakes made of dust from this rock are sold to pilgrims, of which we bought two as specimens.

Bethlehem means the "House of Bread." It was anciently called Ephrath, the fruitful. It had springs of water and fertile fields, very different from the barren regions to the east and south. Here a full supply of food might be obtained from agricultural pursuits.

Bethlehem is now a flourishing Christian town of white stone houses, containing about 8000 inhabitants. A large building, consisting of a church and three convents, stands over the place where Christ was supposed to have been born. Part of it was erected by the Empress Helena, the mother of the Emperor Constantine, in the early part of the fourth century. It is, therefore, one of the oldest monuments of Christian architecture in the world. A short distance from the gate of the city is the well where David quenched his thrist, and whose waters he prized so highly.[1]

Many of the Bethlemites, as they are called, work in mother of pearl and in olive wood and are very anxious to sell their trinkets to the visitors; they hang on so persistently in their efforts to sell that a person feels much relieved when he has left the city. We returned to Jerusalem late in the evening, very weary with our much traveling.

Leaving Bethlehem on the east, the road winds down a rocky slope, past fields of wheat and barley and terraced vineyards. Innumerable sheep and goats are seen on the surrounding hills as in the days of Boaz and David. At the

[1] 2 Sam. 23:15.

BETHLEHEM, MARKET PLACE. (Showing the Church of the Nativiy in the rear.) *(Original Photo).*

CAVE OF ADULLAM.

foot a level plain is reached, affording good pasturage, and dotted over with clumps of olive trees. This is called the "Shepherds' Field," from the tradition that here the shepherds were keeping their flocks by night when the angels appeared to them.[1]

The cave of Adullam lies to the south-east, not far from Bethlehem. The limestone rocks of the district abound in caves, many of them of great size. The cave of Adullam is approached by a wild ravine, after which a narrow path leads up to it by a steep ascent. The entrance to the cave is by a small opening through which only one person can pass at a time. This leads to a series of chambers, some large

BETHLEHEMITE WOMAN. (*From Photo.*)

[1] Luke 2:8.

enough to hold several hundred men. Here David sought refuge from Saul.[1] Here he so longed for a drink of water from the wells of Bethlehem at the gate.[2] To this place there came to him every one that was in distress, and every one that was in debt, and David became their captain.[3] The term "Adullamites" is sometimes applied to discontented politicians.

[1] 1 Sam. 22:1.   [2] 2 Sam. 23:15.   [3] 1 Sam. 22:2.

CHAPTER XXXIII.

FROM JERUSALEM DOWN TO JERICHO.

BETHANY — HOME OF JESUS — HOUSE OF MARY AND MARTHA — LAZARUS' TOMB—STONE OF REST—APOSTLES' SPRINGS— "VALLEY OF ACHOR" — WAY OF BLOOD— MODERN JERICHO-BALSAM GARDENS.

LL arrangements having been made the evening before, we got a timely start in the morning. A party of four of us, accompanied by a Turkish guide, started for Jericho, the Jordan and the Dead Sea.

Coming around from the Jaffa gate and crossing the Kidron, passing Gethsemane and descending the Mount of Olives towards Bethany, we were shown the supposed place where the fig tree stood which Christ cursed.[1]

In a few minutes we reached Bethany which is a small village on the side of the Mount of Olives, not quite two miles from Jerusalem. It lies directly on the road that leads down from Jerusalem to Jericho. It is a poor village, containing about twenty or thirty houses, built of stone. The material which composes them seems to have been the ruins of former buildings. It is now called the town of Lazarus in memory of his having been here raised from the dead. In the center rises the ruins of a crusading castle which was once called St. Lazarus.

[1] Matt. 21:19.

Bethany may be called the home of Jesus. When He went up to Jerusalem, He always stopped here in the house of His friend Lazarus,[1] and his loving sisters Mary and Martha. When He had been teaching in the temple all day, He used to walk over the Mount of Olives in the evening, and go to the house of Lazarus to rest Himself and spend the night.

At one of these visits of Jesus, Martha wished to get up a nice dinner for Him and His disciples. She wanted her younger sister, Mary, to come and help her; but Mary was sitting at the feet of Jesus, listening to His words. Martha came into the room where Jesus was speaking and complained to Him of Mary, saying, "Lord, dost thou not care that my sister has left me to serve alone? Bid her, therefore, that she help me." But Jesus took Mary's part, and said: "Martha, Martha, thou art careful and troubled about many things, but one thing is needful, and Mary has chosen that good part which shall not be taken from her."[2]

Bethany is specially noted as the place where Lazarus was raised from the dead. He had died while Jesus was far away beyond Jordan. Jesus knew that he was sick, and He might have come and healed him, but He stayed away in order to show His power by raising him from the dead. When Jesus returned to Bethany, He went with the sorrowing sisters to the grave of Lazarus. After ordering the stone to be taken away from the mouth of the grave, He cried with a loud voice: "Lazarus, come forth," and he that was dead came forth alive and well. What a happy family that was in Bethany that night!

Going down about twenty steps into a chamber or cave to our left, is a tomb cut into the rock, which is the tomb of

[1] John 11:11.   [2] Luke 10:38 –42.

BETHANY, THE HOME OF MARY, MARTHA AND LAZARUS.

(*Original Photo.*)

Lazarus. Reader do you expect to hear that voice calling you when you have been dead a long while and your poor body turned to dust? O yes, Jesus will call all you fathers and mothers and children.[1] Jesus first calls men who are dead to all that is good and right from the death of sin, when He says, "Awake thou that sleepest, and arise from the dead, and Christ shall give thee light;"[2] also, "and you hath he quickened who were dead in trespasses and sin."[3]

Such as have received this new quickening life, and that everlasting life,[4] though they die,[5] yet shall they live. And again there shall be another call to all in their graves, for Jesus says, "Marvel not at this, for the hour is coming in the which all that are in the graves shall hear his voice." May we all hear that voice, "Come ye blessed of my Father, inherit the kingdom prepared for you."[6]

Some seven or eight rods from the tomb of Lazarus is the place where tradition locates the house of Mary and Martha, and also the house of Simon the leper.[7] A short distance from Bethany is the so-called "Stone of Rest," about three feet long, which pilgrims stoop down and kiss. It marks the spot where Martha met Jesus.[8] A chapel has been erected in memory of the event. About ten minutes further on we come to the watering place, or the "Apostles' Springs," which have been identified with the "Sun Spring"[9]

The country is very hilly and barren, and this district appears quite deserted. It is dangerous for one to travel without an escort. Here the "certain man" who went down from Jerusalem to Jericho, spoken of in the parable of the good Samaritan, was supposed to have been attacked.[10] At

[1] John 5:28. [2] Eph. 5:14. [3] Eph. 2:1. [4] John 3:16. [5] John 11:25.
[6] Matt. 25:34. [7] Matt. 26:6. [8] John 11:20. [9] Josh. 15:7. [10] Luke 10:30.

the place where the inn was supposed to have stood there is at the present time a halting place for travelers.

There is a deep ravine winding down towards the Jordan, which contains water during the wet season of the year. It is identified as the "Valley of Achor."[1] In the distance below us, we saw the valley of the Jordan, and the Dead Sea with its dark blue waters. In about one hour and a half we reached Jericho.

The ancient Jericho lay by the springs at the foot of the hill of Karantel, that is to the west of modern Jericho, and to the north of Jericho of the Roman period. This is proven both by the Bible and by Josephus. The town was of considerable size and enclosed by walls, and its vegetation was very luxuriant. It is sometimes called the city of palms, and down to the seventh century, dates and palms were common, though they have now almost entirely disappeared. Around the town lay a large and flourishing oasis of corn and hemp fields. The Israelitish town at first belonged to the tribe of Benjamin, afterwards to the kingdom of Judah. In spite of many conquests Jericho continued to flourish.

It was especially noted for its balsam gardens, the culture of which probably dated from the period when Solomon received rare spices from South Arabia.[2] The plant has now disappeared entirely, although the plants of South Arabia and India would still flourish in this warm climate. Here, too, flourished the Henna, which yields a red dye. In the time of Christ shady sycamores stood by the wayside.[3]

Antony presented the district of Jericho to Cleopatra, who sold it to Herod, and that monarch embellished it with a palace and made it his winter residence, as being the

[1] Josh. 15:7.   [2] 1 Kings 10:10.   [3] Luke 19:4.

(*Original Photo.*)
TOMB OF LAZARUS AT BETHANY.

    Asleep in Jesus! blessed sleep!
      From which none ever wake to weep;
    A calm and undisturbed repose,
      Unbroken by the last of foes.
    Asleep in Jesus! peaceful rest!
      Whose waking is supremely blest;
    No fear, no woe shall dim that hour
      That manifests the Savior's power.

JERICHO.

most beautiful spot for the purpose in his dominions. He died here, but directed that he should be interred in the Herodium. It was at Jericho that the Jewish pilgrims from Perea (east of Jordan) and Galilee used to assemble on their way to the temple, and Christ also began His last journey to Jerusalem from this point.[1] As early as the fourth century the councils of the church were attended by bishops of Jericho.

[1] Luke 19:1.

CHAPTER XXXIV.

Jericho, Jordan, and Dead Sea.

JERICHO—THORNS—BALM OF GILEAD—APPLES OF SODOM—ELISHA'S SPRING—HOUSE OF RAHAB—FORTY DAYS' FAST—ROBBERS—JORDAN MAN DROWNED—BATHING IN JORDAN—DEAD SEA — CAMELS — MOUNTAINS OF MOAB—AMERICAN PARTY.

EMPEROR Justinian caused the Church of the Mother of God at Jericho to be restored, and a hospice for pilgrims to be erected. About the year 810, a monastery of St. Stephen existed at Jericho. New Jericho, on the site of the present village, sprang up in the time of the crusaders, who built a castle and the Church of the Holy Trinity here. The place was afterwards inhabited by Moslems and gradually decayed. In 1840 it was plundered by the soldiers of Ibrahim Pasha and in 1871 almost entirely destroyed by fire.

The present Jericho consists of a group of low, dirty huts, with a hotel and a few other buildings which are more attractive. The population is about 300 souls. The villagers usually crowd around strange visitors, and there is danger of being robbed. The site of the home of Zaccheus is shown to us here.[1]

The gardens contain many grape vines which in summer yield an abundant supply of fruit. Everywhere the ground

[1] Luke 19:1—10.

is overgrown with thorny underwood. From the formidable thorns of these rhamnaceae, the thorny crown of Christ was made. They are now used by the natives in constructing their almost unapproachable fences.

The Zakkum tree is found here; it is also called the pseudo-balsam tree, or balm of Gilead, having small leaves like the box. The fruit resembles small unripe walnuts, from which the Arabs prepare pseudo-balsam or Zaccheus oil, quantities of which are sold to pilgrims. We find here also the Solanum sanctum, a very woody shrub, three to four feet high, with broad leaves which are wooly on the under side. The fruit looks like an apple, being first yellow, and afterward turning red. It is sometimes called the apple of Sodom, and has been erroneously connected with the wine of Sodom, mentioned in Gen. 19:32. All these are products of a sub-tropical climate, for we are now about 825 feet below the level of the Mediterranean. The barley harvest takes place here in the middle of April.

The Sultan's Spring, by which Jericho was once supplied with water, wells forth copiously from the earth and is collected in a pond twenty-two yards long and six and one half yards wide. Tradition states that this was the water which Elisha healed with salt;[1] whence it is called Elisha's Spring by the Christians. Above the spring is shown the site of the House of Rahab.[2]

A path took us to the Hermits' Caverns on the Jebel Karantel, the grotto in which Jesus is said to have spent the forty days of His fast.[3] This was a fearful place, containing a high mountain and an immense precipice, with grottos and caves, so that no one would like to remain there alone any great length of time.

[1] 2 Kings 2:19—22.   [2] Joshua 2.   [3] Matt. 4:1.

Jericho is about fifteen miles north-east of Jerusalem. In a distance of fifteen miles the road descends about 3,000 feet, hence the phrases, "Going up to Jerusalem," and "Going down to Jericho." On every side the steep mountains and deep ravines, now as formerly, are the haunts of robbers. All travelers passing along it need escorts.

Jericho, the city of palm trees,[1] stood about five miles west of the Jordan. It was the first city to which the Israelites laid siege after crossing the river. The walls fell down miraculously, at the sound of the trumpets.[2] The city was destroyed, and Joshua pronounced a curse upon the man who should rebuild it: "Cursed be the man before the Lord, that riseth up and buildeth this city Jericho. He shall lay the foundation thereof in his first born and in his youngest son shall he set up the gates of it."[3] After five centuries this curse was fulfilled.[4]

In the time of Christ, Jericho was a flourishing city. Herod built a palace here and an amphitheatre. It is now a barren waste with only a few shapeless ruins. The groves of palms which once stretched for miles around the city, and gave it its name, have disappeared.

The brook Cherith, on the banks of which Elijah was fed by the ravens,[5] flows past Jericho into the Jordan. In earlier times it was known as the Valley of Achor in which Achan was stoned.[6]

We crossed the plain of Jordan to where tradition locates the baptism of Jesus by John.[7] Pilgrims come here from all parts to visit this sacred place and many of them are baptized in the Jordan, especially in the spring of the year when large pilgrim tours are made.

[1] Deut. 34:3. [2] Josh. 6:20. [3] Josh. 6:26. [4] 1 Kings 16:34.
[5] 1 Kings 17:1—7. [6] Josh. 7. [7] Matt. 3:13

The water was muddy, caused by the rains. A few days before we were here, Mr. Steffens, from New York, was drowned at this place, and on this account our dragoman did not want to give his consent for us to bathe in the Jordan, but by insisting, Mr. J. C. Mack and myself had a good bath. We took turns in bathing, one of us remaining on shore and supporting the other in the water with the aid of a long pole. What a place for bathing and baptizing! This is also near the ancient Gilgal of the Bible, where the Israelites erected twelve great stones after crossing the Jordan.[1]

To the east of Jericho, a short distance from the Jordan, is a Greek monastery where we were well entertained for the night, by the Greek monks. We felt well secured as all the private rooms, chapels and stables were in one enclosure, as is the custom in that country.

After a good night's rest, we were aroused early in the morning and, after our tea, we again started on our journey. The sky was clear, and the sun shone brightly, and our horses went briskly over the plains. This was a morning that will never be forgotten, we trust. A letter was received from J. C. Mack since our return home stating, "O, what a good time we had going to Jericho, the Jordan and the Dead Sea!"

The Jordan, the principal river of Palestine, rises in the north near Mount Heron, flows through the Sea of Galilee, and then has a very winding course into the Dead Sea. At present the lower valley of the Jordan alone will be described; the upper portion of the river will be noticed hereafter. The entire length of the river, in a direct line, is about 120 miles. From the Sea of Galilee to the Dead Sea the distance is

---

[1] Joshua 4:19.

about sixty-five miles direct, but the river so doubles and winds that its actual course is about 200 miles long. The name means "*flowing down*." It enters the Dead Sea about 3,000 feet below its source. The Jordan issues from the Sea of Galilee, a muddy, impetuous stream. It has cut so deep a channel that throughout the greater part of its course it is hidden from view. From any height, however, it is easy to trace its course by the trees and shrubs which grow upon its banks and overhang its bed. As the river descends about 600 feet between the Sea of Galilee and the Dead Sea, its current is quite rapid. It is also subject to destructive floods. In the time of harvest it overflows its banks. The wild beasts which find shelter amid the jungle in the valley, must then flee to higher ground. Of a predicted destroyer it is said: "Behold, he shall come up like a lion from the swelling of Jordan against the habitation of the strong: but I will suddenly make him run away from her: and who is a chosen man, that I may appoint over her? for who is like me? and who will appoint me the time? and who is that shepherd that will stand before me?"[1]

The breadth of the Jordan varies: the average is about 300 yards. The sunken channel of the river is from a quarter to a half a mile wide and has steep banks of white earth. The river has two banks, a higher and a lower. The water rises to the height of the former, but scarcely ever overspreads the plain. The whole strip of valley on its banks is called El Ghor, which means a valley between hills. In its course the river forms several small islands, and at a number of places it flows over rocks. The northern part of the valley is partly occupied on both sides of the river by fields

[1] Jeremiah 49:19.

THE BANK OF THE JORDAN.

(*Original Photo*).

of barley; but below Jericho, the plain is barren and untilled with only a few low shrubs. From our starting place in the morning the Jordan is about one hour's ride, over a sandy and salty plain. Nothing is seen along the river with the exception of here and there under brush and small timber. We soon reached the shores of the Dead Sea, and as the sun was shining very warmly we bathed our feet in its crystal waters.

The Dead Sea is the lowest body of water on the face of the earth. It lies in a deep hollow, 1,300 feet below the level of the Mediterranean. It is divided into two unequal portions by a tongue of land. The northern portion is very deep, the greatest depth known being 1,308 feet. The southern portion is much shallower, nowhere exceeding twelve feet. The water is clear as crystal and of a deep blue color. The waves are crested with foam of a dazzling whiteness. It is about forty miles long and ten miles broad. It is called the Dead Sea because no animal life can be sustained in its waters.

In the Bible it is spoken of as the salt sea.[1] The water contains more than one part in four, of various salts. It is eight times more salty than the ocean. This makes it very bitter to the taste. Another effect is to make the water very buoyant. Eggs float in it like corks. Swimming is very difficult as the body floats high in the water.

In Joel it is called the East Sea,[2] as compared with the Mediterranean. Along the eastern shore the mountains of Moab stand like a mighty wall, from 1,200 to 2,000 feet above the waters. While the mountains on the west side, though

[1] Josh. 3:16.   [2] Joel 2:20.

seldom rising above 1,500 feet, are more broken. The north shore of the Dead Sea is strewn with trunks of trees, bones of animals and shells of fish, brought down by the Jordan. The trunks of trees, after tossing about, possibly for years, in the bitter waters, are cast on shore so saturated with salt that the wood will scarcely burn. They are also covered with a white incrustation of salt. The north shore of the sea is a large marsh of bullrushes and tall grass, with some bushes. Here the attention of our party was attracted by a large herd of camels, feeding. There were many young ones among them, and they created considerable curiosity as they stood upright, with their heads high in the air. On our return to Jerusalem we met several other parties going down, among them being some from our own state, and others from Chicago, Illinois. We arrived at Jerusalem at about 4 P. M., feeling well paid for our time and investment.

(*Original Photo.*)
RESTING ON THE BANKS OF THE DEAD SEA.

Lo! Death has reared himself a throne
In a strange city lying alone
Far down within the dim East.
Where the good and the bad, and the worst and the best,
Have gone to their eternal rest.
There shrines and palaces and towers
(Time-eaten towers that tremble not!)
Resemble nothing that is ours.
Around, by lifting winds forgot.
Resignedly beneath the sky
The melancholy waters lie.

CHAPTER XXXV.

HEBRON AND CAVE OF MACHPELAH.

SOLOMON'S POOLS—AQUEDUCTS—TOMB OF THE PROPHET JONAH—
VALLEY OF ESHCOL—HISTORY OF HEBRON—GREAT STONES
—TOMBS OF ABRAHAM, ISAAC AND JACOB WITH
THEIR WIVES—JEWISH PRAYER—"CHRISTIANS,"
"DOGS"—MISSIONS—PILGRIMAGES.

FROM the Bethlehem road we turned to our right at Rachel's tomb, and in about one hour we reached the so-called Solomon's Pools. They are three in number, and are situated in a valley at the rear of the castle. They were repaired in 1865. As the valley descends abruptly toward the east, the reservoirs had to be constructed in steps, as an embankment of great size would have been necessary to confine the water in a single large reservoir.

The three pools do not lie exactly above each other. The second is 53 yards distant from the highest, and 52 yards from the lowest, and is about 19 feet below the former and the same height above the other.

The highest pond is 127 yards long, 76 yards wide, and 25 feet deep. It is partly hewn in the rock, and partly enclosed by masonry, flying buttresses being used for the support of the walls. The central pool is 141 yards long, 68 yards wide, and 38 feet deep. It is almost entirely hewn in the solid rock. The lowest pool, the finest of the three, is 194 yards long, 59 yards wide, and is at places 48 feet deep. It is partly hewn in the rock, and partly lined with masonry.

The water from these pools was carried to Jerusalem by aqueducts of which much might be said. Above the upper pool we enter a chamber at the end of which a spring bubbles forth, the water of which is conducted to the pool by a channel supposed to be identical with the sealed fountain mentioned in Solomon's Song 4:12.

The surrounding mountains are barren, but the bottom of the valley is not entirely destitute of vegetation. Further on, on the top of the hill, are the ruins called Burjsur, which answers to the Beth-zur.[1] A short distance from there is shown the site of the Prophet Jonah's tomb, also that of the Prophet Gad who was buried here. Many tombs are cut in the rock at different places in this neighborhood. Shortly before coming to Hebron the country opens out into a rich valley with several fine springs of water and magnificent vineyards. The valley is supposed to be that of Eshcol (cluster), where the spies, Caleb and Joshua, cut down a bunch with one cluster of grapes, bearing it between them on a staff.[2]

Hebron contests with Damascus as to being the oldest city in the world. The ancient name was Kirjath-arba, the city of Arba.[3] Among Mohammedans it is known as El-Khalil, "The Friend," as referring to Abraham who was called by God Himself, "my friend."[4]

Hebron is beautifully situated among groves of olive trees on the slope of a hill at the southern end of the valley of Eshcol. It is solidly built with blocks of grey stone.

[1] Josh. 15:58; Neh. 3:16. [2] Num. 13:23. [3] Gen. 23:2. [4] Isaiah 41:8.

THE LAND OF ABRAHAM.

Not long after Abraham came to Canaan, we find he pitched his tent in the plain of Mamre, which is in Hebron, and he built there an altar to the Lord.[1]

Here no doubt he often sat at the door of his tent, and watched his flocks and herds as they were quietly feeding

ABRAHAM ENTERTAINING THE ANGELS.

on the plains and over the hills of Hebron. While doing so on one occasion, the Lord appeared to him and made known to him the destruction that awaited Sodom and Gomorrah, and the other wicked cities of the plain of the Jordan.[2]

[1] Gen. 13:18. [2] Gen. 18.

At Hebron Sarah, Abraham's wife, died.[1] As a burial place he purchased the cave of Machpelah from the children of Heth.[2] When Abraham himself died at a good old age, his sons, Isaac and Ishmael, buried him beside Sarah.[3]

Here also Isaac and his wife Rebekah were laid. Leah, wife of Jacob, was laid in the same cave, and when Jacob died, far away in Egypt, he "gave commandment concerning his bones," that they should be carried there.[4]

The entrance to the cave seems to have been in the face of a projecting mass of rock. At a very early period a building was erected over the cave. One of the stones is thirty-eight feet in length. It would be interesting to look at the graves of the patriarchs, but the cave is now enclosed in a great mosque and very few Jews or Christians are allowed to enter it.

Hebron is a town of great antiquity. Mediaeval tradition localised the creation of Adam here; and at a very early period, owing to a misinterpretation of Joshua 14:15, where Arba is spoken of as the greatest man among the Anakim (giants), Adam's death was placed here. Abraham is also stated to have pitched his tent under the oaks of Mamre, the Amorite,[5] the place being near Hebron, and opposite the cave of Machpelah.

When Sarah died[6] Abraham purchased from Ephron, the Hittite, the double cavern of Machpelah as a family burial-place, and the narrative is no doubt intended to convey the meaning that an interest in the soil of Palestine was thereby secured to Abraham's descendants. Isaac and Jacob were also said to be buried here.

[1] Gen. 23:2. [2] Gen. 23:3—20. [3] Gen. 25:10. [4] Gen. 49:29—33. [5] Gen. 13:18. [6] Gen. 23.

Hebron was destroyed by Joshua[1] and became the chief city of the tribe of Caleb (chapter 14) which gradually became incorporated with the tribe of Judah. David spent a long time in the region of Hebron. After Saul's death, David ruled over Judah from Hebron for seven and a half years. It was at the gates of Hebron that Abner was slain by Joab, and David caused the murderers of Ish-bosheth, the son of Saul, to be hanged by the pool of Hebron. Hebron afterwards became the headquarters of the rebellious Absalom, but after that period it is rarely mentioned.

These tombs are of intense interest to the Jews, and are frequently visited by them. The only place to which they can come is the great walls that form the enclosure. In this wall is a large opening into which our guide, in the presence of an officer, reached to the full length of his arm, and brought out three papers which he destributed to the visitors, the writer receiving one of them. These papers contain Jewish prayers. The Jews write their prayers and requests on paper, making their wants known to God through Abraham their father, and deposit them in these walls, with the expectation of having them answered. The prayers principally refer to the restoration of Jerusalem, the return of their brethren, and blessings on their wives and their children.

A Jewish family is not happy when they have no offspring, and at this place special request for such blessings are made known to God. The Jews are allowed to put away their wives in case they bear no children and to take another without the least disgrace. We will here give the original prayer as it has been translated from the Hebrew to the English language.

[1] Josh. 10:37.

JEWISH PRAYER.

Praise God, Jerusalem the Holy City, may God rebuild it speedily. Amen!

Reuben, the son of Gittel, may he be helped to refreshness and satisfaction, and to be cured from all his pains, and have a contented, pleasant, honorable living.

My wife, Blume, the daughter of Hench, to a perfect cure, and to get with child of durability and to bring them up in doctrinal education, and to marriage, and benefactions—between all Israel.

My mother, Gittel, the daughter of Rebekah, may be cured from eye-pains, and have a good age, with much pleasure from her children.

Praise God, Sluzka, (another town). My brother, Haim, the son of Gittel, may he be helped to refreshment and satisfaction, and to a perfect cure, and a contented, honorable living. His wife, Malkeh, may she be strengthened in bodily health; his daughter, Sarah Rebekah, may she be married speedily and satisfactorily; his daughter, Libe, to be led in good ways; Para and Sume, may they be brought up in pleasure and satisfaction, with long and good days. Between all Israel.   (*Translated by a converted Jew*).

When Canaan was taken by Joshua, according to a promise given by Moses, Hebron was assigned to Caleb.[1] Afterwards it was made a city of refuge and given to the priests. When David was first chosen king on the death of Saul, he made Hebron his capital, and he reigned there for seven years. Here Absalom conspired against his father.[2] Like Jerusalem, Hebron is looked upon with reverence alike by Jews, Christians and Mohammedans.

We were here on a great feast day of the Mohammedans and it was very unpleasant as they followed the Christians from place to place calling them all sorts of names, such as "Christians" (derisively) "Dogs" and others more vile while several stones were thrown. Had it not been for our Turkish guard we might not have fared so well.

[1] Josh. 14: 6—14.   [2] Sam. 15.

RETURNING TO JERUSALEM.

We called at several Mission Homes where we were very nicely entertained for a short time, and then returned to Jerusalem, on the way passing many pilgrims that were going from Hebron to Jerusalem, most of them with bundles under their arms and staves in their hands, many quite old and hundreds of them in a company. They were principally from Russia.

These pilgrimages are made in the spring of the year by the thousand, and many of the pilgrims are said to be very poor people while others are not.

CHAPTER XXXVI.

Emmaus and Samuel's Tomb.

TOMBS—ROUGH ROADS—SAMUEL'S TOMB—CHRIST MET THE DIS-
CIPLES—EMMAUS—LORD MADE HIMSELF KNOWN—STONE
STRUCTURE—MOUNTAINS AND RAVINES—BROOKS—
WHERE DAVID SLEW THE GIANT—RETURN
TO JERUSALEM—LEAVING THE
HOLY CITY.

PARTY of us, four in number, accompanied by a dragoman, took a tour on foot from Jerusalem to Emmaus and return, taking with us a donkey for the purpose of carrying our coats and lunch. Starting from the Jaffa gate we were soon among the mountains, which hid from our view the Holy City. The country is barren and not much inhabited. Here and there an Arab is seen coming or going with some goats or a camel. Many tombs and caves, cut into the solid rock, are to be seen; while the signs of life are very few, yet there are indications that the country at one time was thickly populated. We soon lost our path and even our dragoman became confused while going over these mountains and hills, rocks and cliffs, that were almost impassible for man or beast. High mountain peaks and immense deep ravines were passed.

At places in the low lands, there were some olive trees, while at other times vines and fruit trees were seen. In the distance a building was seen, and on coming closer, we found

THE TOMB OF SAMUEL. 321

it to be a church or mosque which contained the tomb of Samuel, the prophet. "And Samuel died and all the Israelites were gathered together and lamented him, and buried him in his house at Ramah." What a thought to visit a tomb of one who had been received of the Lord, in answer to prayer!

"So Hannah rose up after they had eaten in Shiloh, and after they had drunk.... And she was in bitterness of soul, and prayed unto the Lord, and wept sore. And she vowed a vow, and said, O Lord of hosts, if thou wilt indeed look on the affliction of thine handmaid, and remember me, and not forget thine handmaid, but will give unto thine handmaid a man child, then I will give him unto

JERUSALEM DRAGOMAN. *(Original Photo.)*

the Lord all the days of his life, and there shall no razor come upon his head.... And Eli said unto her, How long wilt thou be drunken? put away thy wine from thee. And Hannah answered and said, No, my lord, I am a woman of a sorrowful spirit: I have drunk neither wine nor strong drink, but have poured out my soul before the Lord.... Then Eli answered and said, Go in peace: and the God of Israel grant thee thy petition that thou hast asked of him."[1]

And the woman was no more sad, and the child was born unto her, and she brought him unto the Lord. "For this child I prayed; and the Lord hath given me my petition which I asked of him: therefore also I have lent him to the Lord.... And he worshipped the Lord there."[2] What a lesson of faith and perseverance can be learned here from this faithful mother! After 3,000 years we are permitted to visit the tomb of her righteous son.

The road was very rough and we became tired of traveling. We stopped here to rest and eat our lunch and then passed on with the ancient Emmaus in view. What a road to travel! Undoubtedly the Savior walked along this road after His resurrection from the grave, meeting on the way two of His disciples who were earnestly engaged in talking of the things which had happened.

"And it came to pass, that, while they communed together and reasoned, Jesus himself drew near, and went with them. But their eyes were holden that they should not know him. And he said unto them, What manner of communications are these that ye have one to another, as ye walk, and are sad?" And they answered, not knowing to whom they spake, "Art thou a stranger in Jerusalem, and hast not

[1] 1 Sam. 1:9—11 and 14, 15, 17. [2] 1 Sam. 1:27, 28.

known the things which are come to pass there in these days? And he said unto them, What things? And they said unto him, Concerning Jesus of Nazareth, which was a prophet mighty in deed and word before God and all the people."

What an acknowledgement of Christ this was, as they opened their hearts to Him in complaint! He said unto them, "O fools, and slow of heart to believe all that the

"ABIDE WITH US; FOR IT IS TOWARD EVENING."

prophets have spoken: ought not Christ to have suffered these things, and to enter into his glory?" And He began to expound unto them the Scriptures. "And they drew nigh to the village, whither they went: and he made as though he would have gone further. But they constrained him, saying, Abide with us; for it is toward evening, and the day is far spent. And he went in to tarry with them. And it came to pass as he sat at meat with them, he took bread and blessed it, and brake, and gave to them. And their eyes were opened and they knew him, and he vanished out of their sight. And they said one to another, Did not our heart burn within us while he talked with us by the way, and while he opened to us the Scriptures?"[1]

We were admitted into the enclosed walls of the ancient grounds, where, on one side, is a convent. We were well entertained by the priests, and kindly shown the different places of interest. Leading us out into the yards they pointed out to us the place where the ancient buildings stood. There is at present nothing left but ruins of stone structures and immense stone floors. The spot was shown where the table stood when the Lord blessed the bread and vanished out of their sight.[2]

We were all very tired by this time, but while we were thinking of the events of long years ago, when Jesus and the disciples walked over these same roads, we forgot all our weariness.

On bidding the priests adieu, we took our course for Jerusalem. The day was by this time far spent, and we hurried along. Coming down the valley we saw the place, where, according to tradition, David picked up out of the brook the stones with which he slew the giant, while on one mountain were the Israelites and on the other the Philistines.[3]

The country is hilly and barren, and without much interest, were it not for the wonderful Bible facts which make every step so interesting, instructing and inspiring. We soon reached the Jaffa road, very weary and fatigued, but grateful in heart to God for the wonderful blessings and privileges bestowed; we arrived at our hotel about 7:30 P. M.

[1] Luke 24:15—32.   [2] Luke 24:31.   [3] 1 Sam. 17:40.

DAMASCUS GATE, JERUSALEM.

(Original Photo.)

We then spent some weeks in and about Jerusalem, visiting the many places of interest; talking with many people about the country and what happened in different localities; tracing the travels and wanderings of our Lord and Master from place to place; hearing many traditions, some unquestionably of doubtful origin; reading from the Holy Book passages that were appropriate to certain places and occasions; knowing that this is the land which God had promised to His people, and that they lived and ruled here; realizing that here His only begotten Son came upon earth to save fallen humanity, and just where He ought to have found His own He was despised and rejected, but at last overcame His enemies and their conspiracies, ascended to His Father, and now we await His second coming — all these things taken together create an impression upon one which is beyond the power of words to express.

On the 16th of April, in company with our friend, R. Poweck, we started for Joppa. We had formed many pleasant acquaintances during our stay in Jerusalem, and our parting with friends was tinged with sadness. As the train moved slowly out amid the waving of handkerchiefs and the shedding of tears, it reminded us of a funeral procession. A feeling akin to that experienced by a child leaving home for the first time came upon us. The poet expresses a fine sentiment when he says:

> "We will meet you in the city
> Of the New Jerusalem."

On the other hand, after being away from our dear ones at home so long a time, it caused us joy to realize that instead of sailing farther away, we were going in the direction of "home."

CHAPTER XXXVII.
Mount Carmel.

LEAVING JOPPA—HAIFA (ACRE)—MOUNT CARMEL—ELIJAH'S CASTLE—PHŒNICIA—BAAL WORSHIPERS.

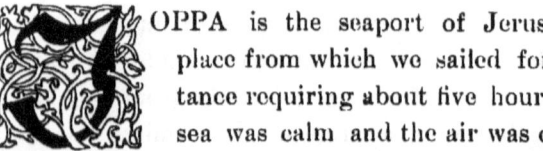OPPA is the seaport of Jerusalem and the place from which we sailed for Haifa, a distance requiring about five hours sailing. The sea was calm and the air was cool. We left Joppa about midnight, arriving at Haifa early in the morning. Haifa is located at the foot of Mount Carmel, across the beautiful bay from Acre, or Accho, as it was called in Bible times.

The tribe of Asher did not succeed in driving out the inhabitants of Accho.[1] A Jewish colony was afterwards established in this town, yet most of the citizens remained heathen. Accho was considered by the Greeks to belong to Phœnicia. It was afterwards called Ptolemais by one of the Ptolemies, and was important as a seaport. By Roman authors, and on coins, the place is represented as a colony of the Emperor Claudius. St. Paul once spent a day at Ptolemais,[2] and during its later Christian period the place became an episcopal see, the names of several of the bishops being handed down to us as members of various councils.

Haifa has about 7,250 inhabitants. A German colony is located here. The Europeon part of the town is very clean

[1] Judges 1:31.   [2] Acts 21:7.

HOUSE OF SIMON THE TANNER, JOPPA. (*From Photo.*)

and attractive, vineyards having been planted on Mount Carmel by the Germans.

Mount Carmel has a very historical connection. It was situated on the south frontier of the tribe of Asher, and is frequently mentioned in the Bible. Mount Carmel is a ridge stretching in a north-western direction for about fifteen miles from the Plain of Esdraelon, till it terminates at the Bay of Acre, which forms its southern boundary. Some of its peaks are 1,700 feet above the level of the sea. Its steep slopes are covered with forests and thick jungles, the dark colors of which make the chain conspicuous among the surrounding white limestone mountains. At its foot the river Kishon enters the sea. Mount Carmel abounds with caves. The prophets Elijah and Elisha frequently found refuge among them. The peak is now called "The place of burning." Here Elijah challenged the priests of Baal to prove by fire from heaven that Baal was the true God; but there was no response, although they cut themselves with knives, crying, "O Baal, hear us." Elijah then offered sacrifice to the Lord, and fire from heaven consumed the whole burnt offering. The people fell on their faces, exclaiming, "The Lord, He is the God." Down below is the river Kishon, to which Elijah told the people to take the prophets, and where he slew them. The ruins of an old castle mark the location according to tradition where the slaughter of the prophets of Baal took place.

While Elijah prayed for rain on top of Mount Carmel, he told his servants to look out towards the sea. At first they saw a little cloud rising from it, "like a man's hand;" but it swelled till "the heaven was black with clouds," and there was a very great rain.

The aboriginal inhabitants regarded the mount as sacred, and at a very early period it was called the Mount of God.[1] The beauty of Carmel is also extolled in the Bible.[2]

PHŒNICIA.

Phœnicia was a tract of country lying north of Palestine, along the coast of the Mediterranean, and extending eastward to Lebanon. Its limits varied at different times. It may be said to have extended 200 miles northward from Acre, with an average breadth of fifteen miles.

Conder says of the Phœnicians: "This strong and clever people, who in the later times had all the trade of the Mediterranean in their hands, are said to have come from the mouth of the Euphrates. They already traded with Egypt before the time of Moses, and it is probable that the introduction of the alphabet, not only into Palestine, but also into Greece, is due to the Phœnicians.

"We know that the Hebrews, at least as early as the days of Hezekiah (726 B. C.), and probably much earlier, together with the Moabites and the Phœnicians, used an alphabet which was so simple and practically useful that it gradually superseded the clumsy characters of the Egyptians and which has spread in various forms westward all over Europe and America, and in the East throughout Asia and India." The Phœnician language very much resembled the Hebrew.

The Phœnicians, like the Hindoos, were a very religious people. Every person bore a religious name, placing himself under the protection of some god or goddess, as Abibaal (Baal is my father), Baleazar (Baal protects). Each city was under the protection of some deity. The ships carried

---

[1] 1 Kings 18: 19—36. [2] Isa. 35: 2; Song of Solomon 7: 5.

RELIGION OF THE PHŒNICIANS.

images of the gods at the prow. Their chief deities we Baal and Ashtoreth supposed to represent the sun and moon, and Molech.

The religion had two horrible rites. Virgins prostituted themselves in the temple as a work of merit. Human sacrifices were frequently made. In times of danger, children were offered by their parents to Molech. This large brazen image was heated to a glow by fire within. The victims were placed by their parents in the arms of the image from which they rolled into the fiery lap below. First-born, or only sons, or virgin daughters were deemed especially acceptable to the divinities. When Carthage, a famous city in northern Africa, founded by the Phœnicians, was besieged, 200 children of the noblest families were thus sacrificed.

The prophet Micah, in the Old Testament, thus described the worship acceptable to God, "Wherewith shall I come before the Lord, and bow myself before the high God? Shall I come before him with burnt offerings, with calves of a year old? Will the Lord be pleased with thousands of rams, or with ten thousands of rivers of oil? Shall I give my first-born for my transgression, the fruit of my body for the sin of my soul? He hath shewed thee, O man, what is good; and what doth the Lord require of thee, but to do justly, and to love mercy, and to walk humbly with thy God."[1]

[1] Micah 6:6—8.

CHAPTER XXXVIII.

TYRE AND SIDON.

ANCIENT RUINS—BIBLE TIMES—CROWNING CITY—ROBBED OF ITS TREASURES—TOP OF A ROCK—ZAREPHATH.

HE two chief cities of Phœnicia were Tyre and Sidon. To these cities the Lord Jesus referred when He began to upbraid the cities wherein most of His mighty works were done, because they repented not: "Woe unto thee, Chorazin! Woe unto thee, Bethsaida! for if the mighty works, which were done in you, had been done in Tyre and Sidon, they would have repented long ago in sackcloth and ashes."[1]

Tyre was a rich and flourishing city in the days of Solomon. Even earlier, in the time of Joshua, it was called "the strong city Tyre."[2] It was a seaport town, with a fine harbor. Most of the sailors in the world at that time belonged to Tyre. The ships of Tyre sailed to every port in the Mediterranean, some went even to Britain for its tin. In the markets of Tyre were to be found the choicest products of every country in the world—fine linen, spices, ivory, gold, silver and other metals, and precious stones.[3] It was called "the crowning city, whose merchants are princes."[4]

While Tyre was in the height of its prosperity, its ruin was prophesied by Ezekiel. He foretold that "they shall break

[1] Matt. 11:21.   [2] Joshua 19:29.   [3] Ezekiel 27.   [4] Isa. 23:8.

TYRE. 335

down thy walls, and destroy thy pleasant houses: and they shall lay thy stones and thy timber and thy dust in the midst of the water."[1] Nebuchadnezzar, king of Babylon, came

(*Original Photo.*)
CONVENT OF ST. ELIAS, NEAR JERICHO.

with a great army and besieged Tyre. The siege lasted thirteen years. When the people found that the city would be

[1] Ezek. 26:12.

taken they went over in their ships to the island, where they built a new city, the present one. They carried everything of value from the old city and left it empty. Nebuchadnezzar in his anger broke down the walls and destroyed the pleasant houses, as the prophet had predicted.

New Tyre became richer and stronger than the old city. Being on an island, an army could not reach it. Some centuries later when Alexander the Great was on his way to the East, he resolved to conquer the island city of New Tyre. As he had no ships he set his army to building a road out into the sea to reach the island on which Tyre stood. In making this causeway he employed the ruins of old Tyre, carrying them away, and throwing them into the sea. Thus were the words fulfilled, "Thy stones and thy timber shall be laid in the midst of the water." Alexander did not entirely destroy the city, and it existed for hundreds of years afterward.

Its utter ruin, however, had also been foretold. God said He would make it like the top of a rock, a place to spread nets upon.[1] This was also fulfilled; for many years it was nothing but a miserable fishing village called Tsur. It now contains about 4,000 inhabitants.

Zarephath was a seaport about fifteen miles north of Tyre. The name means melting place for metals. During a long famine in Israel, the prophet Elijah was miraculously supported by a widow here, whose son also he restored to life.[2] The place was called by the Greeks Sarepta.[3] It is said to have received its name Sidon from the eldest son of Canaan.[4] Sidon appears to have been older than Tyre, for the latter is not mentioned with it in Gen. 10:15—18 and is

[1] Ezek. 26:14. [2] 1 Kings 17:9—24. [3] Luke 4:26. [4] Gen. 10:15.

called her daughter.¹ In Joshua it is called "Great Zidon."² It prospered and was inferior only to Tyre, but its ruin was also foretold.³

It was destroyed by Artaxerxes Ochus, king of Persia, 350 B. C. It was afterwards rebuilt, but it never rose to eminence. The present city is called Saida. The harbor is choked up with sand, and its trade is inconsiderable, being chiefly noted for its fruit.

¹ Isa. 23:12.   ² Josh. 11:18.   ³ Ezek. 28:21—23.

PLOWING AND SOWING IN THE ORIENT.

CHAPTER XXXIX.

Nazareth and Hills of Galilee.

KISHON—HOME OF ZEBEDEE—NAZARETH—HOME OF JESUS—SHEEP
AND GOATS—STREETS—ST. MARY'S WELL—MOUNT TABOR—
HILLS OF GALILEE—BEDOUIN CAMPS—TIBERIAS—
SEA OF GALILEE—A NIGHT OF MISERY.

 PARTY of four was soon organized and with a carriage and a driver left Haifa for Nazareth, Tiberias, and the Sea of Galilee. The distance to Nazareth is twenty-three and one half miles or one day's drive, the road leading through the well cultivated plain of the Kishon; here we went through a grove of oak trees which are very rare in this country. Many ruins of old villages are seen.

About four miles from Haifa we came to the beautiful village of Yafa, the Japhia of Joshua 19:12, on the borders of Zebulun. A tradition arose in the middle ages that the home of Zebedee and his sons James and John was situated here. The ruins of old homes are seen on every hand in which Bible characters were born, lived and died.

Nazareth broke suddenly into view and we descended by a good road into the town. Here we halted for the night. Nazareth lies a few miles north-west of Mount Tabor. It stands on the western side of a valley, and rises a little way up the slope of a hill.

NAZARETH, THE HOME OF JESUS, AS IT IS TO-DAY.

(Original Photo).

One fountain seems to have been the main if not the only source of water supply for the inhabitants. It was to this fountain no doubt that Mary the mother of Jesus came, day by day, among the village maidens, to fill her pitcher. At Nazareth the angel Gabriel appeared to Mary and foretold the birth of her Son.[1] The fear of a cruel king drove Joseph and Mary to Nazareth, and there Jesus was brought up till He began His public ministry. No event in His history while living here is recorded except the journey to Jerusalem.[2]

After the baptism of Jesus and His teaching in Galilee, He came to Nazareth, and, as His custom was, went into the synagogue on the Sabbath day, and stood up to read, His words exciting such anger that those who heard Him "thrust him out of the city, and led him unto the brow of the hill whereon their city was built, that they might cast him down headlong." But He passed through the midst of them and went His way.[3]

The Savior was called "Jesus of Nazareth," because He had lived there so long. The city was small and despised. "Can any good thing come out of Nazareth?" asked Nathanael.[4]

In the time of Christ the hills around were no doubt terraced and cultivated to their summits. They are now bare, but they yield pasture for flocks of sheep and goats. Jesus, in one of His addresses, spoke of the separation of the sheep from the goats.[5] The goats, traveling faster than the sheep and thriving on a scantier vegetation, are driven to the mountain tops, while the sheep feed on the richer herbage below.

[1] Luke 1:26—28.   [2] Luke 2:40—52.   [3] Luke 4:16—30.
[4] John 1:46.   [5] Matt. 25:33.

The town now contains about 5,000 inhabitants, mostly Christians. Two monasteries are here, one of the Greek, the other of the Latin rites, containing a large number of monks. All those given as Christians should be considered as a whole. In the Orient it is not this name or that by which Christians are known, but the principal question is, "Are you a Christian?" because Heathens, Mohammedans and Jews all reject Christ as a Savior, while the Greeks, Latins, Armenians, Coptics, Franciscans and Protestants are all called "Christians" because they believe that Christ is the Savior of the world.

The streets in Nazareth are very poor; in fact this is the case throughout the Turkish domain. In the principal street of Nazareth, the gutter, instead of being one on each side, as is the case in American towns, was in the middle of the street, and, as the traveling was difficult, we were all compelled to get out and walk, one and sometimes two of us being required to hold the wagon to keep it from falling over.

Over these hills and valleys and perhaps on these very streets the blessed feet of Jesus trod during His boyhood, and the well called "St. Mary's well" was no doubt frequently visited by Him when a child.

In a short time after leaving Nazareth we were in a valley with Mt. Tabor in our front, and in about fifteen minutes more we were at the base of the hill. To our right in the valley below we saw the ancient Daberath.[1]

Mount Tabor was situated on the frontier of Issachar and Zebulun. It was here that Deborah directed Barak to assemble an army, and from hence the Israelites marched into the plain and defeated Sisera.[2] In the Psalms, Tabor and

[1] Josh. 19:12.   [2] Judges 4.

Hermon are extolled together.[1] Origen and St. Jerome speak of Mt. Tabor as the scene of the transfiguration.[2] There are three chapels built there in memory of the three tabernacles which St. Peter wished to build.

Passing along we saw many sheep and goats pasturing on the hills of Galilee. The hills were dotted with the numerous camps of Bedouins. The Sea of Galilee was before us, and as we ascended the hills coming around the curves we were in Tiberias. By this time it was evening and the party were much wearied, and arrangements were at once made for night quarters. It was a pleasant evening, the moon and stars were shining, the sea was calm and the water as clear as crystal. Tiberias is built down to the waters, it being only a few rods from the hotel to the sea. We had the pleasure of bathing in that noted body of water. The name Galilee[3] was originally applied to the highlands

BEDOUIN WOMEN. *(Original Photo).*

[1] Psalms 89:13.   [2] Mark 9:2—10.   [3] Isa. 9:1, and Matt. 4:15.

only which extended from north of the lake of Gennesaret to the west. The tribes of Asher, Zebulun, and Issachar who dwelt here were carried into captivity like their kinsmen, but the land was colonized anew after the captivity, by Jews from the South. The population, however, retained its mixed character, and the name Galilee was extended to include the whole province lying between the plain of Jezreel and the river Litany. The north part was called Upper Galilee, to the south of which was Lower Galilee.

The country was famed for its fertility, rich pastures and luxuriant forest trees being its chief features. The tract situated to the west of the lake was the most beautiful part of the country. In the Roman period, Galilee formed a separate province and was densely peopled.

The Jewish element still continued predominant, but was more affected by foreign influences than in Judea. The language also varied from that spoken in Judea.[1] The Jews of this district seem to have been less strict and less acquainted with the law than those of Judea, by whom they were consequently despised. Their revolt against the Romans in A. D. 67 proved, however, that their national spirit was still as strong as that of their brethren.

Galilee attained the height of its prosperity about the time of Christ. Sepphoris had for a time been its chief town; but Herod Antipas, who was not less splendor-loving than his father Herod the Great, determined to build a new and magnificent capital. His dominions at this time embraced Galilee and Perea, which however were separated by the Decapolis. Tiberias has a population of 3,700 which are of different nationalities and different religions.

[1] Matt. 26:73.

A NIGHT IN TIBERIAS.

The night was spent, but not without being disturbed by the noise of the natives, donkeys and dogs, and the attentions of fleas, for which Tiberias is noted. Arabs say the king of fleas resides here; consequently a part of the night was spent in a wakeful state, as is the custom in that country. As they have flat roofs on their houses, and they are easy of access, I spent a part of the time on the roof. My position commanded a magnificent view of the sea, which helped to vary the monotony of waiting for morning.

Finally morning came, and after partaking heartily of breakfast consisting of fish from the Sea of Galilee, which had been ordered the previous evening, the day was spent on the sea and visiting the ancient ruins along its shores.

CHAPTER XL.

SEA OF GALILEE AND ADJACENT POINTS.

GENNESARET—DESCRIPTION—MAGDALA—CAPERNAUM—CHORAZIN—BETHSAIDA—SEA OF GALILEE—PLAIN OF THE FIVE THOUSAND—CANA OF THE BIBLE—SAUL'S BATTLE-GROUND—ARABS PLOWING.

LAKE Tiberias was anciently called the lake of Gennezar or Gennesaret, from the plain at its north-west end bearing that name. This is the place where the herd of swine ran into the sea and were drowned.[1] The greatest length of the lake is thirteen miles, and the greatest width nearly six miles. The banks are beautifully green early in the spring. The hills surrounding this beautiful blue body of water are of moderate height, and the scenery is enlivened by a few villages.

The sea is sometimes visited by violent storms. We learn from the Gospels that the lake was once navigated by numerous vessels, but there are now only a few miserable fishing boats here. The water is used for drinking purposes by all of the inhabitants there about and has a slight brackish taste. It is cooled by being placed in porous jars and allowed to stand over night.

Magdala is a town north of Tiberias and at the south end of the plain of Gennesaret. The name means tower. It was the city of Mary Magdalene, and here Jesus Christ

[1] Luke 8:33.

TIBERIAS AND THE SEA OF GALILEE.

landed after feeding the multitude on the opposite bank. Mary Magdalene, on whom Jesus had performed a wonderful cure, ministered to Him of her substance, stood by His cross, went to His sepulchre, and was the first to welcome Him when He rose from the dead.[1] At present there are in existence only the ruins of a tower and heaps of rubbish, among which about twenty mud-built cottages stand.

Capernaum, Chorazin and Bethsaida were three cities on the northern end of the lake. The exact position of Capernaum is disputed. It is generally supposed to have been not far west of the Jordan inlet, where there are at present many ruins and large blocks of stone. A convent is built here in memory of the ancient Capernaum. Here we ate our lunch, there being six of us besides the boatman.

Jesus Christ was so often in Capernaum that it is called His own city.[2] Here He commenced His public ministry, and often taught in the synagogue.[3] Here He healed Peter's wife's mother,[4] the nobleman's son,[5] the centurion's servant,[6] and raised from the dead the ruler's daughter.[7] The ruins of a synagogue are still visible.

Chorazin stood on a hill about two and a half miles north of the supposed site of Capernaum. The remnants of the houses are partly in a shallow valley with some on a rocky spur.

Bethsaida, "House of Fishing," was the city of Andrew, Peter and Philip.[8] Its exact position is uncertain.

In these three cities Jesus had performed great miracles, yet, on account of their unbelief, they were to be destroyed. Only a few ruins mark the places where they are supposed

[1] Luke 8: 2, 3. [2] Matt. 9: 1. [3] John 6: 59. [4] Matt. 8: 14.
[5] John 4: 46. [6] Matt. 8: 5, 6. [7] Matt. 9: 18—25. [8] John 1: 44.

to have stood. They are an awful warning to those who refuse or neglect God's offered salvation through Jesus Christ. Jesus said: "Woe unto thee, Chorazin! woe unto thee, Bethsaida! for if the mighty works, which were done in you, had been done in Tyre and Sidon, they would have repented..... And thou, Capernaum, which art exalted unto heaven, shalt be brought down to hell: for if the mighty works, which have been done in thee, had been done in Sodom, it would have remained until this day." And now the teachings and prophecies have all been fulfilled.[1]

The weather being very warm and the water clear and cool, there was nothing more enjoyable than a bath in this beautiful lake.

The lake is subject to sudden storms which sweep down from the hills by which it is surrounded. At about 2 P. M. while we were at Capernaum our boatman became alarmed, as the wind began to blow and the waters raged. He called for all the passengers to get aboard and return to Tiberias at once, as it would be impossible to return if the storm became more severe. The storm however soon subsided, and all fears vanished. How often do we read of the storms on the sea of Galilee!

Jesus at one time performed a great miracle at the north end of the lake, east of the Jordan inlet, where there is a beautiful plain sloping towards the sea. Here Jesus fed a great multitude with five loaves and two fishes, and there was enough for all, about five thousand men, besides women and children. After such a great number had eaten, there were twelve baskets full of fragments left.[2]

"And straightway Jesus constrained his disciples to get into a ship, and to go before him unto the other side,

[1] Matt. 11:21—23. [2] Matt. 14:20, 21.

JESUS WALKING ON THE SEA.

while he sent the multitudes away." And Jesus went up into the mountain to pray. By evening the ship in which the disciples were crossing the water was in the midst of the sea, tossed by the waves, "for the wind was contrary."

Towards morning "Jesus went unto them, walking on the sea." And when the disciples saw Him walking on the sea they were afraid and cried out, "It is a spirit," and were

FEEDING THE FIVE THOUSAND.

in trouble; but Jesus, knowing their condition, spoke unto them, saying, "Be of good cheer, it is I, be not afraid." When Peter knew that it was the Lord, he wanted to go to Him on the sea. Jesus said, "Come" and Peter left the ship, but soon began to sink, because he looked at the winds and the roughness of the sea instead of looking to Jesus. So often we, by looking away from Christ to the storms and raging winds of life, lose our hold by doubting, and we sink.

Jesus heard and helped when Peter cried: "Lord save me." And so He will hear us when we call upon Him. Jesus stretched forth His hand, and caught him, and said unto him, "O thou of little faith."

Is it not true, dear reader, that Jesus has often grasped our hands just in time to keep us from sinking; if it were not for this Holy One we would soon be lost in despair. He grasps the sinking, heals the sick, feeds the hungry, opens the eyes of the blind, and brings back to life the dead, and through Him all may receive the forgiveness of past sins, and become heirs of God and joint heirs with Christ. Then we can say with the Apostle Paul: "He that spared not his own Son, but delivered him up for us all, how shall he not with him also freely give us all things?"[1] "Nay, in all these things we are more than conquerors through him that loved us."[2]

The next day, April 23d, we started over the hills of Galilee towards the Cana of the Bible, where Jesus performed His first miracle, turning water into wine. Cana of Galilee is a small town near Nazareth, where Jesus with all His disciples and His mother were invited to a marriage. They had no wine, and Jesus, knowing what was to come, waited until they had set six water pots of stone, after the manner of the purifying of the Jews. Then "Jesus saith unto them, Fill the water pots with water," and they filled them to the brim. Jesus told them to "draw out now," and when it was drawn and tasted, it was wine. The ruler of the feast saith, "Every man at the beginning doth set forth good wine, but thou hast kept the good wine until now." This

---

[1] Rom. 8:32.   [2] Rom. 8:37.

AGRICULTURE IN THE ORIENT.

miracle did Jesus in Cana of Galilee and then went to Capernaum and from there to Jerusalem, for the Passover of the Jews was at hand.[1]

The village of Nain, where the Lord Jesus raised the widow's son and gave him to his mother, is located to our left.[2]

The valley is cultivated in a very indifferent manner, but crops, wheat principally, looked well. Many stones the size of a peck and a half bushel measure are very thickly scattered over the cultivated land; but they could easily be removed by a little work.

Arabs plow with bullocks, while plenty of good horses are seen on pasture. The plow is a very simple structure, a bent beam or pole which extends forward to the cattle with an upright piece perpendicularly attached to which is fastened a kind of point that throws the ground on both sides. In this country of systematic plowing, and farming, it would be condemned at once. The Arab walks along with one hand to the plow. In the other he carries a whip with which to drive the bullocks. This is the oriental way of plowing, being used in Palestine, Asia Minor, Egypt and India.

We returned to Haifa on the third day, in the evening, where we expected to take the steamer for Beirut. We felt grateful to God for what we had seen and heard. Often the desire arose that we might have with us a number of our beloved ones at home to help us store the information to be gathered in these travels.

[1] John 2.   [2] Luke 7: 11—13.

CHAPTER XLI.

BEIRUT AND DAMASCUS.

BEIRUT—DILIGENCE—RAILROAD—LEBANON MOUNTAINS—MOUNT HERMON—DRUSES—MASSACRING MARONITES—EUROPEAN COMMISSION—DAMASCUS—HISTORY.

EIRUT is the seaport of Damascus, which is about seventy miles distant, beyond the Lebanon mountains. It was one of the ancient Phœnician towns where the so-called dwellers on mountains had one of their strongholds. Berytus and Byblus were their two towns located at the foot of Mt. Lebanon. In 1840 the population of Beirut was only about 8,000; it is now about 80,000, chiefly Christians. The increase is largely due to the settlement here of refugees after the Mohammedan massacre of Christians in Damascus and Lebanon, in 1860.

Beirut is the most flourishing seaport on the coast of Syria. It has a regular service of Egyptian, French, and English steamers. A French company is constructing a new railway from Beirut to Damascus.

American missionaries have established in Beirut the Syrian Protestant College, and a large printing office in which books are printed in Arabic and other languages. English missionaries have an institution here in which to train teachers for the Lebanon schools.

BEIRUT, THE SEAPORT OF DAMASCUS.

(*From Photo.*)

The railway from Beirut to Damascus was not yet completed, and the easiest way of making the trip was by the "Diligence," a system operated by a French company, that runs regular conveyances every day and night. Leaving Beirut in the morning, we were at Damascus in the evening of the same day. They have six horses attached to the omnibus or hack, and drive at a recklessly high rate of speed, changing horses about every five miles. The change is quickly made, the driver giving the signal of his approach to one of the stations with a series of blasts on a horn. The fresh horses are made ready and brought out before our arrival; then they are quickly attached and the journey is resumed. Horses were changed twelve times between Beirut and Damascus.

The applications for transportation are so numerous that a passage must be procured a day or two and sometimes a week before going over the Lebanon and the Anti Lebanon mountains.

It was from these mountains that the timber was brought to Jerusalem for the construction of the temple. The tops of the mountains were covered with snow, especially Mount Hermon with its snowy peak 9,050 feet high. The Arabs say that Lebanon carries winter upon its head, spring upon its shoulders, summer in its bosom, while autumn lies sleeping at its feet.

The range is composed of four distinct courses of mountains, rising one above the other. The first, or lowest, is fertile, and abounds with grain and fruit; the second is barren and burned; the third enjoys perpetual spring, while the fourth, or highest, is covered with perpetual snow, where winter, with its cold and frost, continuously reigns.

Sannin, the most conspicuous summit, is about 8,500 feet high, and generally snowclad, while clear cold water flows down its sides, very refreshing in a hot country. Hence the Scripture comparison, "Will a man leave the snow of Lebanon which cometh from the rock of the field, or shall the cold flowing waters that come from another place be forsaken?"[1]

Lebanon was famous in ancient times for its cedars, a noble tree somewhat like the walnut, the poplar, and oak in our country for size and usefulness. Some of these cedars have been measured, showing forty-five feet in girth, while their huge branches stretched out fifty-eight paces from side to side. The wood is firm and very durable. It also has a fragrant odor which seems to have been alluded to when speaking of the smell of Lebanon.[2] At present there are only a few groves of the trees; in ancient times they were far more abundant.

The inhabitants of Mount Lebanon are principally Druses and Maronites. The belief of the Druses is that when men die they are born again in a human birth according to their merit. Unlike the Mohammedans, they do not pray, this being regarded as an interference with the works of the Creator. Mutual protection and hatred of all others is their animating feeling. In some respects they resemble Mohammedans. They never taste wine or tobacco, a practice which would be a credit and a blessing to the people of this country. Women are veiled; they are divorced by telling them three times that they had better go back to their mothers.

Damascus, with Hebron, is claimed to be one of the oldest cities on the earth, and dates back very near to the flood. It is claimed by many to cover the site of the Garden of Eden.

[1] Jer. 18:14. [2] Hos. 14:6.

HISTORY OF DAMASCUS.

Jews, Christians and Moslems have different legends regarding the origin of the city.

David conquered the town after a bloody war, as it was allied whith his enemy the king of Zobah, and placed a garrison in it.[1] During the reign of Solomon, an adventurer, called Rezon, succeeded in making himself king of Damascus. The history of the northern kingdom of Israel, as regards its foreign policy, is almost exclusively occupied with its relation to Damascus.[2] Several of these princes bore the name of Benhadad.

The most formidable enemy of Israel was Hazael, whose usurpation of the Syrian throne appears to have been promoted by Elijah and Elisha.[3] Owing to the hostilities between the two Jewish kingdoms, the Damascenes could attack Israel unopposed. Hazael devastated the country east of Jordan, crossed that river, captured the town of Gath, and made the king of Judah pay dearly for the immunity of Jerusalem from siege.[4] Benhadad III., the son of Hazael, was less successful than his father had been.[5] Jeroboam II. succeeded in recapturing the former Jewish territory from Damascus.[6] Shortly afterwards we find Pekah, king of Israel, in alliance with Rezin of Damascus against Jotham, king of Judah. They marched against Jerusalem, but had very little success against Ahaz, although he was compelled to restore the seaport of Elath on the Red Sea to the Syrians.[7] Ahaz invited the Assyrians to aid him against the Syrians. These allies subdued one after the other of the three kingdoms in detail, the rulers of which should have united their forces against the common enemy.

[1] 2 Sam. 8:5, 6. [2] 1 Kings 15 and 20. [3] 2 Kings 8:8—15. [4] 2 Kings 12:18.
[5] 2 Kings 13:25. [6] 2 Kings 14:28. [7] 2 Kings 16:5, 6.

CHAPTER XLII.

DAMASCUS.

POPULATION—NAAMAN—SAUL'S CONVERSION—STREET CALLED STRAIGHT—HOUSE OF ANANIAS—TOMB OF ST. GEORGE—WINDOW FROM WHICH PAUL ESCAPED—VISITORS IN DAMASCUS—DOGS—MONEYS—OVER THE LEBANON MOUNTAINS BY MOONLIGHT—TURKISH FUNERAL.

IT is extremely difficult to estimate the population of Damascus, but according to the government statistics in 1888, there were 120,750 inhabitants. The Moslems have in all 248 mosques and schools.

Damascus is noted for its rivers and streams from the mountains. It was from here that Naaman went to Elisha. Naaman was a great man and very honorable, but he was a leper. The little maid that was taken captive in the land of Israel, and waited on Naaman's wife, said unto her mistress, "Would God my lord were with the prophet that is in Samaria! for he would recover him of his leprosy." So Naaman, the captain of the host, went, and took with him a great price to pay for the service of the prophet. Undoubtedly he expected a great reception and much favor; but he was disappointed. Elisha sent a messenger unto him, saying, "Go and wash in Jordan seven times." Naaman was wroth and said, "Are not Abana and Pharpar, rivers of Damascus, better than all the waters of Israel? may I not wash in them

DAMASCUS. MINARET ST. ELLENE. (Original Photo.)

and be clean? So he turned and went away in a rage." But his servants reasoned with him and he went and washed according as the prophet had told him and he was healed.[1] So all of us, by coming as the Lord requires, may be healed from the leprosy of sin.

It was to Damascus that Saul came to take prisoners all such that professed to be followers of the Lord Jesus Christ. As we were going around visiting these different places of interest we were taken to the supposed place according to tradition where Saul was struck down with the great light.[2] It was about half a mile beyond the old walls. We also went through the street called "Straight,"[3] and indeed this street has the proper name as it is very straight and principally under roof, or covered over with arches made of timber and straw or thatch. The spot was shown to us where tradition locates the site of the house of Ananias, where the Lord appeared to him in a dream, saying that he should go to the street called Straight, to the house of Judas, and inquire "for one called Saul, of Tarsus: for, behold, he prayeth." Ananias came and put his hands on Saul, that he might receive his sight.

We were led to the tomb of St. George, which is much revered by the Christians. This saint is said to have assisted St. Paul to escape from Damascus, and the window above the Turkish wall is still pointed out where the apostle was let down in a basket by night.[4]

Many curious things are to be seen in the streets of Damascus. Donkeys and camels frequently crowd the way, while numerous hack drivers and dragomen offering their services are met on all sides.

[1] 2 Kings 5. [2] Acts 9:3. [3] Acts 9:11. [4] Acts 9:25.

One peculiar thing here in Damascus, as in all other oriental towns, is the large number of dogs on the streets. In front of the hotel eleven were counted at one time, and, in going through the town, at another place where the street makes a curve thirty-five were counted, and by going a little further fifty dogs of all sizes, colors, descriptions and ages were seen, nearly all having the appearance of being half starved. These dogs have no owners and no homes but are simply roving round town in search of food, and lying around in the sunshine in front of some of the shops and business houses, while pedestrians must either go around or step over them, without disturbing them in the least. Occasionally when one is accidentally trampled upon you hear a growl, and at times they are engaged in fighting each other. On the whole, this is a very unpleasant thing with which strangers have to contend. In Palestine, as in India, dogs are considered sacred to some extent.

It is no wonder the Scriptures refer so often to dogs. As in the case of the poor man Lazarus, "moreover the dogs came and licked his sores." They are also referred to in terms of abomination and reproach, and as enemies, imprudent and false. The apostle admonishes,[1] "Beware of dogs," as false teachers, ignorant and dumb, sleeping, lying down, loving to slumber. Isaiah speaks of them as "greedy dogs which can never have enough."[2]

Through the entire dominion of Turkey the value of money is very deceptive as there are so many different kinds in circulation and it varies in value at almost every point we visited—Cairo, Joppa, Jerusalem, Haifa, Beirut and Damascus. While there are a number of money changers in

[1] Phil. 3:2. [2] Isa. 56:11.

all these towns, yet many, if possible, will take advantage of travelers. The principal moneys are given in the list of money tables in this book; but there are many more in circulation not mentioned. Here English, French, Swiss and Italian money is used at its current rates of exchange.

As we were somewhat tired on our arrival at Damascus, a part of our two weeks' stay at this place was spent in resting. The day hack to Beirut being full, it was necessary for us to take the night mail, which meant a ride of

(*Original Photo.*)
A TURKISH FUNERAL PROCESSION.

about seventy miles over the Lebanon mountains by moonlight. The nights are chilly, especially in the spring, in consequence of the snow on the mountains.

On Sunday, May 5th, at Beirut, we attended a Turkish funeral of high order. The procession, which consisted exclusively of men, no women being seen, halted at a large church or mosque, and the corpse was taken inside, where burning lights were placed all around the casket. Here a

Greek service was held, the priest burning incense. Many of the spectators exhibited anything but a reverential manner. After the services in the church, the corpse was put into a hearse similar to those in our country, and taken to the place of burial. The horses were all covered with blankets up to their ears, and each of them was led by a footman. No tears were shed by the friends, but a few of those in the rear showed expressions of grief.

Many peculiar looking Jews are seen all through the Holy Lands, with their black wooly hats and a long curl of hair hanging down at each side of their heads, in front of the ears.

SAUL OF TARSUS STRUCK WITH THE GREAT LIGHT.

CHAPTER XLIII.

BEIRUT TO SMYRNA AND EPHESUS.

TRIPOLI—ORANGE MART—ISLAND OF CYPRUS—LARNAKA—SIMASOL—MAN OVERBOARD—ISLAND OF RHODES—CARRYING THEIR BEDS—ISLAND OF CHIOS—SMYRNA—BY TRAIN TO EPHESUS.

FOUR hours after leaving Beirut on the steamship Achille, we reached Tripoli, a town of about 17,000 inhabitants where the steamer stopped for a time to load and unload freight. The weather was warm and the sea calm, while the mountains in the distance were seen to be covered with snow. In the valley there is an abundance of fruit grown, such as lemons, oranges, etc. Here 2,000 boxes of oranges were taken on board and it was thought that each box contained about two bushels.

Our next objective point was the island of Cyprus. We arrived at the town of Larnaka, and stopped a short time. Cyprus is one of the largest islands in the Mediterranean. It is about 140 miles long, and from five to fifty broad. It lies in the east of the Mediterranean. In ancient times it was noted for its copper, which is named after the island.

When Paul and Barnabas were living at Antioch, they were appointed to be the first Christian missionaries to the heathen. They went first to Cyprus, to which place Barnabas belonged, landing at Salamis, a large city on the east of the island. A great many Jews lived at Salamis, and the apostles preached in their synagogues. They then went preaching all through the island, till they came to Paphos. Near this place stood the temple of Venus, the goddess of love. This

SEAPORT OF SMYRNA. *(Original Photo.)*

temple was so celebrated that it was sometimes called the "Paphian Goddess," her priestesses were prostitutes.

The Roman governor, whose name was Sergius Paulus, lived at Paphos. He was not satisfied with the false gods of

(Original Photo.)
THE RUINS OF THE PRISON OF ST. PAUL, EPHESUS.

"The keynote of life's harmony is sacrifice."

What though on peril's front you stand?
  What though through lone and lonely ways,
With dusty feet and horny hands,
  You toil unfriended all the days,
    And die at last with man's dispraise?

Would you have chosen ease, and so
  Have shunned the fight? God honored you
With trust of weighty works. And O,
  The Captain of the heavens knew
    His trusted soldier would prove true.
          —Joaquin Miller.

his country, and wished to learn the truth. When he heard of the preaching of Paul and Barnabas, he sent for them. A sorcerer, called Elymas, tried to withstand the apostles, but he was struck blind.[1]

The last mention of Cyprus in the New Testament is in connection with Paul's voyage to Rome. He sailed under Cyprus.[2] This island now belongs to Turkey, but the administration of public affairs is in the hands of the British government.

Sailing along Cyprus we soon reached another town called Simasol. Near this town the country is charming, but viewed from the sea it looks mountainous. At this place an aged man fell overboard while being transferred to a smaller boat. It seemed for a time that he would surely be drowned, but by his own heroic struggles and the assistance of others, he was finally rescued. The poor man was completely exhausted and seemed very grateful for the aid he had received.

Out at sea again, sailing toward the island of Rhodes. The morning of May 9th was pleasant, and we gave to God all the honor for our safety and His care for us while going from one point of Bible interest to another. There were several other Americans aboard including Gen. J. C. Smith and daughter, of Chicago, Ill., and Mr. Gibson from Georgia, U. S. A. We sailed through the Grecian archipelago, where many islands were seen on either side. The eastern side belongs to Asia Minor, and the western side to Europe.

On the ship there were many that carried their beds with them. It is the custom among many in the Orient for each one to carry his own bed, consisting of a blanket or two;

---

[1] Acts 13:4—13.   [2] Acts 27:4.

some carry only pillows to lay their heads upon. This is doubtless what is meant when Jesus commanded certain ones to "take up thy bed and walk." The customs were not the same, however, in the time of Christ as they are in our country nor as they are in that country at the present time.

Passing on past the island of Rhodes without stopping we arrived at the island of Chios,[1] and in about six hours more we arrived at Smyrna, Asia Minor, the location of one of the seven churches.[2]

Smyrna is the largest city in Asia Minor. Christianity was early planted here and Polycarp, a disciple of John, and bishop of Smyrna, suffered martyrdom about 166 A. D. Smyrna is a flourishing commercial city, with many foreign merchants. Christians are so numerous that the Turks call it "infidel Smyrna."

About the year 96 A. D., there was a church at this place and God was so pleased with its faithfulness that the angel spoke to His servant John, on the island, and said, write: "I know thy works, and tribulation, and poverty, (but thou art rich)." They were poor, stripped, perhaps, of all temporal possessions, because in their attachment to the gospel, yet rich in faith in the kingdom of Christ; and "I know the blasphemy of them which say they are Jews, and are not, but are the synagogue of Satan. Fear none of those things which thou shalt suffer: behold, the devil shall cast some of you into prison, that ye may be tried; and ye shall have tribulation ten days: be thou faithful unto death, and I will give thee a crown of life."[3]

From here we went to Ephesus, about two hours ride from Smyrna, on the railroad. There is a beautiful country

---

[1] Acts 20:25.   [2] Rev. 2:8.   [3] Rev. 2:8--10.

between Smyrna and Ephesus — hills and valleys and beautiful landscapes on all sides with here and there ruins of castles and forts, and the ruins of ancient aqueducts running for miles supported by immense pillars of stone. This being my forty-second birthday made it specially interesting to me to visit the ruins of this ancient city.

(*Original Photo.*)
RUINS OF THE AQUEDUCT, EPHESUS.

CHAPTER XLIV.

Ephesus.

TEMPLE OF DIANA—PAUL IN EPHESUS—HOME OF ST. JOHN—TOMB OF ST. LUKE—RUINS OF MARBLE—MODERN EPHESUS—LEAVING FOR GREECE.

THE most celebrated temple in ancient times was that of Diana, or Artemis, at Ephesus. The city stood on a hill side, sloping gradually into a plain not far from the seacoast. The temple was built of white marble, so bright as to dazzle the eye. It was 425 feet in length, 220 feet broad and supported by 127 columns. The temple was filled with most beautiful statues and pictures.

The first temple was destroyed by fire at the hands of a man named Eratostratus, on the same night on which Alexander the Great was born (356 B. C). When it was asked why the goddess allowed such a famous temple to be destroyed, it was given out that she was so busily engaged with the mother of Alexander, aiding in bringing her son into the world, that she had no time or thought for anything else.

Alexander offered to rebuild the temple, if he were allowed to inscribe his name on the front, but the Ephesians refused. With the help of all the states of Asia Minor, they built a temple still more magnificent than that which had been destroyed. It was decorated with gold, jewels and precious stones and the roof was supported with columns of green jasper. The second temple was destroyed by the Goths, 260 A. D.

The apostle Paul came to Ephesus when the temple was in all its glory, and preached for about three years. There were many pretended magicians in the city. They said that certain words, called Ephesian letters, copied from the image of the goddess, would charm away evil spirits, heal diseases and do other wonderful things. Some of these magicians came to Paul confessing the tricks they had played and burned their books of charms in the streets before all the people. Had they decided to dispose of them by sale, they might have received 50,000 pieces of silver for them.[1]

Once a year a great feast was held in honor of the goddess, and people flocked to Ephesus from all parts to join in it. Strangers often bought small silver models of the temple with the idol inside. They looked upon these as charms, able to keep them from harm and bring good fortune. The sale of these things brought great gain to the silversmiths of Ephesus.

Demetrius, a silversmith, was afraid that he would lose his business through Paul's preaching. He persuaded the silversmiths to get up a cry, "Great is Diana of the Ephesians." The whole city was in an uproar. The services of the chief magistrates were required in quieting the people, telling them that there was no need of their out cry, for every one knew that Diana was great.[2] Paul afterwards left to visit other churches.[3]

When Paul was a prisoner at Rome, he wrote a beautiful letter to the Ephesian Christians which is recorded in the New Testament. He thanked God that they who were

---

[1] Acts 19:19. [2] Acts 19:24—41. [3] Acts 20:1.

once in darkness were now in light in the Lord. They were to walk as children of light, giving up all their former evil doings.

There is not now throughout the whole world a single worshiper of the goddess "Diana" or of the image which is said to have fallen down from heaven.

The apostle John, the beloved disciple of Jesus, lived at Ephesus, both before his banishment to the island of

RUINS IN EPHESUS. (Original Photo).

Patmos and after his release. St. Luke also lived at Ephesus and died there, and his tomb is to be seen at the present day among the ruins. (See illus., p. 77.)

There were seven churches in the Roman province of Asia to which John, at the command of Jesus, wrote an

EPHESUS AS IT IS TO-DAY. (Original Photo.)

epistle or letter.[1] He first addressed the "angel," or minister, of the church at Ephesus. The church at Ephesus was in good standing; they had borne, and had patience, and for Jesus' sake had labored and had not fainted, and yet there was something wrong. "I have somewhat against thee, because thou hast left thy first love." And the warning was: "Remember therefore from whence thou art fallen, and repent, and do the first works; or else I will come unto thee quickly, and will remove thy candlestick out of his place, except thou repent."[2] "To him that overcometh will I give to eat of the tree of life, which is in the midst of the paradise of God."[3]

To-day there is not one in Ephesus to read the epistle to them that was written for them by the apostle. She lost her first love, and her candlestick was removed forever. Ephesus is a heap of ruins of the finest kind of building material. The modern village consists of a few small huts made of the poorest material in the midst of the very best with which to construct houses, as the illustration shows. (See illus., p.377.)

The country is hilly and the valleys very fertile. The sun shone very warmly and all were about exhausted when we returned to the station. Accommodations at the station are very poor.

We returned to Smyrna which is a beautiful city. Much of the material and marble to build it has been brought from the ruins of Ephesus. Its population is about 300,000 souls, comprising people of all nationalities. It has a fine seaport, and many war ships are anchored in the harbor. We visited Smyrna, and Ephesus with its ruins, and many

[1] Rev. 1:11. [2] Rev. 2:4, 5. [3] Rev. 2:7.

380   AROUND THE GLOBE.

points of interest; but we concluded to leave although much more time could have been profitably spent in Asia Minor visiting Pergamos, Thyatira, Sardis, Philadelphia and Laodicea, the others of the seven churches. As the way is hard and traveling very laborious in connection with the expense, we bid adieu to this ancient country of Bible interest.

RUINS OF THE THEATRE AT EPHESUS. (Original Photo)

It was a beautiful morning in May and the sea was very calm when at 9:30 we went aboard the ship and moved out into the deep. We sailed across the straits which are dotted with small islands which make very attractive scenery.

CHAPTER XLV.

Athens, Greece.

PAUL IN ATHENS — MARS HILL — THE UNKNOWN GOD — NEW DOCTRINE — PAUL'S SUCCESS.

ATHENS is situated in the southern part of Greece, about three miles from the seacoast and is reached by train, going through a splendid country along the sea. The city stands on a plain, but there are four small hills all of which formed part of the city. One of the hills, called the Acropolis or citadel, is a square craggy rock, on which stood the Parthenon, the famous temple of Athena, the goddess supposed to watch over the city. It was built of white marble. The image of the goddess, celebrated for its size and beauty, was made of ivory and gold. Not far from the Acropolis is another rock called "Mars Hill," where important cases were tried by judges. The plain below was covered with houses, temples, and other public buildings. Statues everywhere met the eye.

Athens was noted for its idlers. Both the people of the city and strangers who came to it spent their time in nothing else save either telling or hearing of something new. The chief place of resort was the market place, a square, surrounded with temples and shady porticoes. Near it were some famous schools of philosophy.

Paul was alone in Athens. He went through the city from street to street. His attention was chiefly taken up with the numerous temples and images. His spirit was stirred within him when he saw that the city was wholly given to idolatry.[1] Athens was so full of idols that it was said to be easier to find a god in it than to find a man. He felt sad that men should forget their great Creator, and give the honor due Him to the works of their own hands.

ATHEN, AKROPOLIS

Paul went first to the Jews who were in the city, and reasoned with them in their synagogue or church, but his chief work was in the market place, where he went every day to speak with any who were willing to hear what he had to say. Among those whom he met were two classes of Athenian philosophers from the schools near at hand. One class, called Epicureans, took their name from Epicurus, who lived more than 300 years before Paul visited Athens. Epicurus taught that the world was not made by a Creator, and that

[1] Acts 17:16.

THE STOICS.

pleasure is the chief good. He himself was much better than his followers, whose motto, in later years, may be said to have been, "Let us eat and drink for to-morrow we die."

The Stoics were the other class. Their name is from *stoa*, a porch, in which Zeno, their founder, first taught. Virtue was held to be the highest good, and they pretended to be indifferent alike to pleasure and pain. Many of them, however, were hypocrites, indulging in vice, and some were

MARS HILL, ATHENS. (Original Photo.)

tempted to suicide. Paul did not talk with the philosophers about the questions which they were fond of discussing, but about Jesus and the resurrection from the dead. The feelings thus excited were mingled with curiosity and contempt. Paul seemed to them as putting forth strange gods, a mere "seed picker," one who picks up scraps of knowledge which he does not understand. As far as they could make out, Paul appeared to be preaching a new religion. As it was difficult to hear in the crowd, they proposed to go to Mars Hill, close at hand.

They went up from the market place by some steps, to the top of the rock, where there was a level spot encircled by a stone bench. Some of Paul's hearers sat, others stood around him. The blue sky was above his head, the earth under his feet and in front was the Acropolis, crowned with temples. Stretching out his hand, Paul spoke as follows: "Ye men of Athens, I perceive that in all things ye are too superstitious. For as I passed by, and beheld your devotions, I found an altar with this inscription, *To the unknown God*. Whom therefore ye ignorantly worship, him declare I unto you, etc.," as found in Acts 17:22—31.

Like the greatest of the Greek orators, Paul began with, "Ye men of Athens." He acknowledged that they were religious. The Athenians confessed by the inscription on the altar that there was a God whom they did not know. He was the God whom Paul preached. Pointing, perhaps, to the splendid Parthenon, Paul taught that God dwells not in temples made with hands; He is the great Creator of all things, and does not need anything from us.

The Athenians claimed to have sprung from the earth. Paul taught, on the contrary, that all men were equally made by God. He has given them power to find Him though they have but dimly groped after Him in the darkness. In support of what he said, Paul made a well known quotation from a Greek poet, "For we are also His offspring." The Athenians were proud of the beautiful statues of their gods, but Paul declared that the Godhead is not like to gold, silver or stone, formed into images.

After teaching the "Fatherhood of God," and the "Brotherhood of Man," Paul said that the time of ignorance God had overlooked, but that now He commanded all men everywhere to repent. He also spoke of a coming judgment, of which God had given a pledge by raising from the dead the ordained judge, the Lord Jesus Christ. He, before whom we must appear at the last day, now invites us to come

TEMPLE OF ATHENA. *(Original Photo.)*

to Him as our Savior. When Paul spoke of the resurrection, some, probably the Epicureans, broke into open mocking, while others, probably the Stoics, with a show of politeness said, "We will hear thee concerning this yet again."

Still some believed and were baptized. Among them was Dionysius, one of the judges of the court of Areopagus, a woman named Damaris, and others with them. It must have been a great trial to take this bold step in a city wholly given to idolatry; but they sought the truth, and were not content simply to walk according to custom.

Although Paul never again visited Athens, a Christian church was established which afterward produced some eminent men. The temple of Athena was converted into a place of worship for the One True God, and on Mars Hill there now stands a church, called after Dionysius.

(*Original Photo.*)
A GRECIAN COSTUME.

CHAPTER XLVI.

ATHENS AND CORINTH.

GRECIAN FUNERAL—PRIEST BEGGING ALMS—KING'S GARDENS AND PALACE—TOUR TO CORINTH—CORINTHIAN CANAL.—PAUL AT CORINTH.

WHILE attending a Grecian funeral in Athens we noticed many things in their customs that differ from those we have in this country; and yet it is interesting to know that we have adopted many of the Greek customs as our own.

On this occasion a young man led the procession, carrying the lid of the coffin, holding it erect. He was followed by a number of boys with banners, after which came about a dozen priests with their long garments. Following these was the coffin, borne by six men, and containing the corpse which was exposed to view. Then came the friends in carriages, while in the rear was the funeral car drawn by four black horses, each horse covered with a mourning blanket, and led by a man. These men, including the one sitting on the car, all wore high silk hats.

Thus the procession left the house of the deceased, proceeding through the streets of Athens to the church, a fine structure. The king and queen were present at the funeral and occupied seats in their special enclosure by the side of the pulpit and the patriarch. After the ceremony was performed, the procession left the church in the same manner as it had come.

(From Photo.)
GRECIAN COSTUME AND UNIFORM.

Dr. Becker, in his Charades, gives an exhaustive sketch of Greek customs in funerals. It is interesting to observe how many of these we have adopted in America, such as the anointing and washing of the body and the use of the white shroud, the employment of garlands of flowers, the laying out of the dead and the attendance of the relatives and friends, the burial on the third day, the procession following the bier, which is borne by relatives or friends, and the final burying in a wooden or stone coffin. But we have Christianized the ordinary Greek ceremonies in this country by omitting a part of what they regard as essential.

We noticed at the outside of a church door an aged priest wearing his priestly garments, leaning on his crutches, begging alms of those who went in and out. Such men, who have served in the churches and given their best days to the

ATHENS.—THE KING'S PALACE.

Lord and His cause, ought not to be brought where they bring disgrace upon the cause, by being neglected on the part of the Christian church.

We visited the king's gardens and went through the palace. On entering the grounds and coming towards the palace, one of the king's stewards came and after the dragoman had introduced us we were taken through the palace.

The first door we entered brought us into a large hall, where we turned to our left passing through double doors that opened at the foot of a grand stairway leading to the second floor. As we came to the top of the stairs there were a number of cannons pointing directly toward us, seemingly daring the enemy. Passing through another door we came into a room where the banners and flags were kept that had passed through all their battles and wars.

(Original Photo.)
GRECIAN LADY'S COSTUME.

Here we were told to halt and the king's servant withdrew, as he was dressed in a citizen's costume and dared not appear without wearing the costume of the king's servants and officials. The king's guards and those around the palace all wear the national costume, which is shown in the illustration.

After a few minutes he returned, dressed in his kingly garment or uniform which was as follows: Trousers black,

(Original Photo.)
RUINS OF THE ACROPOLIS.

coat black, Prince Albert cut, but short in front, trimmed with black braid, the vest was red; the whole made a fine appearance. Thus attired he led us on through the banquet halls of immense size, grandly finished and furnished, and thence to the reception room.

In this department there were some very fine seats. The throne consists of an elevation or rostrum about ten feet square, two steps high and very finely carpeted, on which there is an elegant chair for the king; a canopy over the seat makes a most imposing appearance. Yet this is simply nothing to be compared with the throne of the Great King of all the earth, before whom all must appear. May the Lord grant to all the dear readers that blessed reception: "Come, ye blessed of my Father, inherit the kingdom prepared for you."

A ride of about three hours on the train brought us to Corinth. A part of the country through which we went is very barren, while the remaining portion is cultivated. Many vineyards are seen all through Greece.

We crossed the Corinth canal, which connects the sea with the Gulf of Corinth. This is a masterly piece of work cut through the solid rock. The modern town of Corinth is about two miles from the ancient ruins.

Paul left Athens and came to Corinth perhaps by very nearly the same route that we took. Corinth was at that time a wealthy city and the capital of Greece, located between two seas. The people were very fond of pleasure. There was a famous temple to Venus with many priestesses. At Corinth Paul found lodging with a Jew, called Aquila, who, with his wife, Priscilla, had come from Italy. The emperor had ordered all Jews to leave Rome, because they were so often making disturbances. One reason why Paul went to them was because they were tent-makers like himself, and he worked with them for his daily bread. It is wrong to live in idleness, if we are able to work. Paul says: "If any would not work, neither should he eat."[1]

The unbelieving Jews were so enraged at seeing numbers become Christians that Paul feared lest he should be beaten

[1] 2 Thess 3: 10.

and imprisoned. God comforted him in a dream at night. He said to Paul: "Be not afraid, but speak, and hold not thy peace: for I am with thee, and no man shall set on thee to hurt thee, for I have much people in this city."[1] This encouraged Paul, so that he stayed more than a year longer in Corinth, and went on teaching.

(Original Photo.)

RUINS OF THE ACROPOLIS.

After this a new governor named Gallio came to Corinth, and the Jews seized Paul and dragged him before the governor. "What has he done?" asked Gallio.

The Jews answered: "He has been teaching us to worship God in a wrong way." Paul was just going to defend himself when Gallio said to the Jews, "If this man had done anything wicked, I would have judged him; but as it is only a question of words, I will not hear you." Then he drove them away from the court. Upon this the Greeks took Sos-

[1] Acts 18:9, 10.

thenes, the chief ruler of the synagogue, and beat him even before the judgment seat, but Gallio cared for none of these things.[1]

About a month later, Paul took leave of the brethren, and sailed for Syria. He afterwards wrote two long letters to the Christians in Corinth.

[1] Acts]18.

CHAPTER XLVII.

From Corinth to Naples, Italy.

HARVEST IN GREECE—PATRES—BUSINESS HOUSES OPEN ON SUNDAY
—A FIGHT—OUT ON THE DEEP—AMERICAN PARTY—ISLAND
COFU—BRINDISI, ITALY — COUNTRY — NAPLES—
MOUNT VESUVIUS—POMPEII — ELECTION —
FUNERAL PROCESSION—TOUR
TO ROME.

LEAVING Corinth by train we arrived at Patres, one of the main seaports of Greece, in about four hours. We traveled through a fine country along the sea and the farmers were in the midst of harvest, reaping their wheat and oats with sickles, as many as one dozen following each other, and binding their sheaves as they cut them. Many vineyards were also seen. The climate is fine and the sea breeze is very invigorating.

Sunday, May 29th. All business houses are open and no church bells are heard, but crowds of people are on the streets, all intent upon amusement.

Just as we were to go aboard the ship, there was a great excitement and it was reported that four Greeks had fought with knives and that all were stabbed and one killed. The police, followed by a large crowd, took them away to prison. O, how sad to see that sin and vice does so abound everywhere one goes!

BRINDISI, ITALY.

Soon we were on the ship and met with several young gentlemen from America, one from Ohio, one from Pennsylvania and one from Michigan. Two of them were young ministers visiting Bible points of interest, and they were all having a pleasant time together.

We soon sailed for Brindisi, Italy. The next day we arrived at the island of Cofu, belonging to Greece and formerly in the possession of the English. The weather was very pleasant and the sea calm. We arrived at Brindisi where we had longed to be on account of our baggage having been forwarded to that place. Fortune favored us and we found all in a proper condition, having made the long journey from Yokohama, Japan, to Brindisi, Italy, in the most satisfactory manner, for which the Lord received all honor. Here our steamship ticket expired. We felt consoled that the longest sea voyages were over and that now we were drawing towards home.

Brindisi is located on the eastern coast of Italy and is the principal Mediterranean seaport, and, as usual in all seaports, there is much vice and sin here. Boys from eight to ten years old were staggering around on the streets in a beastly state of intoxication. In the evening the streets are crowded with people. While they have police officers they also have soldiers who march through the streets to preserve order.

Leaving for Naples, the western seaport, nigh to Puteoli where the apostle Paul landed, a distance of about ten hours' ride by train, we passed through some very fine country, highly cultivated, yet much of it very mountainous. Many tunnels were passed through. We arrived at Naples in the evening and were soon ensconced at a good hotel with our friends, Messrs. Fultz and Jacobs, from America.

Naples and Vesuvius.

Naples is a magnificent city located a short distance from Mount Vesuvius and not far from Pompeii. The sky is generally clear, and the climate temperate and pleasant. Through the country, grain, the olive and grapes are the principal agricultural productions. Cattle are raised in large numbers.

Sunday, May 26th, was election day at this place and no observance of Sunday was noticeable and most of the people were out in the parks. A funeral procession passed which was as follows: six men carrying on their heads a kind of platform about eight feet wide by ten feet long. Over this platform hung a large black cloth trimmed in gold embroidery, the cloth hanging down about four feet below the platform all around. On each side were three men holding the cloth as it hung down; making in all twelve men, all wearing peculiar garments and having their faces covered with white cloths. On the platform stood the casket finished in gold. About a dozen carriages followed in the procession.

A visit to Mount Vesuvius, a distance of about thirty minutes by train, was made by three of us and a dragoman. This proved to be one of the hardest days of our entire tour. It is almost impossible to give a description of the great volcano. It is about 4,000 feet high and covers an area of about two square miles. It appears as though the whole mountain were on fire as the heat and steam escape from the stones and cracks when the lava runs out.

Ascending the mountain and getting above the clouds, with the sea far below us, we saw a wonderful sight. Hearing the rumbling beneath us and the thundering above us, we were almost terrified, and felt as though we were on for-

INN OF THE GOOD SAMARITAN AS IT IS AT PRESENT, BETWEEN JERUSALEM AND JERICHO.
(*Original Photo.*)

MOUNT VESUVIUS.

bidden grounds. At places the stones were so hot that you could not sit on them, while the lava came down all around us whenever the crater discharged. In the center, the crater was probably one hundred feet high. Around it was a gulf perhaps fifty feet deep and one hundred feet wide which fed the crater. About every five or ten minutes the rumbling and thundering began and a wonderful explosion took place when lava was thrown hundreds of feet high. As it came

(Original Photo.)
NAPLES, ITALY, AND MOUNT VESUVIUS.

down on the crater and scattered all around, it made a noise as though car loads of stone were being dumped. O, what a terrible place this is; and yet so many visit it.

In noticing the amount of water on the face of the earth it seems as though it was but a small thing for the Almighty to have destroyed the world by water or a flood; and it is but a small thing for the Almighty to destroy this world by fire, because He has it all in His own hands.

Pompeii is but a short distance from here. It was destroyed by the great eruption centuries ago. Great excavations are made at the present time.

Rome is distant about ten hours ride on the train. There are all along the route caves cut into the rocks and mountains in which natives live. Many women are employed as guards at the crossings, with flags in their hands. A chain is stretched across the road to prevent accidents. Railroad traveling is cheap in Italy. We arrived at Rome in the evening.

CHAPTER XLVIII.

ANCIENT ROME.

CENTER OF THE ANCIENT WORLD—OTHER NATIONS ROBBED OF THEIR TREASURES—PAUL IN ROME—PUTEOLI—THREE TAVERNS—PAUL'S IMPRISONMENT.

ROME was, in ancient times, the greatest city in the world, and the capital from which the then known world was controlled. In the time of Augustus the Roman Empire was the greatest the world ever saw. It extended from the Atlantic to the Euphrates, and from the Danube to the Sibyan desert. The Mediterranean was a Roman lake. Other empires have exceeded it in territory and population, but there never has been a second empire which so united in itself all the cultivated nations of its time.

Rome was situated in the centre of the central sea of the ancient world. From this point the world, known to the ancients in Europe, was conquered and controlled. It seems wonderful that one country should govern so many nations. This was done by placing Roman governors over these various kingdoms, the governors being sustained by a multitude of Roman soldiers. A net-work of roads extended from Rome to every part of the empire, like so many cords binding the conquered world to the centre.

The various generals who conquered other nations robbed them of their choicest treasures; these were brought to Rome to decorate and enrich the capital. There were beautiful statues from Greece, obelisks and columns from Egypt, and a variety of curious and costly manufactures from Asia. Gold, silver and precious stones had been gathered from every part of the earth. The city was embellished with temples, many of them beautifully sculptured. There were also theatres, amphitheatres, baths, triumphal arches

WATER FOUNTAIN IN ROME. (*Original Photo.*)

and aqueducts. Augustus boasted that he had found Rome of brick and left it of marble.

All religions were tolerated in Rome except Christianity. It was thought that the prosperity of a country depended upon the worship of the gods. Christians had no images and did not offer sacrifices, so they were regarded as atheists, men without any religion. In Tinnevelly, where numbers had become Christians, an outbreak of cholera was attributed to the anger of the demons at no longer being worshiped.

THE APOSTLE PAUL IN ITALY.

The Christian church at Rome was probably founded by the "strangers of Rome" who were in Jerusalem on the day of Pentecost.[1] Paul had often purposed to visit Rome, but had as often been hindered.[2] To make up in part for this failure, he wrote from Corinth the present epistle and sent it by Phebe, a servant of the church at Cenchrea, the eastern port of Corinth.

At last Paul was sent to Rome to be tried before Cæsar. The ship in which he sailed came to Puteoli, on the west coast of Italy, the great port of Rome, where corn ships unloaded their cargoes. The centurion allowed Paul to remain seven days with the Christians who were living there. From Puteoli Paul went to Rome by a famous highway, called the "Queen of Roads," along which were inns for travelers every twenty miles.

When the Christians at Rome heard of Paul's landing at Puteoli, several set out to meet him on the way. Some of them had seen him before in other countries. When he was at Corinth, he wrote a long letter to the Christians at Rome. Aquila and Priscilla were now again living in Rome, and very likely they would be among those who went to meet Paul.

Some came out to a place about forty-three miles from Rome, called Appii Forum, and others to a place called Three Taverns, ten miles nearer Rome. They saw a little gray-headed old man, a chained prisoner, but they received him as an ambassador of Jesus Christ. Paul thanked God and took courage.[4] At Rome the centurion delivered over the prisoners to the captain of the emperor's body-guard who allowed Paul

[1] Acts 2:10. [2] Rom. 1:13. [3] Acts 28:13, 14. [4] Acts 28:15.

to live by himself in his hired house, in charge of a soldier.[1] Paul first sought to make known the Gospel to the Jews in Rome, some of whom believed and some believed not. Afterward he labored among the Gentiles, no one forbidding him.[2]

The church at Rome must have increased largely, for only a few years later great numbers of Christians were put to death by Nero. Converts were made even in the palace. During his confinement Paul wrote several of his epistles. He was comforted by the presence of several kind friends, as Luke, Timothy, John and Mark.

After two years' confinement at Rome, Paul was declared innocent and set free. When he left Rome he visited the churches where he had first made known the Gospel. He may have gone to Spain.[3] In a letter to Titus, he wrote that he hoped to spend the winter in Macedonia,[4] but before it was over he was arrested on a new charge, and sent back to Rome to stand a new trial.

Since Paul had been last in Rome more than half the city had been burned down. It was generally thought that the cruel and wicked emperor Nero had given orders to his servants to set fire to the city in several places, but he laid the blame on the Christians who were now numerous. He ordered large numbers to be crucified; others were wrapped in the skins of wild beasts and torn by dogs; some were covered with pitch and set on fire at night to burn as torches in the emperor's gardens.

The second imprisonment of Paul was very severe. Now, too, he was almost alone. Luke only remained.[5] When Paul appeared before the blood-thirsty Nero, the murderer of

[1] Acts 28: 16. [2] Acts 28: 17–31. [3] Rom. 15: 24.
[4] Titus 3: 12. [5] 2 Tim. 4: 11.

his own mother, no man stood by him. It was dangerous for any one to help a Christian in those evil times; but Paul says that the Lord Jesus Christ stood by him and strengthened him.

While Paul's trial was going on he wrote a second letter to Timothy who had taken charge of the church at Ephesus. Timothy was like a dear son to Paul, and this letter is full of wise and loving counsel. He urged him not to be afraid of shame and suffering as a Christian, but to endure hardness, as a good soldier of Jesus Christ.

Paul expected to be put to death, but he looked forward to it with peace and joy. He wrote to Timothy, "I am now ready to be offered, and the time of my departure is at hand. I have fought a good fight, I have finished my course, I have kept the faith. Henceforth there is laid up for me a crown of righteousness, which the Lord, the righteous judge, shall give me on that day." Paul felt that the fight was nearly over now. Unrighteous judges would condemn him to a disgraceful death, but the righteous judge would give him a crown of life. Paul adds: "Not to me alone, but unto all them also that love him."[1]

Paul tells Timothy how greatly he desired to see him. He asked him to bring the cloak which he left at Troas to protect him from the damp of his prison, and the cold of winter, also his books and parchments.[2] We do not know whether Paul ever saw Timothy again. When an old man, about seventy years of age, Paul was led out beyond the gates of Rome to die. Luke, his faithful friend, was no doubt with him, and cheered his weary march to the place of execution. Above all, the Lord Jesus Christ would be with him, so that

[1] 2 Tim. 4:6—8.   [2] 2 Tim. 4:13.

when the axe was raised to sever his head from his body he could triumphantly exclaim, "O death, where is thy sting! O grave, where is thy victory? Thanks be to God who giveth us the victory through Jesus Christ."

Eighteen hundred years have passed away, and Paul is enjoying unspeakable happiness in heaven. How much better it is to spend life like Paul in trying to do good, than to live a life of sin and ease! We need men like Paul to carry the Gospel of salvation to the people, and turn them from serving the idols of sin and the world to the God of love and mercy. Will you all take part in this noble work? The crown of righteousness may be ours also. It is however a prize which must be won. There is a race set before us, which we all must run. We must lay aside every thing that hinders us, and we must run with patience, looking unto Jesus. Thus enter upon the race, and so run that you may obtain the victory.

CHAPTER XLIX.

Modern Rome.

ART PRODUCTIONS — GREAT CATHEDRALS — ST. PETER'S CHURCH — ANCIENT RUINS.

MODERN Rome has a population of 500,000 souls. It is the center of the Roman Catholic church and the seat of the Papal government.

Wherever one may go in Rome, the pictures and statues that are seen are entirely different in their nature from those of any other place. The show windows are full of art productions illustrating Bible subjects and events, making a very attractive appearance. The Virgin Mary, Jesus, and the Twelve Apostles are favorite subjects and are frequently seen reproduced in life size.

There are many schools and colleges in Rome and many young men, divinity students, with priestly garments, are seen on the streets. They usually appear in groups, each group being accompanied by an older man.

The great cathedrals here are among the finest and most wonderful in the world. They are made of the finest materials, are supported by immense columns of marble and granite of different colors, and are embellished with various images, paintings, curtains and draperies. The altars and confessional boxes are very highly finished. There are many attendants at these places of worship. Some are coming, some are going, while others are worshiping, many of them on their knees praying, and wiping the warm tears from their eyes. Their devotion commands the utmost respect, although in many particulars they are in the dark regarding their eternal welfare. The attendants who escort visitors through the different cathedrals show to strangers the utmost kindness.

St. Peter's church is considered the greatest in the world, and covers an area of 18,000 square yards and is

(*Original Photo.*)
ST. PETER'S CHURCH, ROME.

claimed to have cost about $50,000,000, and according to tradition it is located on the spot where St. Paul suffered martyrdom. The church contains a great deal of mosaic work. One stone is so finely polished that it appears like glass. May not this give some idea of the grandeur of the temple of Solomon in Jerusalem? In the center is a large bronze canopy under which the pope reads mass on high festival occasions, and around this are eighty-six ever burning lamps, the annual expense of which is said to be $3,750,000.

The question may be asked, "Is not many a poor man and woman taxed to the utmost to raise the money with which to pay these enormous expenses? Yet, these poor people feel greatly consoled by believing that by making confessions, and paying their dues, they will enter heaven.

O that the light of the Gospel might shine, and make such to see that by going to the Lord Jesus Christ, confessing and repenting of their sins they shall find mercy and pardon by believing in Him.

Rome is a very interesting city and is built in modern style with churches and other buildings of high order. There are also many ancient ruins to be seen of aqueducts, walls, and columns that have been standing for centuries. Like Jerusalem, about all that is seen and heard here is of a religious tendency.

CHAPTER L.

Homeward Bound.

FLORENCE, ITALY—BASEL, SWITZERLAND—PARIS, FRANCE — LONDON, ENGLAND—CROSSING THE ATLANTIC—NEW YORK, U. S. A.—HOME.

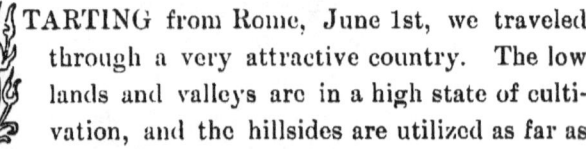STARTING from Rome, June 1st, we traveled through a very attractive country. The low lands and valleys are in a high state of cultivation, and the hillsides are utilized as far as possible. Many tunnels are passed through and many bridges are crossed by the railroad. The people are very sociable and talkative, yet their language is very difficult for an American.

We arrived at Florence, Italy, and spent some time there. Florence is a grand city with churches surmounted by domes, and magnificent structures of all kinds and statues such as can be seen in no other country. The Sabbath day was spent by the people in having a drawing-lottery, at which there was great excitement. This day is not observed by them as it is in America. Bands were playing, soldiers were marching, and many of the people were promenading the streets, while others were attending the services in the magnificent cathedrals surmounted by immense domes hundreds of feet high.

From Florence we went to Milan. We were now getting into a more mountainous country as we came nearer Switzerland. After spending some time in Milan, and after having our money exchanged into the currency of Switzerland, we traveled toward Basel, going through as many as ten tunnels in an hour's time. We noticed that the railroad companies employed principally women as guards at the crossings. The mountain scenery was grand, the tops of the peaks being covered with snow, and waterfalls hundreds of feet high being

LUZERN, SWITZERLAND. *(Original Photo.)*

seen on all sides. In the valley many of the peasantry were making hay.

One very encouraging feature to us was the fact that the railroad employees spoke principally the German language; this was especially appreciated after having traveled through so many countries where strange languages were used. We went through the St. Gothard tunnel which is nearly three miles long.

AROUND THE GLOBE.

Basel is a city of about 600,000 inhabitants, and shows the results of the peculiar business characteristics of the thrifty Swiss people. These few latter cities compare very favorably with our American cities.

Leaving Basel by rail we went to Paris. The country through which we traveled is well improved; the inhabitants own fine stock of all kinds, their horses being similar to the large draft horses of our country.

Paris is without any exception, to our best judgment, the finest city in every respect on the face of the earth. It con-

(*Original Photo.*)
SISIKON, AT THE URNER SEA.

tains about 2,500,000 inhabitants. Here many of the railroad coaches and street omnibuses are two stories high; and they are nearly always filled to their utmost capacity. They are entered at the end and are calculated to hold about forty passengers on the upper story.

While general information goes to show that a great deal of sin and vice exists in this city, many of the customs of the people, especially their manner of doing business, and the way in which they wear their garments, are being copied by the other civilized nations of the world. Hundreds of interesting things might be said about the French people,

SHIP OF THE AMERICAN LINE.

but space and time forbid. The customs and manners of all the civilized European countries are so well known to the average reader that their repetition here would be comparatively uninteresting.

On the 7th of June we left Paris, our next objective point being London. At Calaix we took a steamer across the English channel which was very wild and rough. We landed on English soil at Dover, about four o'clock in the morning. The air was quite cool, there being considerable snow along the coast.

In about two hours after leaving Dover by rail we arrived in London where we had been ten years before. We noticed a great change in that part of the city called "Ludgate Circus." Here I again met my friend J. C. Mack, of Boston, with whom I had roomed while at Jerusalem, and with whom the interesting journey to Bethany, Jericho, the Jordan and the Dead Sea was made.

About one week was spent here visiting special places of interest in this great metropolis, among which was Spurgeon's tabernacle, where the son of the eminent Charles H. Spurgeon is at present preaching. A very interesting service was held at this place. We were here permitted to meet for the first time Dr. C. Day, of Chicago, with whom we afterwards spent many pleasant hours, and with whom we visited the ex-prisoners' home, where we, together, took part in a service under the auspices of the Salvation Army of London.

On returning from religious services and places of interest in the evening, we met many women of a very low character on the streets. It is stated that there are over 600,000 prostitutes in the city of London, who accost men on every side. We noticed that the drinking houses were full of both men and women. This is no doubt the most wicked city of the civilized world. These statements have been made by officers of the Salvation Army. O, what a sad condition of affairs, that people prefer darkness rather than light!

Arrangements were now made to leave London; our baggage was inspected by the custom officers, and was allowed to pass. Much more might be said but as it would not be new to our intelligent readers, we refrain. Leaving London, we went by rail to Southampton, the main seaport of the American steamship line. Our friend J. C. Mack accompanied us from here to New York.

Our voyage was a very pleasant one, and it was especially cheering to know that our journey's end was so near, and that we would soon have the pleasure of meeting our dear ones again.

We arrived at New York on the 25th of June, feeling grateful to God for His protecting care and the grace given us during these long voyages. After our baggage had landed and passed the custom offices without any difficulty, we spent a few days with relatives and friends in the eastern states.

We arrived at home on the 4th of July, 1895; and were met by our family and a host of friends that had gathered at the railroad station to welcome us home. The time which we had been looking forward to, during our entire journey, had now come.

We were grateful to God for His special grace during all these wanderings. The Lord cared for us both on land and sea; and the earnest longing of the writer is that he might be able to share with his fellowmen the information and experience obtained; and that some one may be benefited through these lines.

A PETITION.

The writer concludes with a petition in which he wishes the readers could heartily join:

O GOD, THOU WHO HAST MADE OF ONE BLOOD ALL NATIONS OF MEN FOR TO DWELL ON THE FACE OF THE EARTH, AND DIDST SEND THY BLESSED SON TO PREACH PEACE TO THEM THAT ARE AFAR OFF, AND TO THEM THAT ARE NIGH, SPEED THE TIME WHEN ALL THE NATIONS OF THE EARTH MAY CALL ON THEE AS THE TRUE GOD, AND JESUS CHRIST AS THE REDEEMER OF THE WORLD. GRANT THAT ALL THE PEOPLE OF THESE DIFFERENT LANDS MAY FEEL AFTER THEE AND FIND THEE, AND HASTEN, O HEAVENLY FATHER, THE FULFILLMENT OF THY PROMISE, TO POUR OUT THY SPIRIT UPON ALL FLESH, THROUGH JESUS CHRIST OUR LORD, TO WHOM BE ALL HONOR AND GLORY FOREVER. AMEN.

THE NEW YORK HARBOR OF THE AMERICAN LINE.

List of Illustrations.

Steam ship	22
Gethsemane and Mount of Olives . .	23
Ship's upper deck	29
Honolulu	31
European funeral procession in Turkey .	35
Japanese conveyance	38
Japanese temple	40
Daibutsu . .	41
Turkish festal day . . .	43
Japanese dinner—eating macaroni .	47
St. Anna's church, Jerusalem . .	49
Miyanoshita, hot springs and bath houses .	51
Japanese jinrikisha and tea house .	52
Japanese mode of greeting . .	53
Tea plantation	54
Japanese dray—Fujiyama in the distance	55
Street scene in Yokohama .	56
Japanese idol	57
Ruins of St. John's church, Ephesus	59
Japanese worship	63
Light house . .	65
Two seated jinrikisha . .	67
An oriental burden bearer . .	68
Bristol hotel, Colombo, Ceylon	70
A scene in the tropics .	71
Madras harbor and pier .	73

LIST OF ILLUSTRATIONS.

Madras Post Office	75
Tomb of St. Luke, Ephesus	77
Madras catamarans	81
Coolie girl	83
Women cleaning heads	85
"Ninety to ninety-five percent are poor people"	86
The Field of Blood, or Valley of Hinnom	87
The Hugli river	90
Ship in storm	91
High Court, Calcutta	93
The valley and tombs of Jehoshaphat	95
Hindoo festival	98
Prayer Mill	99
Burning Gnatt	101
Monkey temple	102
Dancing girl	104
Upper Kidron and Mount Calvary	105
Sacred tree	109
Brahmans drowning themselves	110
Mount Zion and the Mount of Olives	111
View of Bombay harbor	115
Child in jewels	117
Interior of the cave of Elephanta	119
Gates of the church of the Holy Sepulchre	123
Rock of the Apostles	127
Child studying nature	129
Birds of India	131
Towers of Silence and vultures	133
Church of the Lord's Prayer on Mount Olivet	139
Map of Canaan and part of Egypt	141
Children of Israel crossing the Red Sea	144

LIST OF ILLUSTRATIONS. 421

Suez canal	146
Karnak, Egypt	150
Oriental women veiled	153
Water carriers	155
Mohammedans praying	157
Dancing dervishes	161
Ruins of the temple of Diana, Ephesus	163
Palm trees, Egypt	165
The flight to Egypt	167
Pyramid and Sphinx	171
Sphinx	172
Egyptian well near Cairo	174
Apis tombs	178
Interior of the Apis tombs, principal passage	180
Hours of meditation	181
Seaport of Joppa, Palestine	189
Jonah and the whale	191
Ruined church at Lydda	193
Jaffa gate	198
Mosque of Omar	203
Palestine in the time of Christ	211
Abraham offering up Isaac	214
Interior of the Mosque of Omar	217
Stables of Solomon	221
Church of the Holy Sepulchre	225
Mary Magdalene at the tomb	229
Interior of the Coenaculum	237
Pool of Siloam	241
Greek ceremony of feet washing	245
Arc De L'Ecce Homo via Dolorosa	248
Crucifixion	251

LIST OF ILLUSTRATIONS.

The last supper	255
Mount Zion and tomb of David and Solomon	258
Leper hospital, Jerusalem	261
Tomb of the Virgin	267
Interior of Gethsemane as it appears at the present day	271
The descent of the Holy Ghost	273
The Golden gate, Jerusalem	275
St. Stephen's gate, Jerusalem	281
Cave of the nativity: the manger	283
Bethlehem	287
Bethlehemite woman	289
Bethany	293
Tomb of Lazarus at Bethany	297
Jericho as seen to-day	303
The bank of the Jordan	307
Resting on the banks of the Dead Sea	311
Abraham entertaining the angels	315
Jerusalem dragoman	321
"Abide with us; for it is toward evening"	323
Damascus gate, Jerusalem	325
House of Simon the tanner, Joppa	329
Convent of St. Elias, near Jericho	335
Plowing and sowing in the Orient	337
Nazareth, the home of Jesus, as it is to-day	339
Bedouin women	343
Tiberias and the Sea of Galilee	347
Feeding the five thousand	351
Beirut, the seaport of Damascus	355
Damascus. Minaret St. Ellene	361
A Turkish funeral procession	365
Saul of Tarsus struck with the great light	366

LIST OF ILLUSTRATIONS.

Seaport of Smyrna	368
The ruins of the prison of St. Paul, Ephesus	369
Ruins of the aqueduct, Ephesus	373
Ruins in Ephesus	376
Ephesus as it is to-day	377
Ruins of the theatre at Ephesus	380
Athen, Akropolis	382
Mars Hill, Athens	383
Temple of Athena	385
A Grecian costume	386
Grecian costume and uniform	388
Grecian lady's costume	389
Ruins of the Acropolis	390
Ruins of the Acropolis	392
Inn of the Good Samaritan	397
Naples, Italy, and Mount Vesuvius	399
Water fountain in Rome	402
St. Peter's church, Rome	408
Luzern, Switzerland	411
Sisikon, at the Urner sea	412
Ship of the American line	413
New York harbor of American line	418

INDEX.

Abraham entertaining the angels	315
Absalom's tomb	277
Aden, Arabia	140
Allahabad, India	108
American cemetery in Japan	56
American mission in Beirut	354
American mission in Cairo	165
Apis tombs	178
Apostles' Springs	295
Application for passport	18
Arabs plowing	350
Baptism of Jesus	302
Bath houses of Japan	51
Bathing in the Jordan	305
Beirut	354
Benares	101
Bethany	291
Bethlehem	282
Bethsaida	349
Bitter lake	147
Bombay	114
Brahmans' suicide	110
Buddhism threatened	46
Buildings in India	75
Burning Gnatt	94
Cairo, Egypt	157
Calcutta, India	92
Cana of Galilee	352
Capernaum	349
Caste marks	83

INDEX.

Cave of Adullam	291
Cave of Machpelah	316
Chapels of Holy Sepulchre	232
Chicago visit	25
Child training	129
Chinese customs	64
Chinese steward	28
Chorazin	349
Christmas in India	84
Christ weeping over Jerusalem	274
Church of the Holy Sepulchre	227
Church of the Lord's prayer	274
Church of nativity	285
City of Palms	302
Climate of Jerusalem	213
Colombo, Ceylon	70
Communion service in Bombay	121
Country town on shipboard	29
Crossing the meridian	37
Daibutsu	41
Damascus	361
Dancing dervishes	160
Dead Sea	309
Degradation in Benares	107
Diligence	357
Distances in India	104
Distinction of women	47
Doctors as missionaries	34
Dogs of Damascus	364
Down to Jericho	295
Easter festival	234
Egyptian costumes	153
Egyptian water carriers	155
Elephanta cave	118
Elijah's Field	302
Elisha's Spring	301

INDEX.

Emmaus	320
Ephesus	373
Evangelical mission in Japan	47
Farewell to India	139
Field of Blood	279
Field of Pease	281
First impression in Jerusalem	200
Foreign moneys	21
Fujiyama, Japan	55
Garden of Gethsemane	266
Gates of Jerusalem	210
Gennesaret	346
Globe trotter	92
Goddess of Mercy	42
Gods of War	40
Golden Gate, San Francisco	27
Greek feet-washing	244
Haifa	328
Hebron	314
Hebron Mission Homes	319
Heliopolis, city of On	183
Hermits' Caverns	301
Herod's reign	208
Hezekiah's reign	207
Hill of evil counsel	280
Hills of Galilee	343
Hindoo child widows	116
Holy fire	235
Home of Mary, Martha and Lazarus	292
Hong Kong, China	64
Honolulu	31
Hospital for bullocks	114
House of Ananias	363
Houses of Jerusalem	213
Howling dervishes	162
Hugli river	89

Infant weddings	97
Inscription on a tombstone	97
Island of Cyprus	367
Island of Rhodes	372
Island of Roida	166
Island of Sumatra	70
Ismalia	147
"I will be a Christian"	45
Jairus	116
Japanese crematory	48
Japanese hotel	48
Japanese idols	57
Japanese mode of building	56
Japanese politeness	53
Japanese productions	53
Japanese sandals	46
Japanese war spirit	52
Japanese women	58
Jericho, ancient	296
Jericho, modern	300
Jerusalem	196
Jerusalem missions	240
Jerusalem not a place of amusement	201
Jewish resort for prayer	317
Jewish prayer	318
Jinrikisha	39
Jonah's tomb	314
Jordan river	302
Joseph's well	169
Jubulpore	113
Judas' tree	280
Kamakura	39
King David's reign	202
King Solomon's reign	205
Kobe, Japan	62

INDEX.

Land of Goshen	185
Last judgment	274
Last supper	254
Lazarus' tomb	291
"Learn to know thyself"	45
Leaving home	25
Lebanon Mountains	357
Leper hospital	265
Leper island	30
Leper physician	33
Lepers	260
Licensed prostitutes	48
Madras, India	72
Madras mission work	81
Madras penitentiary	76
Madras population	74
Madras wages	75
Mamilla pool	253
Mariette	180
Mars Hill	381
Memphis	174
Milk grotto	285
Mission meetings	84
Miyanoshita	51
Mohammedan feast day	318
Monkey temple in India	102
Moslem's prayer	156
Mother and child parted	62
Mrs. Besant on Theosophy	82
Mrs. F. A. Nalor	61
Mt. Calvary	228
Mt. Carmel	328
Mt. Moriah	215
Mt. Olivet	270
Mt. Tabor	341
Mt. Zion	259
Museum of Gizeh	182

INDEX.

Nagasaki	62
Nain	353
Nazareth	338
Ninety percent poor	86
Parsee funeral	132
Parsee marriage	130
Parsees	122
Passport	19
Paul in Athens	381
Paul in Ephesus	375
Paul's escape from Damascus	363
Penang	69
Plains of Sharon	195
Pool of Bethesda	213
Pool of Siloah	278
Population, Jerusalem	213
Port Said	187
Prayag	110
Prayer Mill	99
Products of India	100
Public buildings, Jerusalem	255
Pyramids	170
Ramses II & III	177
Rachel's tomb	282
Railway to Jerusalem	195
Ramleh	195
Red Sea	143
Religious services in Singapore	69
Rev. Halicham Bannagee	85
River Kishon	381
Religious services on shipboard	63
Sacred tree	109
Sagar island	90
Sailing for Joppa	187
Salt Lake	26

INDEX. 431

San Francisco	26
Sea of Galilee	346
Sea rough	37
Seasickness	29
Shepherds' Field	289
Simasol	371
Singapore	66
Smyrna, Asia Minor	372
Solomon's pools	313
Solomon's temple	214
Sphinx	172
Stables of Solomon	220
Stephen stoned	266
Strait of Malacca	69
Street called Straight, Damascus	363
Streets and shops in Jerusalem	252
St. James' tomb	278
St. Mary's well	342
Suez canal	146
Sakkara, Egypt	173
Table of time	22
Tea houses, Japan	52
Temple of Diana	374
Thos. Cook & Son	17
Tiberias	393
Tokio	46
Tomb of King David	256
Tomb of King Solomon	256
Tomb of Samuel	321
Tomb of the Khedives	165
Tomb of the Virgin	266
Tripoli	367
Turkish funeral	365
Tyre and Sidon	334
Valley of Achor	296
Valley of Eschol	314

INDEX.

Valley of Hinnom	279
Valley of Jehoshaphat	274
Valley of the Kidron	260
Via Dolorosa	248
Walls of Jerusalem	210
Wheelbarrows in Japan	54
Wonders of the sea	30
Worshiping the river	93
Yokohama	39
Zacharias' tomb	278

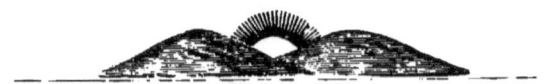

www.ingramcontent.com/pod-product-compliance
Lightning Source LLC
Chambersburg PA
CBHW051726300426
44115CB00007B/489